'An insightful, compelling and thor[c]
of some of the deepest problems w
the progressive policies that co[u]
Grace Blakeley, author of *Vulture Capitalism*

'With the Labour Party timidly reversing even modest
commitments, this book is full of ideas that can fill the vacuum.'
Guy Standing, author of *The Politics of Time*

'A really valuable attempt to do something different –
thoughtful, clever and timely.'
**Henrietta Moore, Founder and Director,
UCL Institute for Global Prosperity**

'People know we can't go on as we are. So the more ideas
pouring out like this will greatly help set the direction of travel
of our political debate.'
John McDonnell MP

'An inspiring, imaginative and radical vision for Britain's
future, equal in ambition to the challenges the country faces.'
**Peter Jones, Emeritus Professor of
Political Philosophy, Newcastle University**

'This is a coherent, radical and feasible manifesto for
government. Given the chance, it would ignite enthusiasm, win
the young back to politics and enable people to enjoy security
and freedom in their life with one another and with the powers
that be. It calls us back to a realistic image of the good society.'
**Philip Pettit, L. S. Rockefeller University Professor of
Human Values, Princeton University**

'*Act now* identifies a new direction where need replaces greed
in a social contract that would protect the British public and
guarantee freedom from the preventable harm created
by ideology.'
**Mo Stewart, author of *Cash Not Care: The Planned
Demolition of the UK Welfare State***

ACT NOW

Manchester University Press

ACT NOW

A vision for a better future
and a new social contract

Common Sense Policy Group

Manchester University Press

The right of Common Sense Policy Group to be identified as the authors of this work has been asserted in accordance with the Copyright, Designs and Patents Act 1988.

Published by Manchester University Press
Oxford Road, Manchester M13 9PL
www.manchesteruniversitypress.co.uk

British Library Cataloguing-in-Publication Data
A catalogue record for this book is available from the British Library

ISBN 978 1 5261 8075 9 hardback
ISBN 978 1 5261 8076 6 paperback

First published 2024

The publisher has no responsibility for the persistence or accuracy of URLs for any external or third-party internet websites referred to in this book, and does not guarantee that any content on such websites is, or will remain, accurate or appropriate.

Typeset by Newgen Publishing UK
Printed in Great Britain by CPI Group (UK) Ltd, Croydon, CR0 4YY

CONTENTS

Part III: Making it happen

COMMON SENSE POLICY GROUP

Chair

Matthew Johnson, Professor of Public Policy, Northumbria University

Author team

Danny Dorling, Professor of Human Geography, University of Oxford

Jamie Driscoll, Mayor of North of Tyne Combined Authority

Irene Hardill, Professor of Public Policy, Northumbria University

Cat Hobbs, Founder and Director, We Own It

Elliott Johnson, Vice-Chancellor's Fellow in Public Policy, Northumbria University

Neal Lawson, Director of Compass

Jennifer Nadel, Co-Director Compassion in Politics

Daniel Nettle, Professor of Community Wellbeing, Northumbria University; Research director at Institut Jean Nicod, CNRS, Paris

Kate Pickett, Professor of Epidemiology, University of York; Academic Co-Director of Health Equity North

Zack Polanski, Deputy Leader of the Green Party and London Assembly Member

Allyson Pollock, Clinical Professor of Public Health, Newcastle University

Diane Reay, Professor of Education, University of Cambridge

Howard Reed, Senior Research Fellow in Public Policy, Northumbria University, Landman Economics

Ian Robson, Associate Professor, Social Work, Education and Community Wellbeing

Graham Stark, Senior Research Fellow in Public Policy, Northumbria University and Virtual Worlds

David Taylor-Robinson, Professor of Public Health and Policy, University of Liverpool and Honorary Consultant in Public Health at Alder Hey Children's Hospital; Academic Co-Director of Health Equity North

Richard Wilkinson, Professor Emeritus of Social Epidemiology, University of Nottingham

CONSULTATION GROUP

Joanne Atkinson, Nurse and Associate Professor in End of Life Care, Northumbria University

Amy Barnes, Senior Research Fellow, University of York

Jane Betty

Hugo Fearnley, Mayor's Political Adviser, North of Tyne Combined Authority

Simon Duffy, Citizen Network

David Hall, Visiting professor, Public Services International Research Unit (PSIRU), University of Greenwich

David Hall, Modify Productions

Michael Hill, Associate Professor in Nursing, Northumbria University

Julia Hines

Leah Jennings, Chief of Staff, Office of Jon Trickett MP

David Littlefair, Associate Professor in Education, Northumbria University

Jason Madan, Professor in Health Economics, Warwick Medical School

Courtney Neal, Population Health Sciences Institute, Newcastle University

Roweena Russell, Big Local Jarrow

Matthew Smith, Professor in Health History, University of Strathclyde

Lena Swedlow, Campaigns and Projects Officer, Compass

Simon Winlow, Professor of Social Science, Northumbria University

Suggested citation: Common Sense Policy Group (2024) *Act Now: A Vision for a Better Future and a New Social Contract*, Manchester: Manchester University Press.

Find out more about the Common Sense Policy Group's work at: www.commonsensepolicygroup.com.

FOREWORD

In countless ways, the United Kingdom of 2024 is not the country its citizens want it to be. It is deeply ironic that, eight years on from a political upheaval that promised to restore 'control' of its affairs to the population of the UK, the prevailing sense in British politics is of anger and despair at the lack of accountability in government – and of endless displacement activity by government itself, fanning a set of highly coloured anxieties about small boats and culture wars while floundering more and more in addressing the chronic deficit in corporate and individual wellbeing that we are living with.

The pervasive degradation of public services has left us with massively indebted or bankrupt local authorities, a fragmented, exhausted health service, demoralised schools whose teachers are routinely undermined by bullying rhetoric from politicians as much as by anxious or violent or alienated students, a public transport system that is overpriced and under-maintained, a prison estate that is overcrowded to the point of squalor – the catalogue of failures goes on, intensified by the staggering reluctance to plan realistically for whatever is involved in transition to an economic model that will mitigate the effects of climate crisis. Within all of these areas, there continues to be an astonishingly high number of people working with dedication and integrity but pushed to near collapse by the stress of dysfunctional systems and spiralling demands. Does anyone seriously want things to be like this?

One of the deepest problems is that the frustration that such a question generates is all too easily diverted into destructive words and actions – another kind of displacement activity. As is more nakedly the case in the United States, politics on the streets can become 'performative', a ritual of insistent slogans and mutual demonising, theatricality replacing the hard work of argument and actual change. And with a dismally predictable logic, those in government reply with hostile caricatures, with the repression of protest and an encouragement to moral panic. We need to focus on engaging politicians around structural issues over which they have actual capacity to enact reform.

Can politics be rescued from this shadow-battling and become again a means of naming, understanding and resolving the crises that most affect people's ability to organise their lives with dignity, generosity and hopefulness? That is the question this book sets out to answer.

It does so with a sharp critical eye on both major political parties, implicitly challenging them to ask a bit more seriously what has happened to their foundational values and why they have so often bought in to the assumption that a boot sale of national public services is the way to make them work better for the population as a whole. Behind much of the argument is the research – now 15 years old – of two of this book's authors, Richard Wilknson and Kate Pickett, demonstrating how the absurdly mechanical models of growth with which we have been living destroy the sense of shared wellbeing by allowing an indefensibly accelerated widening of the economic gap in society between the secure and the insecure. To pick up their focal image, this fantastical, feverish process has created a spiritual catastrophe – if we understand the word 'spiritual' as essentially about the capacity to live in a frame of reference larger than desperate anxiety for losers and frantic acquisitiveness for winners.

Plenty of voices have been raised in the last decade or so – those of Michael Sandel, Lyndsey Stonebridge, Robert Skidelsky, David Olusoga, Adrian Pabst, Tim Jackson and Daniel Chalmers, to mention only a few – to push back at the toxic assumption that there is no alternative to the reduction of social need to a global market opportunity. The experience of the pandemic, the more we look back on how it unfolded and was handled, showed just how readily this model could corrupt and distort public health provision – but also how deep and passionate was the longing to see some kind of resetting of the way we value and reward public service. We are still waiting to see how clapping for the NHS translates into the kind of institutional transformation that would genuinely secure humane, effective healthcare and health education as an achievable shared good for our society. And while on the subject of education, we urgently need another kind of reset based on grasping the fact that education is something to do – once again – with creating frames of reference that are spiritually nourishing and durable, not only with the mechanisms of acquiring a tradeable set of results.

The proposals in this book are detailed and pragmatic, set out with careful attention to how they might be implemented and how they might be funded. These chapters are not an idealistic rant demanding some sort of total recalibration of how we live. But they are unmistakeably radical, in the sense that they interrogate what the political establishment of both left and right take for granted, what they think is achievable and acceptable. One of the striking features of what follows in these pages is the accumulation of sober evidence for how widespread is the appetite for solutions that might seem drastic to many.

But this opens up a final and crucial dimension to what this book offers. On the day I write this, the Welsh government has published its response to the recent report of the Independent Commission on the Constitutional Future of Wales, a cross-party document that unanimously argued (on the basis of two years of extended and in-depth consultation) not only for further localisation of significant powers but for a continuing investment in 'democratic innovation' – that is, in creating and enabling grassroots deliberative consultation, supported by a commitment to effective civic education both in and beyond our schools. If any of what is found in the pages following is to happen and to become part of our common political wisdom, it will need just this commitment to 'democratic innovation'. It is about inviting citizens into processes of discussion, discovery, scrutiny, at a level well beyond the focus group or the occasional polling exercise. It is to take seriously the often rather muffled and indistinct urge in our country towards a fairer and more hopeful settlement that provides a genuinely secure environment for all.

Is this an unrealistic dream? Apparently the Senedd doesn't think so. The response included the commitment to a substantial sum budgeted for taking this work forward. Who knows what level of effectiveness this will have? We can hope – but it will depend on a climate in the UK at large that is more receptive than it currently is to this kind of thinking. The chapters that follow look towards just that kind of shift in the imagination – the spirit – of Britain, returning repeatedly to that fundamental challenge of how we sustain a social order that does justice to the most humane, generous and grounded instincts of our communities.

Time for action.

Rowan Williams

ACKNOWLEDGEMENTS

We have received support from a wide range of colleagues over the past few months. All of your support is greatly appreciated. At Northumbria University, Joanne Atkinson has provided endless support as Head of the Department for Social Work, Education and Community Wellbeing, while we are extremely lucky to have Gemma Brown as a brilliant Press Officer. At Compass, Lena Swedlow has provided invaluable insight into the various challenges to overcome within the text as well as support with regard to launches and policymaker engagement. Finally, Jane Betty has produced, extraordinarily quickly, an index with a rare degree of complexity and depth. We recognise and value all of your support enormously. Thank you.

INTRODUCTION

We are living through a period of long-term stagnation and decline marked by overlapping crises. The overwhelming evidence for this can be seen in a wide range of statistics. Real incomes are falling for everyone but the rich. The same is true of life expectancy. Our municipal facilities are crumbling, and the National Health Service (NHS) is struggling to meet people's needs. The most immediate result is that a huge number of ordinary people have, in recent years, suffered a noticeable reduction in the liveability and pleasantness of their everyday lives.

Cutting through this uninspiring general pattern are discrete crises: the financial crash, the pandemic, the cost-of-living crisis. Each of these has inflicted terrible suffering on individuals while putting enormous strain on society as a whole. As we look to the future, the stagnation seems set to continue, while the frequency of crises is only likely to increase.

Crises, however, can also be opportunities. They expose the inadequacy of the status quo, making people more receptive to bold, new solutions.

For years, the right-wing and centrist political consensus has presented the same, failed solutions, contributing to a downward cycle in which desperation leads to despair. For those of us who want to see society get better, this situation has been a political disaster. But progressive politicians, narrowly focused on obtaining respectability on the terms of a settlement that is not working, have failed to recognise the urgency of people's need, as well as their willingness to consider alternative solutions. In fact, people outside politics are hungry for stability, security and the prospect of a future better than the present.

Given the rapid pace of scientific and technical advancement, the challenge of transitioning to a sustainable future, and our unparalleled practical interdependence with each other, we need to construct a society that is more cohesive, adaptable and equitable. The pro-market policies of the recent past have led in the opposite direction, failing even on their own terms. They have fostered greater inequality, division and social fragmentation without making most people's experience of everyday life much better. And they have failed to prepare us for future environmental challenges. Rather than embracing and benefiting from change, people have become more insecure. Insecurity heightens apprehension and resistance to change.

This is not the right path. Modern societies can flourish only if people feel they can work confidently together, knowing that wellbeing and participation are shared and that the future can be embraced without fear.

Progressive policymakers, such as the leaders of the UK Labour Party, appear incapable of doing and unwilling to do what their institutions were set up to do: present a transformative vision of how progressive politics addresses people's needs. In an almost homeopathic approach to our crisis, political

2

parties seem to believe that the stronger the ailment, the weaker the medicine needs to be. Even if Labour wins the next general election, its leadership is explicitly committed to maintaining our dysfunctional system, both for ideological reasons and because they claim that the public oppose change.

Yet the evidence shows the contrary: millions of people have thrown their support behind proposals for dramatic transformations, from Brexit to the furlough scheme. The position is disastrous. If elected, Labour will be unable to resolve crises, because they have not articulated a way of doing so or built popular consensus around such a way. Capture of power is hollow if it leads only to greater disaffection or increasingly regressive rule.

What we need is a comprehensive vision of a secure, stable and prosperous Britain, picked out with clear, popular policy pathways leading towards it. The neoliberal and authoritarian right have presented their visions, but their policies have not led where they promised. Instead, they have produced an insecure, unstable and unliveable Britain, one that fails to meet collective – and for many people, individual – needs. The centre left has often accepted the terms of the right's vision. Britons need to be able to imagine a specific alternative. Britain needs a distinct progressive vision, evidence-based but speaking directly to lived experience, sweeping in ambition, scale and significance. What Britain needs in 2024 is what the Beveridge Report offered Britain in 1942.

The Beveridge Report – which, let us remember, was not produced within any single political party – filled a huge gap between what Britons wanted and what they had been offered by their politicians. It captured the popular imagination, fostered consensus and created the foundations for a new settlement. It became a popular weapon that forced politicians to act, for example by committing to its principles ahead of the 1945 general election. But it also gave those parties a legitimate appeal and an organising vision.

The new settlement that was led by the Labour government of 1945 and sustained by subsequent governments of both parties was popular not because of some abstract appeal to values, but because it made concrete changes to people's lives. We need to identify changes today that are as powerful as the image of doctors' bills being removed from people's hands by the creation of the NHS. Reductions in child poverty and inequality are crucial, but we need to show how progressive change will make everyday life concretely better for the vast bulk of ordinary people. Otherwise, progress is seen as irrelevant − change in some abstract statistical quantity, or something that only benefits others. We need to show how we can free people from the daily experience of extortionate energy bills, choosing between heating and eating, traffic jams, municipal decline and anti-social behaviour.

In this report, we demonstrate that by implementing practical and pragmatic policy reform in ten areas, we can achieve these transformations and so much more. The plan we set out envisions Britain run as a business: investment leading to the generation of wealth to transform our lives. While politicians over four decades have consistently justified reform through reference to business, there are few businesses that have succeeded by giving away their assets, withdrawing all essential investment and making themselves dependent on hostile competitors for essential supplies. Yet this is how Britain is run today. The short-, medium- and long-term prospect is ever-increasing poverty, inequality and private indebtedness. The investment we present

4

is entirely feasible, will not generate inflation and is precisely of
the type used by businesses to generate wealth.

We show how claims that investment is unpopular are wholly
wrong. It's time to make progressive policy popular again. This
sounds like a bizarre point to make: progressive parties were created specifically to ensure that government acted in the interest
of the vast bulk of society. That they have become associated
with 'metropolitan elites' or technocratic political classes speaks
to the total failure of those institutions to understand the needs
and interests of most people, or the bases of their policy preferences. *Act now* – our attempt to produce for 2024 something
like what Beveridge was able to achieve in 1942 – provides an
alternative vision to get us out of this historical cul de sac. And
it is overwhelmingly popular.

For this book, we conducted a large survey between 20 and 26
January 2024 with two groups of adult UK voters: 851 residents
with postcodes within 'Red Wall' constituencies in the North
and Midlands of England and Wales that were lost by Labour
to the Conservatives in 2019, and 1,052 participants across
Britain.[1] Before running the survey, we used a screening survey
with 693 Red Wall voters to identify strong opponents of the
10 individual policies within this report by those who reported
ratings of less than 20 out of 100 for each policy. We worked
with some of these opponents to understand and co-produce
arguments that would persuade people like them to support
the policies. We then organised four arguments for each policy around three categories that were consistent across all 10
policies: absolute gains (everyone benefits), relative gains (some
benefit at the expense of others) and security (that our needs
are secured). We also developed another category that was specific to each policy.

We then presented each of the two groups of participants with descriptions of the policies and a co-produced argument at random for each policy. We analysed the survey to identify levels of support for the policies among Red Wall voters who voted Labour or Conservative in 2019 and among national voters according to their voting intentions as of the date they completed the survey. We found overwhelming levels of support for each of the policies, alongside high levels of uncertainty about voting intentions. Thirty per cent of national voters either do not know who they will vote for or intend not to vote. These potential voters strongly support each of the policies and are there to be persuaded by parties of the merits of voting. Parties need to act now.

Parties that endorse the policies we set out have scope to create a new settlement, re-establishing the boundaries of government across the UK and resetting the remits of the public and private spheres. Instead of rolling back the state, we argue that we should roll it forward as public cooperation, based on active citizenship and economic democracy, manifested in plural, robust and resilient institutions.

The policies outlined in this book – which in honour of Beveridge we henceforth refer to as our report – are both feasible and popular. We offer them as a contribution to the conversation that will provide the pathway to that secure, democratic and prosperous Britain.

PART I

THE SETTING

CHAPTER 1
WHAT DID BEVERIDGE DO FOR US?

Chapter in 30 seconds

In the 1940s, Britain was facing the acute crisis of the Second World War against the background of inadequate provision of the means for a good life for most people. The tumult led to reform and the creation of better institutions and demonstrable social progress. An important stimulus for change was the Beveridge Report. Originating outside any one political party, the report spelled out a tangible pathway to a better future, in the form of specific policy proposals that also added up to a coherent vision. It was widely disseminated and immediately understood by the country. The Labour Party's endorsement of it contributed to the Labour landslide in the 1945 general election. In this chapter, we set the scene for 2024 by revisiting the Britain of the war. We need a progressive programme of the same scope, scale and ambition as that of the 1945 government to deal with our current challenges. To make this happen, there needs to be broad national consensus around concrete, common-sense, timely, implementable ideas.

Introduction: the historical context for Beveridge

In May 1940, Neville Chamberlain's government fell and was replaced by a cross-party coalition under Winston Churchill. As leader of the opposition, Clement Attlee was brought into the Cabinet. The new National Government placed renewed emphasis on post-war planning and reconstruction. This was a key part of boosting civilian morale at a pivotal moment in the Second World War,[1] which was being fought on several fronts.[2] At home, daily life was regulated by food rationing through the Board of Trade, which actually improved the population's diet. Unemployment had also been almost eliminated,[3] but the pressures of war meant that life was a tremendous struggle.

The social upheaval caused by the war and particularly by the large-scale evacuations from major cities revealed serious shortcomings in existing social services.[4] The war led to recognition that people could end up in poverty through no fault of their own, which accelerated a move away from traditional, piecemeal welfare provision.[5] Media coverage about the inadequacies of existing services together with heightened public interest in social issues meant that pressure for reform began to build across several policy areas.[6]

The Old Age and Widow's Pensions Act was introduced in summer 1940 and prompted what *The Times* called a 'remarkable discovery of secret need' among older people.[7] Meanwhile, a forceful letter written by Lady Allen to *The Times* in July 1944 called for government investigation into the 'repressive conditions that are generations out of date' in voluntary and local authority children's homes. This prompted a public outcry.[8]

We find ourselves in a similar position today, in spite of all the technological advances of the intervening decades.[9] COVID-19 exposed how vulnerable Britain had become after 15 years of austerity politics and spending cuts. Even the voluntary sector, which Beveridge saw as critical to the functioning of society, has been degraded and overwhelmed.[10] In 2020, almost all British people found themselves in need of at least some support from public services. What they initially received was deficient in the extreme, leading to a crisis response at odds with four decades of government practice: massive emergency funding in order to prevent mass unemployment, destitution and illness. Hugely ambitious government programmes such as the furlough scheme, which effectively nationalised 11.7 million jobs, were seen as not only desirable but essential by the very politicians previously committed to cutting budgets to the bone.[11]

Some 80 years ago, Labour members of the National Government were looking ahead to recovery and reconstruction during their own period of crisis. They were mindful of the mistakes made a generation earlier during the First World War and the hollow promises of then-Prime Minister Lloyd George's 'Homes Fit for Heroes'.[12] They recognised a need to present a future in different terms from the past.[13] Even industrialists were planning for change: 120 of them published a statement titled *A National Policy for Industry* in 1942 that called for a community-first approach, favouring consumers, promoting partnership with workers, protecting small producers, accepting regulation by parliament and contributing to public welfare.[14]

The timeliness of Beveridge

Today, the lessons of the past appear to be rapidly falling by the wayside as we return from new normal to old normal.[15] Post-pandemic, the Conservative leadership rapidly signalled a

11

renewal of austerity politics while Labour committed to matching Conservative spending plans should they be elected. The main contenders for government speak of recovery and reconstruction, but there is little evidence that anything other than continued stagnation and decline are possible under their current policy positions.

There were a couple of key moments that ensured that the post-war period was different. William Beveridge was a long-standing expert in unemployment. In 1941, while working on wartime workforce requirements for the Ministry of Labour, he was asked by Arthur Greenwood, Labour Minister for Reconstruction in the National Government, to chair an inter-departmental committee on the coordination of social insurance. Social insurance at that time was uncoordinated, having developed gradually and organically across seven Departments since the Edwardian era.[16] Beveridge did more than 'tidy up' that system. Instead, he presented 'social insurance … as a contribution to a better world'.[17]

Beveridge identified the five 'giant evils' of squalor, want, ignorance, idleness and disease, which he argued had to be slain on the road to reconstruction. His plan foresaw a society with full employment. He proposed a national health service that would be free at the point of use, comprehensive social insurance through the state and non-means-tested family allowances. Beveridge's own caution about the 'revolutionary' changes he proposed is significant. Maintaining some continuity with pre-war institutions, his plans were to be a 'natural development from the past'. As he put it: 'it is a British revolution'.[18]

The committee of civil servants consulted widely, met on 48 occasions and received representations from 127 different organisations,[19] though the eventual report bore Beveridge's name alone. Mass Observation (MO), a project with a remit to monitor public opinion, captured how interest in the forthcoming report and its role in creating what it called 'A New Britain' grew during 1942.[20] Beveridge's courting of such advance publicity was far from welcomed by the government. Publication of the report was delayed by several weeks as some in Churchill's Cabinet considered it 'too revolutionary'.[21] Published just after the important military victory at El Alamein, the report signalled 'a new phase of optimistic restructuring of social policy'.[22]

Why Beveridge was popular

There was tremendous interest in the report, which Beveridge described as a 'public boom'.[23] MO captured how more than 600,000 copies of the full report and its summaries were sold by February 1944. Its survey found that 92 per cent of those questioned knew about the report the day after publication.[24] Reception among politicians was more mixed, with some Conservatives terrified at the cost of the prospective policies.[25] The National Government was divided, and Beveridge described a lack of engagement, including from the Prime Minister.[26] This was a significant misjudgement from Churchill, whose Tories continued to lose by-elections as the country expressed its desire for change. The incumbent politicians had failed to see that a time of great adversity brings forth an appetite for change, an optimism to which Beveridge appealed successfully. 'The purpose of victory', he wrote, 'is to live in a better world than the old world … each individual citizen is more likely to concentrate upon his war effort if he feels that his government will be ready in time with plans for a better world'.[27] He argued that 'democracies, like Cromwell's armies, need to know what they fight for and to love what they know'.[28]

The May 1945 general election was framed around post-war reconstruction but was bitterly fought, with little sign of consensus between major parties.[29] It was Labour's ambitious programme of social and economic reconstruction, including a promise to implement much of the Beveridge plan, which helped to secure its first landslide majority.[30] Its manifesto, *Let Us Face the Future*, had a clear message that victory in war must be followed by a prosperous peace, and Labour offered the electorate a vision for the future. Attlee, like Beveridge, had worked at Toynbee Hall, the pioneering attempt to integrate wealthier university students within the poor communities of London's East End.[31] He had been a social worker and in 1920 published a visionary book, *The Social Worker*. He also taught at The London School of Economics before entering local and then national politics. Then as now, Britain needed a leader who could create coalitions between figures from different political traditions to secure the comprehensive overhaul of policies across the whole of government. Then as now, Britain needed a visionary and effective leader committed to transformative policies to put clear, evidence-based plans into action. Then as now, Britain needed a new approach to politics.

Implementation of the report and impact on the 'five giant evils'

Alongside the nationalisation of key industries and utilities, Attlee's new government introduced a swathe of reforms which set up the key institutions of what Beveridge termed the 'social service state',[32] but which we now know as the welfare state.[33] Nye (Aneurin) Bevan spearheaded the establishment of the NHS while George Griffiths tackled social security.[34] In England and Wales, important legislation included the National Insurance Act 1946, the National Health Act 1946, the Children Act 1948, the National Assistance Act 1948, and the Town and Country Planning Act 1949. Entire industries were national-ised and houses built *en masse*, radically improving the working conditions and access to services of tens of millions of Britons. The achievement of the post-war Labour administration in establishing the enduring institutions of the British welfare state, notably the much-loved NHS, and in extending the social 'safety net', should be seen in the context of both austerity and the mixed economy of welfare. Public spending on welfare grew, but growth was at a rate which 'both contemporaneously and retrospectively has been exaggerated'.[35]

Progress on the five giant evils was rapid. There followed a period of around 30 years of unparalleled economic and state expansion, low inequality and poverty, and rapid recovery fol-lowing two devastating world wars. Life expectancy at birth, which had been below 61 prior to the war in 1935, reached almost 71 by 1960.[36] People could expect to live 10 years more because the government addressed the social determinants of health. The welfare state was largely maintained by both Labour and the Conservatives as part of the post-war consensus which held that a high-tax, well-funded state sector was essential to ensuring the health and wellbeing of the nation.[37]

The five giants have shrunk and grown over subsequent years. While Guy Standing and others have rightly emphasised new or distinct giants,[38] and while we identify our condition as one of ultra-insecurity, it is important to understand the ways in which policies implemented to address Beveridge's five giants had a manifest impact on society, and how removing those policies has had a dramatically damaging effect.

Idleness

'Idleness' was addressed through record low unemployment. The 1944 employment white paper put forward by Ernest Bevin, Minister of Labour in the National Government, was a turning point.[39] It proposed a stable, collaborative but regulated environment for international trade. It suggested interest rate rises to slow excessive inflation, and government spending to stabilise a slowing economy through increased demand for private investment. It planned funding to support retraining for a more flexible employment market in cooperation between employers and trade unions. And it suggested support, including government investment, for areas of the economy that required specific development.

The paper effectively set out the principles of employment policy for the period of the post-war consensus. Years later this progress would be undone, at first slowly due to macroeconomic circumstances rooted in fluctuating commodity prices and the overvaluation of the pound. It was further reversed through a relatively short-term union outlook that saw wage increases as a higher priority than inflation reduction at a time, as now, of rapid increases in energy costs due to international conflict. Finally, the Thatcherite reforms of the 1980s resulted in the unemployment rate more than doubling from the end of the 1970s to a peak of 11.9 per cent in early to mid-1984.[40] This occurred as nationalised utilities were privatised or dispensed with and government investment reduced in other sections of the economy.

While the technical unemployment rate has returned to relatively low levels since, it is heavily skewed by the failure to include the large number of 'economically inactive' people, underemployed people whose skills and potential productivity are going to waste, and people working in the bits-and-pieces 'gig economy', which seldom provides living wages.[41] The New Labour focus on financialisation of the economy and reliance on service industry jobs only temporarily masked a long-term failure to enable people to achieve their potential.[42]

Ignorance

'Ignorance' was addressed through the 1944 Education Act's introduction of universal, free, compulsory secondary education to the age of 15 and the expansion of university places with zero tuition fees. This would be carried further through the 1962 Education Act, which introduced maintenance grants.[43] There were also greatly increased opportunities for technical education through, for example, the Industrial Training Act of 1964, which obliged employers to pay a training levy, with Industrial Training Boards established to coordinate technical education in particular industries.[44] This progress was rolled back in different ways by the actions of successive governments. Thatcher's reforms asserted firm control over university spending and funding that had previously operated almost totally independently, doing away with support for courses which the government felt were of little relevance to the economy they desired.[45] The Conservatives attempted to reduce the control that local authorities – often led by parties other than the Conservatives – had over schools through the introduction of direct central funding.[46] This had little impact at the time but later provided the

17

basis of reforms in the 2010s. Thatcher's government also abolished the majority of the mandatory levy system of Industrial Training Boards and the trade union involvement it entailed, instead leaving such training to employers.[47]

In 1992, under Prime Minister John Major, the Further and Higher Education Act transformed polytechnics, most of which had been established in the 1960s and had a vocational focus, into universities, with a broad academic remit very different to their history and expertise.[48] With Tony Blair aiming to greatly expand university attendance to 50 per cent of young people, beyond any economic requirement for non-vocational academic qualifications, the New Labour government introduced tuition fees of £1,000 in 1998.[49] As with many New Labour reforms, this initial, apparently modest, rolling back of state support opened the door to radical increases. Fees were raised to £3,000 in 2006, and to £9,000 in 2012. This radical approach attempted something of an accounting trick, by displacing national spending onto individual students, even though the resulting debts would likely never be repaid.[50] The failure to fund even the most essential vocational degrees, especially in nursing,[51] resulted in an inability to fill posts without depending on ever-increasing migration.

Today, 'ignorance' is fostered by a failure to provide and fund functioning schools, effective vocational training in general and support for those without family resources to attend higher education. 'Ignorance' is a precursor to a whole host of corrosive problems. Illiteracy effectively excludes the individual from large expanses of mainstream society. It is often trans-generational and precludes engagement with various sectors of the economy. And while illiteracy doesn't necessarily cause crime, it features heavily among those who receive custodial sentences in the

British prison system. As we will see in Chapter 8, we have a system that refuses to tackle this giant.

Disease

'Disease' was addressed urgently by the introduction of the NHS, available free at the point of use to anyone on the basis of need. Its downstream functioning improved in tandem with the upstream mitigation of social determinants, both contributing to improved living standards and life expectancy.[52] The rolling back of progress occurred in distinct periods. Following a relatively modest NHS overspend in its early years, charges for dentures and spectacles were introduced in 1951, which led to the resignation from the government of the NHS's architect, Nye Bevan.[53] Prescription charges for medicines were introduced by the Conservative government the following year.[54]

Conservative governments from 1979 took a different approach by drastically constraining NHS spending increases to an average of just 2.6 per cent per year.[55] Increases more than doubled under New Labour,[56] but this came alongside large increases in the role of private provision. This included expansion of the Private Finance Initiative, which saw new hospitals and other health facilities built and maintained through up-front private investment.[57] The NHS was then required to pay large, often unsustainable and unjustifiable, rent and service fees to the companies that owned the buildings. Since 2010, austerity budgets set by Conservative-led administrations have limited increases to below or around the same level as the last period of Conservative government,[58] while also expanding further the role of private providers[59] and removing bursaries for trainee nurses.[60] As we will see in Chapter 6, the acute assault of the

COVID-19 pandemic and the effects of 15 years of decline in social determinants mean that the NHS now struggles to maintain even core emergency services.[61]

Today, 'disease' is rising rapidly, particularly in the form of socially determined long-term conditions, such as cardiovascular and mental health conditions, resulting in impairment and suffering. The proportion of the UK population with a long-standing impairment is estimated to have risen from 19 per cent in 2011/12 to a record 24 per cent in 2021/22, an increase of 3.9 million people.[62] Indeed, the estimate increased from 14.1 million in 2019/20 to 16 million in 2021/22.[63] The proportion among adults of state pension age remained the same between 2011/12 and 2021/22 at 45 per cent, while for working-age adults it increased from 16 per cent to 23 per cent and for children from 6 per cent to 11 per cent.[64] This suggests that increases in prevalence are not simply the effect of an ageing population. As the government's own 'Levelling Up' report has shown, there is a gap of up to 19 years in life expectancy between those born in different postcodes, and those postcodes are often close to one another.[65] We need policies that address those fundamental material social determinants of wealth, housing, education and employment that shape our health outcomes.

Squalor

'Squalor' was tackled by an enormous process of council house-building,[66] which meant that people could find good-quality, affordable housing against which the private sector had to compete. *Homes for Today and Tomorrow*, published in 1961 and better known as the Parker Morris report, established thorough standards for house-building.[67] Although never mandatory for private developers and only made compulsory for all local authority housing in 1969,[68] this raising of the bar affected the whole sector. The result was the private sector developing its own standards in 1967 and the largest houses, on average, being built in the 1970s.[69]

The Thatcher government's 1980 Housing Act abandoned the Parker Morris standards and facilitated the mass selling off of public housing to tenants at below market value under the Right to Buy scheme.[70] It also made it effectively impossible for local authorities to provide new public housing at scale by heavily constraining (increasingly through subsequent relevant Acts in the 1980s) their ability to reinvest in new public housing the relatively small share of proceeds they did receive.[71] This resulted in both a reduction in the average size of houses and a collapse in public house-building with little compensation through private provision.[72] In addition to this lack of adequate public housing, the feudal system of leasehold homeownership in England and Wales continues to stifle improvements in living conditions, as Conservative Secretary of State for Levelling Up, Housing and Communities Michael Gove has acknowledged.[73]

Today, 'squalor' is a stain on the country, with good housing out of reach of many younger renters and prospective owners.[74] It is the result too of a poorly built housing stock due to a complete failure of vocational training and regulation,[75] and the near absence of the public and social housing sector that previously competed to keep private standards high. Even Richard Blakely, Former Conservative Deputy Mayor of London under Boris Johnson and current Housing Ombudsman, has articulated the need to 're-establish the link between housing and health', claiming that 'The scale of the challenge hasn't been

21

grasped'.[76] Neither the voluntary nor the private sector has proven capable of addressing that challenge.

Squalor is also linked to the degradation of council service provision, leading to everyday incivility and perceptions of disorder. Public cleaning and refuse collection services have been cut back.[77] Long gone are the once free council services that enabled us to dispose of large items of household waste – the mattresses, beds, cabinets and fridges that now litter our landscape.[78] When services that are free at point of use are withdrawn, people find alternatives, such as dumping items in back lanes. Fly-tipping is a national disgrace that stems directly from the rolling back of the state.[79] The broken windows theory suggests that relatively small signs of disorder and squalor – such as a broken window – lead to further, sometimes much more serious, forms of disorder and crime.[80] An overflowing bin leads to dumping of litter around the bin, which leads to a feeling that the area isn't cared about and that graffiti and arson are fair game. A basic understanding of, and commitment to, community wealth, which we set out in Chapter 2, highlights the fundamental need for effective services as the basis for dealing with these social determinants and ensuring that our communities function.

Want

'Want' was rapidly addressed through the introduction of a comprehensive welfare system of unemployment, sickness and family benefits.[81] Coupled with a booming reconstruction-based economy, such systems were so effective that inequality and poverty were at historic lows by the 1960s and remained so for approximately the next 20 years.[82] Because deprivation and inequality are social determinants of physical and mental health,[83] success in addressing 'want' secured a range of other beneficial outcomes for the population. Public support for the welfare state was high. Beveridge predicted this, and it is tragic that so many recent public figures have failed to grasp the basis of health in our country. The re-emergence of want has come from both main parties, though ironically the Conservative government in 1979 regarded a freeze on benefits as too politically toxic.[84] Indeed, much of the rapid increase in inequality and poverty in the 1980s occurred through other mechanisms – for example, large cuts in tax rates for the highest earned and unearned incomes, disproportionate increases in private sector pay for the highest earners, and large-scale lay-offs of more highly paid public sector roles in nationalised industries, leading to mass unemployment.[85]

When New Labour gained power in 1997 after 18 years of Conservative government, it initiated a radical process of benefits reform which set us on the pathway to the present through increasingly stringent and demanding means- and needs-testing.[86] For example, Employment and Support Allowance began to replace Incapacity Benefit in 2008 and was fully underpinned by the new Work Capability Assessment.[87] Even where attempts at redistribution were made, such as through Working Tax Credits, the process was laborious, required significant time investment and high levels of administration, and was unable to respond rapidly to fluctuations in income, meaning that millions did not receive payments they were entitled to or were forced to pay back overpayments at short notice.[88] The underpinning motivation was consistent: an easily accessed, less-conditional system that emphasised entitlement and benefit of the doubt supposedly encouraged fraud, deception, fecklessness and dependence and was unfair to working people.[89] Only a more adversarial approach of claimants being assessed and reassessed could reduce both these social pathologies and the size of the welfare budget.

But this approach initiated by Labour, and the subsequent real-terms cuts in benefit levels driven by the austerity policies of the Conservative-led administrations since 2010, have done nothing to reduce the numbers of people who require government assistance. They have, however, reduced the wellbeing of those in poverty, many of whom are now in work.[90] In 2021/22, 22 per cent of people were in relative poverty after housing costs are taken into account, and the child poverty rate is returning to around a third after a brief dip as a result of the additional state support offered during the COVID-19 pandemic.[91] A failure to support the population during a cost-of-living crisis has resulted in even middle and higher earners experiencing material deprivation. And the welfare system keeps people in poverty, disincentivises activity and fails to support people in work.[92] While food banks represent an incredible civic effort in voluntary action, they ought to be reformed out of existence.[93] As we will see in Chapter 3, there is an obvious alternative way to tackle this giant.

Decline since 2010: the interconnection of the giant evils

Having implemented a decade of austerity in the 2010s, recent Conservative governments have sought to shape policy around a 'prevention agenda' in order to challenge the conceptualisation of the NHS as the 'National Hospital Service'.[94] This has provided renewed focus on the need to achieve better health outcomes by affecting wider social determinants through upstream interventions. This is a recognition that, in effect, the giant evil of disease cannot be tackled independently of the giant evils of want and squalor. However, the policies proposed by these governments have rarely matched the scale of the task. Indeed, on most fronts, they have actively harmed outcomes.

As with Beveridge, only radical policy that captures the mood of the nation can deliver the changes we need.[95] And despite the rhetoric of common sense and pragmatism, the fact is that the two main parties have both engaged in radical policy over the past four decades. Years of rapid progress on the giant evils that had plagued Britain for centuries were undone by intentional policy changes since the late 1970s. This policy process has escalated since the global financial crisis, with the past 13 years of Conservative-led government producing unprecedented shifts in wealth since 2010.[96] Beveridge and his report were the product of a particular era, but the issues he was confronted with are no less relevant today. We may use different words now, but we can ascribe contemporary issues to the giant evils, and we need to understand that the policies that have undone the Beveridge consensus have served only to feed those five giants.

The issues are every bit as urgent and desperate today as they were in 1942. As then, they can be solved only by a comprehensive, ambitious, coherent and common-sense plan. While the moral argument for such a plan is strong, the pragmatic argument is stronger. Just as in that period with Attlee, there is clear need for effective political leadership committed to coalition-building and adopting the best ideas from across the political spectrum. Tinkering around the edges simply will not cut it any longer. George Osborne was fond of saying that he wanted to fix the roof while the sun was shining. Instead, he sold the roof and the tools we needed to fix it, and we now need to rebuild the whole house. As you will see in this report, there is a fully costed, fully funded plan that is available, now, for a government brave enough to follow the course charted by the Labour government of 1945.

Recommendations

Beveridge, Attlee and governments for the three decades that followed them recognised that only comprehensive, broad reforms could deal with the crisis as it then existed. Britain experienced a period of unprecedented growth and success alongside unprecedented low levels of inequality and poverty. To deal with the much greater issues we now face, we must:

1 Accept that we are in a position of crisis as significant as the Second World War
2 Face up to the fundamental condition of ultra-insecurity to which we are all exposed individually and realise that we can only achieve security collectively as a nation
3 Understand that headline economic growth, which is of little relevance to the vast majority of the population, cannot be an excuse for damaging living standards and undermining the collective basis of a good life
4 Be bold in advocating policies that will enable us to live successfully, advance civic action and rebuild our nation
5 Vote for politicians and parties that want to make change

The rest of this report is devoted to putting forward specific, timely, implementable policies that enable us to move forward. They do not belong narrowly to any party or political tradition. They are not ideological or utopian, and they are not like the ideological experiment to which we have been exposed for decades. The policies you will read are just common sense.

CHAPTER 2

WHAT GOVERNMENT SHOULD DO

Chapter in 30 seconds

Since the 1970s, the view has been put forward that the state is inefficient, obstructive or powerless. This view is an ideological smokescreen endorsed by people who recognise the state's power and want to control it for their own interests. In fact, the modern state, appropriately plural and democratically account-able, is a very effective institution, the only kind of institution that can underpin the social order and ensure a fair distribu-tion of resources. Political parties have banked on the idea that growing the size of the gross national product (GDP) will increase wellbeing for everyone, through 'trickle-down', even if inequality grows and communities are destroyed. The unsus-tainability and failure of this idea is evident. The state is having to mitigate an ever larger accumulation of downstream social and health problems that this approach has generated. We out-line five principles against which a reformed state should assess every potential policy: will it increase equality, will it promote freedom from domination, will it tackle the social determinants of ill health, will it build community wealth and will it help to level up places?

Introduction: a fresh start
shaped by fresh principles

The two important political settlements of the past 100 years – those of 1945 and 1979 – were based on contrasting understandings of what role the state ought to play in our lives. Both achieved public support, for a while, in large part because they delivered significant improvements in material conditions for a large proportion of the population. Our new settlement will require another reconfiguration of the state, of similar scale. Only the state, as an institutional expression of public cooperation, has the capacity to address the material basis of our present ultra-insecurity.

We need a new vision of the government's remits and responsibilities and new structures that are responsive yet eliminate the current pervasive forms of corruption and dysfunction. We have to dispense with abstract concepts of economic growth that have little or no bearing on our actual lives. This implies a comprehensively different economic model at odds with existing orthodoxies. Instead, we must focus on the state's role in reducing exposure to risk and providing services that enable us to flourish. Only this degree of innovation can free us from insecurity, indignity and domination and enable us to realise our potential, form families, create businesses, build communities and live good, long lives. At the heart of this settlement is a commitment to equality, something that has been actively dismantled over the last four decades.

In Part II of this report, we will lay out specific policies that should form part of this new settlement. Here, we give the more general principles on which it should be based. These are the following:

29

Principle 1: Equality is at the heart of public policy
Principle 2: The freedom that should be pursued is freedom from domination
Principle 3: Tackle the social determinants of health directly
Principle 4: Build up community wealth
Principle 5: Level up places

Before outlining each of these principles in more detail, we need to say a little more about the state and why it is the only actor that can drive the new settlement.

The role and remit of the state

The modern state is a remarkable institution. There are those who see it as a nineteenth-century relic and have argued either that it will dissolve into continental or global super-federations or that it should be rolled back to the point of invisibility so that the private sector can provide people what with they want. However, reports of its demise have been greatly exaggerated. The UK state controls roughly as large a share of activity now as it did at the beginning of the neoliberal settlement because, as it turns out, we need it. States are actually remarkably good at making changes that impact people's lives, as the example of the rapid levelling of health between former East and former West Germany after reunification shows.[1] Those who think the state just gets in the way should examine quality of life in countries that don't have one, such as Somalia.

Only the state can order and guarantee the just distribution of essential resources and provide the basis for our freedoms. Both its supporters and its detractors understand this. Those who decry the state as evil, corrupt and inefficient nonetheless spend their lives attempting to control it. It is by capturing the state that they acquire privileges and resources: this is exactly how certain individuals and groups have been able to acquire and concentrate destructive and monopolising amounts of wealth over recent decades. Claims that the state is weak and ineffectual, or that extreme wealth comes from merit alone, are ideological window dressing. The most effective and damaging ideological element of the neoliberal settlement has been its ability to persuade workers – that is, the vast bulk of society that needs to work in order to live – that the state cannot promote their interests and is some sort of inefficient anachronism, all while using the power of the state to advance the narrow interests of a small sub-group of society. As the Austrian millionaire Marlene Engelhorn has put it, to 'not redistribute wealth is as much of a distributional decision as to redistribute it'.[2]

Controlling the state is essential to promoting any specific set of interests. Decades of neoliberal reform have not actually rolled back the state – they have only changed who it serves. At present, it enables the concentration of wealth in ever fewer hands, protects that wealth from economic shocks, and facilitates the exploitation of cheap labour at home and overseas. It does not protect the vast majority of us who do not live from wealth, and it does not control the exploitation of finite resources that need to remain unexploited in order for us to avoid human extinction.

The state should be the representative of the people and the embodiment of their social interests. This means that it needs to be responsive to the vast bulk of us: our lives, our needs and the things we value. This is not the case at present: it mainly serves the interests and preferences of capital, particularly financial capital, and the ultra-wealthy.[3] No matter how many equality, diversity and inclusion initiatives are used to market the state differently, this remains the case. As the former Prime Minister Gordon Brown has stated, we need to 'face up to the fact that' our country 'is in the throes of a crisis'.[4] Whenever our society has improved, it has been because the state has represented larger numbers of people across the areas, regions and backgrounds of Britain. It can still do this. To end a decades-long slide towards alienation, we need to grab hold of the state and remake it in our image: plural, devolved, responsive and socially beneficial.

Principle 1: Equality is the basis for the new settlement

Britain's commitment to greater equality has a chequered history. The policies of the 1945 settlement were grounded in a commitment to redistribute from the wealthiest to the vast majority of society. The Great Depression and the Second World War had led to an understanding that improving the interests of the majority could only be achieved by redistributing resources, since unchecked resources accumulate to the better off at a cost to the general good. In time, poverty, inequality and insecurity reduced substantially. In almost all areas of society, outcomes rapidly improved. In the post-war consensus, successive Conservative governments continued to run nationalised industry, to implement tax rates of 98 per cent on passively earned wealth and to sustain institutions that would have been rejected out of hand at any time prior to Beveridge's report. This was because those reforms worked and were popular.

The breakdown of consensus in the 1970s can be attributed to various causes. The most significant was the strain on finances caused by inflation associated with geopolitical conflict among states rich in fossil fuels. Younger people from the baby boomer generation who had grown up with unprecedented social security and opportunity faced their first obstacles to personal development. Having not experienced war or life before 1945, they had expectations around continuous improvements in individual circumstances. These were stifled by inflation in prices and a militant, at times short-termist, approach by trade unions.

Neoliberal policy entrepreneurs such as Milton Friedman and Friedrich Hayek had worked for decades to present the fringe position of rolling back the state and massively reducing taxation as a sensible alternative to the post-war settlement. Those ideas, for which Friedman received the Nobel Prize in Economics in 1976, provided a readymade menu of policies for opposition politicians in the UK and US to present as clean breaks from the malaise. This set the scene, throughout the 1980s, for an increasingly radical Conservative government that privatised the public wealth accumulated over the previous decades, resulting in increased house prices and wages for some groups, but also in wealth inequality and poverty and eventually a decline in public services. Nonetheless, the neoliberal settlement garnered loyal support in those age groups who materially gained most – the baby boomers.

The neoliberal settlement celebrated increased inequality, taking it as evidence of dynamism, freedom and just rewards for activity. To the extent that it had to respond to public concern about the least well-off, it argued that they too would eventually benefit, indirectly via 'trickle-down'. It is surprising how widespread and unquestioned an assumption this has remained. Contemporary policymakers, including both 2022

Conservative Prime Minister Liz Truss and current Labour Shadow Chancellor Rachael Reeves, share the commitment to the primary goal of creating numerical growth, even at the expense of equality. Increased economic activity will 'trickle down' to improve the welfare of those in all subsequent strata.[5] 'The resulting inequality between rich and poor' does 'not matter since the concern of the poor' is 'their absolute position and … inequality' is 'distinct from poverty'.[6]

The neoliberal hypothesis has failed on its own terms. As we note in Chapter 12, rather than accelerating, numerical economic growth has slowed since 1979. The slice going to the less well-off has indeed been getting proportionately smaller, but without the overall pie growing faster. Poverty has in many cases increased.[7] These obvious failures mask deeper philosophical ones. Greater inequality is associated – independently of average gross domestic product (GDP) – with a whole range of worse outcomes in health, education, social order.[8] Rather than freeing the state from responsibility for people's wellbeing, inequality-increasing growth obliges the state to mitigate an ever larger flood of health and social problems, affecting ever more people, at great expense.

Greater inequality also undermines the formal equality, and equality of opportunity, of citizens. This means not only that people have less opportunity to pursue valued freedoms but also that we end up with worse public institutions. As the gaps in material resources become larger, so do disparities in the ability to capture the state and use it for partial benefit, whether through lobbying, political donation, currying state contracts or informal social pressure. Public institutions that are partial – that systematically privilege one set of interests – also become less effective and garner less democratic engagement and support. Great inequality creates distorted power relation-ships between different social groups. And let us not forget that committing to making ever larger pies in order for most people to maintain their standard of living with an ever smaller share is ecologically nonsensical. The myth of infinite growth on a finite planet has contributed to the existential threats we cur-rently face.

In place of maximising growth, or some abstract projection of growth, the state needs to be organised around an equality principle. *Every* policy ought to be informed by a commitment to directly reducing the material basis of inequality. Doing this necessarily reduces the inequalities attached to race, gender and disability, since discrimination on that basis fundamentally intersects with material processes and outcomes. While there have been previous attempts at such a formulation,[9] there has been insufficient understanding of the fundamental processes by which it might be borne out. The equality principle means that wealth from the richest ought to be redistributed to fund transformative policies to improve the material conditions of paid and unpaid workers and those who cannot work, gradu-ally and irreversibly eliminating poverty. This principle is con-sistent with providing adequate material incentives for fulfilling socially valued roles, but not consistent with the levels of wealth inequality we currently see.

The equality principle is the keystone of our other princi-ples. Promoting greater equality also promotes freedom from domination (principle 2). Inequality is the headwater of all the social determinants of health; by taking it on, you gradually and necessarily improve population health and wellbeing (prin-ciple 3). With the resources created by redistribution, you can create community-level wealth, in the form of local services and institutions, and places that are good to live in (principle 4). Finally, a commitment to equality necessarily means levelling up by geography (principle 5).

Principle 2: The freedom that should be pursued is freedom from domination

The arguments for the neoliberal settlement were based partly on the idea of increasing freedom – surely a good thing. Neoliberal intellectuals argued that taxation is coercion, as is monopoly state provision of certain public services. As such, these represent restrictions on freedom. If the state were rolled back, all members of society would be freer than they had previously been.

However, no society accords its members absolute freedom to do as they wish without regard to the consequences for everyone. In practice, we value some freedoms as fundamental to protect. Chief among these is freedom from domination.[10] Domination arises where people have to accede to the wishes of others, through desperation: they cannot say no and cannot walk away. A world of desperate poverty and insecurity is one where people have to accept bad jobs, bad relationships or bad housing because they have no alternative but to starve or freeze. People who are dominated cannot relax their guard; they must always adopt tactics to protect their interests, no matter how demeaning or unnatural those tactics may appear.[11] A world where people are nominally equal before the law but only some people can afford legal fees is not a world of freedom from domination. The practical extent of freedom in society cannot be separated from the degree of material and power inequality, or the level of social and environmental protections.

36

Freedom is not necessarily increased by cutting taxes or 'rolling back red tape'.

A state that promotes freedom as non-domination, then, can legitimately tax people to reduce inequality and poverty, can legitimately restrict certain types of action that imposes domination on others, and can and should provide the sort of social and economic resources we set out in this report. What it cannot do is interfere with people's affairs on an arbitrary basis: there have to be reasons for these state actions. The decision to restrict or oblige citizens must be made within a resilient institutional framework that is impartial, in the sense that everyone's interests are equal, and responsive, in the sense that it reflects processes of public argumentation and debate. Just as every policy needs to be measured against its ability to promote material equality, every policy needs to be confronted with the question: does this free more people from potential domination?

Principle 3: Tackle the social determinants of health directly

The neoliberal gambit was that people would be better off if the state got out of, or at least reduced its role in, setting the distribution of income and wealth. As a result of the dynamism this would unleash, they would have fewer problems and the demand for state services would melt away. This has not turned out to be the case. High rates of non-communicable disease, obesity, anxiety, depression, addiction and despair cause problems that society has to address, and the state ends up highly occupied with these. Ironically, the state has ended up ever more heavily involved in the lives of many people: dealing with drug addiction and controlling the narcotics business,

37

providing cognitive behavioural therapy, spending more and more on a healthcare system that has to deal with massive rates of non-communicable disease, providing benefits to people too depressed and anxious to work. We can see all of these outcomes as downstream consequences of the material inequality of society.

We would like the state to be rolled back in many of these areas. But that is only going to be possible if the problems are addressed upstream, closer to the source. This source resides in what have become known as the social determinants of health. This refers to the set of social or political factors that have been shown to predict morbidity and mortality, including poverty, inequality, food insecurity, access to housing and transport, employment conditions, legal support, and protection from violence.[12] We would add the availability of cultural opportunities, green space and municipal facilities.

Government is, reluctantly, beginning to understand this imperative. The UK government's Prevention Agenda is intended to shift understanding of the NHS away from the 'National Hospital Service'.[13] It is aimed specifically at reducing, rather than just treating, early morbidity and mortality. But it has yet to advance substantive policy measures to that end, beyond the Soft Drinks Industry Levy,[14] a limited and indirect intervention via taxation on business.

Either the government fails to understand the material basis of health, wellbeing and prosociality – behaviours that are intended to benefit others – or radical policy implications are too unpalatable for the people who fund political parties. Perhaps there is a fear that people's material needs are limitless, and so taking any responsibility for them represents the opening up of a claim that can never be fulfilled. But this is not so: humans share a common set of basic needs, and we intuitively understand which ones are basic and which are not. Our current system tacitly recognises this, providing personal tax allowances and conditional welfare benefits. We just need to be bolder. We need stronger policies that do not just catch people when they fall but hold people back from falling, such as those proposed in Chapter 3. These policies will pay for themselves because of their desirable downstream effects.

Ironically, the intellectual forebears of the neoliberal settlement were perfectly happy with the idea that the government should provide enough to assure good health and avoid domination. For Hayek,[15]

> There is no reason why in a society that has reached the general level of wealth which ours has attained, the first kind of security should not be guaranteed to all without endangering general freedom ... [T]here can be no doubt that some minimum of food, shelter, and clothing, sufficient to preserve health and the capacity to work, can be assured to everybody.

Rather than pursuing an abstract statistic of financial growth such as GDP and hoping in an ill-defined way that this has collateral good effects on health and wellbeing, policies need to be evaluated directly against their effects on the social determinants of health.

Principle 4: Build up community wealth

Policymakers pay sporadic lip service to the importance of community, but meanwhile communities decline as living entities and social practices. David Cameron's Big Society policy, for example, attempted to delegate responsibility for the bulk of social goods to communities without providing them with the means or powers to succeed. As austerity measures reduced service provision and employment, welfare freezes and increased conditionality reduced purchasing power in many of our most vulnerable communities. Most of these communities had had welfare provision forcefully substituted for industrial activity during the 1970s and 1980s, and they have now seen their local authorities starved of resources and stripped of decision-making latitude.

Communities need to be able to build up not just capacity to make everyday life better but genuine community assets. This is a particular priority for those communities outside London, the home counties and the largest city centres that have come to be described as 'left behind'. These communities have been increasingly dominated by chain supermarkets, fast food and franchise betting outlets, and pubs. Each of these entities has national and international procurement policies and centralises profits, meaning that, aside from wages, very little wealth is retained locally. This had the effect of local economies resembling impoverished monocultures, bereft of the rich diversity capable of keeping and nurturing people and skills where they are needed and wanted. The brain drain of young people drifting away from their loved ones to lives of precarious employment and multiple occupancy in metropolitan centres is tragic and represents a callous rupturing of families and social networks. It also reflects the necessarily inefficient and damaging contribution that our economy makes to climate change by dismissing local investment.

In our left-behind communities, the state remains the most important source of economic stimulus through limited public sector employment, health and educational services, and welfare payments. Thus, the state can lead the way in building up community wealth. The 'Preston Model' provides a precedent for how this could work.[16] Under the Preston Model, local government bodies plus educational and health institutions were identified as anchor institutions, meaning they were responsible for a large share of local spending. Yet they were spending most of this with national companies outside the region, and moreover were holding assets that were providing no benefit to the community. Over a decade, these institutions changed their procurement to make it easy for smaller local enterprises to compete. They encouraged the formation of social enterprises and cooperatives, including local pension schemes and mutual financial institutions. They improved the jobs they provided, encouraged the widest possible use of the assets they held, and in some cases democratised the ownership and control of those resources.

While the Preston Model is not a panacea – many issues can be addressed only through the intervention of national government – it does illustrate how community wealth can be built without inward investment from outside, in ways other than through GDP growth. Many other local authorities are now committed to community wealth-building.

Community wealth-building requires devolution to and rejuvenation of local government of the sort we outline in Chapter 12. It requires reversing the decades-long orthodoxy of the favoured method of procuring public services being outsourcing to large national or international corporations. That outsourcing has often not produced value for money or greater efficiency, even narrowly defined. It is certainly not optimal from the point of view of community wellbeing. Concern for fair employment and just labour markets almost inevitably means that cleaning, catering and support services in schools, hospitals

41

and leisure facilities are better provided through secure, public sector employment than by the private sector. As we will see in Chapter 9, activities of house-building, management and maintenance are productively managed by councils and local cooperatives. Building up community wealth ought to underpin all public sector activity and reform of governance.

Principle 5: Level up places

Just as inequality between individuals has grown, inequality between places has grown. These are both aspects of the same process. Inequality between individuals becomes greater because those who already have wealth are better able to make their influence felt on subsequent decisions, and because financial assets have been allowed to grow faster than productive activity. Inequality between places grows because regions and sectors that are producing income for government are able to attract more infrastructure investment. In both cases, the solution is the same. The government needs to act as a fair arbiter, and in many cases an active redistributor, as much between places as between people. This is a direct consequence of principle 1, and it is to everyone's advantage in the long term.

Devolution of power is related to levelling up but not identical to it. Devolution to UK nations and regions is important because it serves community wealth-building and ensures the responsiveness of the local state to people's needs. Competition between devolved entities, such as that following devolution in Scotland and Wales, can be beneficial as regions seek to provide outcomes in security and liveability that are as good as those available elsewhere in the UK. But the fundamental concern shared by most citizens lies not in process but in outcome. All government policies should be assessed against their ability to reduce the gaps in employment, infrastructure, cultural opportunities and healthy life expectancy between the different places in the UK.

As for the importance of prevention rather than treatment for ill health, the UK government has belatedly, under Boris Johnson in particular, endorsed the importance of levelling up. However, the actual policies – local authorities competing for limited amounts of discretionary funding that are distributed in ways that resemble the notorious 'pork barrel politics' of the US – come nowhere near the scope and scale of what is required.

Conclusion

In Part II, we will set out the policies recommended by this report. In this chapter, we have sketched the design principles that underlie them. The new settlement they add up to recognises that we are socially interdependent, we need to be sufficiently equal, and we need to be free from domination. Solidarity, equality and non-domination are three core values and outcomes without which institutions will always be deficient. Solidarity ensures that we recognise interdependence and the effect that we have on one another. Equality ensures that we uphold the basis for healthy relationships. Non-domination ensures that our interdependence is not abused and that we can pursue our interests without fear of arbitrary interference. These are simultaneously values, goods and outcomes, and they point us towards a very clear account of what government should do for us.[17] The settlement we suggest is a radical departure from the recent past.

While the issues humans face share consistent features globally, and while solutions are likely to have universal implications, Part II will focus directly on developing a programme of domestic policy specifically to rebuild the UK. In doing this, we will draw comparatively on examples of successful innovation from elsewhere, as well as presenting innovative proposals that are uniquely tailored to the UK, as Beveridge did in 1942. Throughout, we will focus on demonstrating clear impacts on people's everyday lives, emphasising that the reasons for obstacles and challenges are ideological: that things can and should be different.

Recommendations

There is a compelling and overwhelming body of evidence that certain policy programmes are better than others, and that the better ones are grounded in concern for a cluster of principles. Policymakers need to scrutinise every policy against five key principles:

1 Will it increase equality?
2 Will it promote freedom from domination?
3 Will it tackle the social determinants of health?
4 Will it build community wealth?
5 Will it level up places?

These are fundamental questions that can be applied easily. It is the duty of government, as the embodiment of the social interest, to apply them in every case.

PART II

THE POLICIES

CHAPTER 3

A SOCIAL SAFETY NET

Chapter in 30 seconds

The government should introduce a basic income for all per-manent UK residents, initially set at £75 per week for over 18s, with £50 for each child. This starter scheme requires only mod-est tax changes and no increase in government borrowing, yet it will have a dramatic effect on poverty and a host of other advantages. There is a strong argument for increasing the basic income over time, to the point where it becomes the main plank of our social safety net. Achieving this longer-term project will require larger changes to taxation, and we return to this below. The arguments for the starter scheme are compelling, and it can be introduced immediately, with a longer-term pathway providing us with the social security we need via more generous levels of basic income payments. This represents a sea change in the way we are protected from wholly avoidable risks and enables us to take the sort of action we need to take to rebuild our society.

Introduction: basic income as the best
way to provide social security

A basic income is a regular – we suggest weekly – payment made by the government to all citizens. Its important features, compared with more familiar allowances and benefits, are that it is *universal*: with very few exceptions, everyone will receive it; it is *unconditional*: you don't have to lose your job to get it, or go on training schemes, or show that your earnings fall below a certain level; Aad it is *individual*: a husband cannot receive it for his wife, and a landlord cannot receive it for their tenant. A basic income is the most efficient way for the government to reduce poverty and insecurity, improve people's freedom, and allow them to take a fuller part in society. A starter basic income breaks the ground.

You might be wondering why the government should give people money with no strings attached, and indeed whether it can afford to do so. The answer to the second question is yes, as we will show. The answer to the first question is that the government should, and already does, transfer a lot of money to certain groups of people. Basic income is just a more efficient and effective way of achieving the goals of redistribution and social security that lie behind those transfers.

In all industrialised societies, the state provides a social safety net. In fact, social safety nets of one kind or another date back way beyond the Industrial Revolution; they are a deep feature of what it means to live in a society. Members of a society recognise that there are grave risks – destitution, hunger, homelessness – against which they should come together to insure themselves. For over a hundred years, in the UK as in other countries, we have centralised this function in the national government, to ensure a system that is uniform and impartial.

Social safety nets enjoy broad public support. Some people support them because they think providing protection from the worst storms that life can throw up is part of our basic moral duty towards our peers. Some see it as enlightened self-interest: if our peers are not starving or desperate (and are assured that they cannot become so), they are more likely to obey the law, contribute productively to the economy, be healthy, take part in community life, and buy products and services from us, and that makes us all better off, so everyone has a direct stake in making sure that everyone else is at least minimally protected.

In market-based economies like ours, social transfers are made on several basic grounds. Sometimes people are unable to gain enough money to live on due to the vagaries of the labour market: either they are underemployed or their jobs do not pay enough to live on. Sometimes people are unable to gain a living due to ill health. Some people are too young to gain a living, and their living costs fall onto their families. Finally, people are entitled to live out their later years in retirement. Our existing system is a complex patchwork of sometimes overlapping schemes designed to capture these different cases.

Broadly speaking, there are two ways of targeting social transfers on the groups we wish to support. Let us call these *absent by default* and *present by default*. In an absent-by-default scheme, the transfer is not made unless the person applies, and succeeds in demonstrating their eligibility. For example, they might need to show that they don't have enough money to live on, or that they are sick. In a present-by-default scheme, the transfer is made to everyone, and we use the tax system to claw it back (and more) from the people who are not currently in need. Our existing system is mostly absent by default. Basic income is a present-by-default system, which is the source of its main advantages.

Absent-by-default schemes have several drawbacks. From the administrative side, you need an army of assessors and officers to examine people's applications and try to keep track of their changing circumstances. But this is hard: how can you tell how much need someone is in, or how sick they are? It means the state getting intrusively involved in people's personal lives and making judgements that are exceedingly difficult to make. From the user side, demonstrating eligibility is difficult and often humiliating.

Even in terms of what they set out to achieve, absent-by-default systems fail. The point of the social safety net is to provide *security* and *certainty*. These are the things that people in adversity most need, and which help them to make good decisions in life. Yet our current system provides only insecurity, because rulings on eligibility can change at any time, and uncertainty, because applicants don't know if their application is going to succeed or be knocked back, or even when a decision will be made. The insecurity and uncertainty of the current benefits system make the welfare of claimants, by definition already hard pressed, worse.[1] And in an absent-by-default system, even when support is approved, it comes through only retrospectively, after a delay while the application is assessed. By this time, the person's circumstances could have changed again, or they could have got into an even worse predicament of homelessness or debt, which will cost even more to sort out.

The other great drawback of absent-by-default systems is that they always generate perverse incentives. If you have to demonstrate unemployment in order to continue to qualify, then you have an incentive *not* to take some part-time work. If you have to demonstrate poverty, you have an incentive never to build up savings. And if you have to demonstrate ill health, you have an incentive to remain sick. It is extremely hard to

50

avoid these perverse incentives in an absent-by-default system, and our current patchwork of benefits is full of them.

How, then, have we ended up with so much absence by default in the system, when it has such obvious drawbacks? The great architect of our current welfare system, Sir William Beveridge, was aware of the drawbacks.[2] He favoured presence by default for child benefit and for pensions, and this has largely been maintained. He was against means testing, for some of the reasons described above, but more means testing has crept into the UK system over the decades. He did, however, make more use of absence by default than a basic income scheme would. This was because the situation we faced 80 years ago was so different from the one we face now.

Seventy years ago, people of working age tended to have single, stable jobs that paid them the same wage over time, and this wage was sufficient for their families to live on. The two circumstances in which they needed the social safety net were cyclical unemployment and inability to work due to illness or accident. These circumstances were rare, exceptional and easy to detect: it is easy to see if a factory has been shut down or someone has broken a leg in an industrial accident. Even then, initiatives such as the Emergency Medical Hospitals during the Second World War provided radical, preventative healthcare and social security to the workforce because policymakers recognised that prevention was better than cure.[3]

By contrast, today, many people are involved in multiple concurrent or consecutive economic activities. The income from these fluctuates wildly and unpredictably, as in the gig economy or zero-hours contracts. It is often insufficient to live on: 61 per cent of working-age adults in poverty in the UK today live in a household where at least one person is in paid employment.[4]

The situations of need that Beveridge's systems were designed to respond to were rare and exceptional. In the UK today, need is frequent, can crop up anywhere, and waxes and wanes over time. An absent-by-default system cannot keep up with, or even assess, situations like this in any kind of reasonable or efficient way. Perverse incentives also loom large, as people avoid taking on more hours or activities so as not to trigger withdrawal of benefits. This is the current situation; it will get worse in the future, as industry, climate and technology continue to change.

Essentially, our lives have become insecure and unstable in ways that Beveridge could never have predicted. This insecurity and instability will only increase. Our current welfare system has been continuously patched up to try to keep up. This increases its administrative complexity over time; and the patches, in addressing one problem, often introduce another one elsewhere. We cannot keep going like this: no amount of patching is going to be sufficient. A basic income is a bold and comprehensive tactic to tackle that uncertainty head on. Basic income offers a path to reclaiming stability.

Basic income is targeted

You might still be stuck on the fact that basic income will go to doctors and lawyers as well as delivery riders. Surely it would be cheaper, as well as more morally right, to not give it to the people who don't need it?

This is a misunderstanding. Doctors and lawyers will receive their basic income, but they will more than pay it back in income tax. The reasons for doing it in this slightly roundabout way – giving to everyone and then taking it back from all those who don't need it – are the mirror image of the drawbacks of absent-by-default schemes described above. The state does not need to directly assess need (only liability for tax, an assessment it makes anyway); there are no perverse incentives; and assistance is there the moment someone needs it, instead of maybe there (or not) after a lengthy and stressful assessment process.

When we consider how well a basic income is targeted to those in need, we need to consider the net effect of the basic income received minus the income tax paid. Once you make that calculation then, combined with a progressive tax system, the impact of basic income is extremely well targeted at those with the lowest incomes (see Figure 1 for the case of our starter

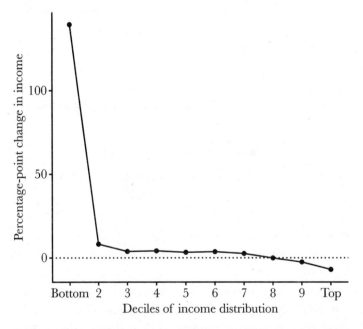

Figure 1 Effects of the introduction of the starter basic income scheme on the incomes of households in different income deciles in the UK (percentage-point change on the status quo).[5]

scheme). Because it is not suddenly withdrawn at any threshold, it is also fairly good for the 'squeezed middle' – those who are struggling to get by but earn a bit too much to be eligible for current forms of welfare assistance. And the richest in society are indeed net payers-in.

Seventy-five pounds does not seem like very much, but the starter scheme would have a dramatic short-term impact on poverty. Using the conventional definition of poverty as receiving 60 per cent or less of the median income, the proportion of working-age adults in poverty would fall by 23 per cent, and the proportion of children by 54 per cent.[6] The wellbeing impact would be larger than these figures imply, because people would have the predictability of a regular amount coming in each week that they would know would always be there. The long-run distributional consequences could be even more positive, as certainty and lack of perverse incentives allow people towards the lower end of the income distribution to be more active and become more productive.

Basic income is affordable

The starter basic income scheme for everyone would cost £274 billion a year. This is a large sum, but there will be large immediate savings. Notably, the state already makes a large present-by-default transfer to working people: the personal income tax allowance. The state opts not to take income tax off people's first £12,570 of earnings, recognising the importance of people first having enough to meet basic needs. This costs £91 billion a year. But it is a bad way of recognising the need, because richer people benefit more than poorer people: if you earn less than £12,570, you don't benefit from the allowance, and if you are a higher-rate taxpayer, you benefit more.

Our starter scheme is a more progressive way of funding basic needs, and so we would reduce the personal allowance to £750 a year. This would save almost all of the £91 billion, a third of the total cost of the basic income. In addition, our starter scheme would save tens of billions on the benefits bill, because other benefits would be reduced correspondingly.[7]

Personal income tax rates would all rise by 3p (to 23p basic, 43p higher, 48p additional), though large numbers of basic-rate taxpayers would immediately benefit from the conversion of the personal tax allowance into a cash transfer. Even after these changes, UK tax rates would be well within their historical range, and within that of other European countries. There would be no need for increased government borrowing or novel sources of revenue.

And these calculations are based on everything carrying on as before, whereas the whole point is that things would not carry on as before. Because of the lack of perverse incentives, and because they could use their basic income to support training or to change sectors, many people would become more active and productive. A strong case can be made that the increased security would reduce mental and physical illness.[8] At present this is a huge cost to society, as well as to individual sufferers: 5.8 million people currently receive one of the benefits related to disability and ill health, with mental illness the largest contributor to this total.[9]

The longer-term prospect

Our starter basic income scheme would reduce poverty immediately, but it would not be enough to eliminate it or guarantee universal freedom from want. It is thus just a first step.

We live in an affluent society. In an affluent society, people should be free from the fear of not being able to meet their basic needs. Such freedom would have many advantages. When people's basic needs are guaranteed, they are freer to lead the lives they value; to spend time creating, innovating and caring; and to participate constructively in political and community life.[10] There is simply no evidence that basic income would lead to idleness: it is the current conditional system that creates perverse incentives for inactivity.[11] Crimes of desperation would be greatly reduced.[12] So, plausibly, would stress-related mental illness and the cynicism and destructiveness that goes with frustration and insecurity.

This is a long-term project, but it is not a pipe dream and there are already pilots in Wales and England, alongside a Scottish government commitment to reducing conditionality. Gradually increasing the basic income to around £295 per adult per week would essentially abolish poverty (as defined by household income of less than 60 per cent of the median), and guarantee everyone a Minimum Income Standard (MIS) – a sufficiently high floor to stand on.[13] Conditional benefits could be largely withdrawn, simplifying the state and making savings elsewhere.

The benefits from improved health and dynamism are difficult to estimate but plausibly large. Contrary to some fears, evidence shows that people would not withdraw from work and simply live on their basic incomes.[14] In fact, the quality and productivity of labour would increase, as people would have the freedom to seek more training and move to work they cared about. Employers would have to make jobs better in order to attract people who had more options. Nor is there any evidence that the greatly reduced inequality would stifle economic innovation; on the contrary, the evidence tends to point the other way.[15]

To fund a full basic income like this from income tax alone would require a basic rate of the order of 65 per cent: high, but again, everyone would be starting from a better position. But as we will see in Chapter 12, there is a compelling and popular case for funding policies through wealth taxes, along with increasing taxes on corporate profits, removing amoral tax reliefs and introducing carbon taxes to incentivise reduced emissions.

Taxes on wealth are particularly attractive because capital has tended to grow faster than incomes over recent decades.[16] That is, private fortunes have grown faster than the revenues of an average household; indeed, it is capital accumulation that has captured much of the numerical 'growth' in economic activity. Since private fortunes are concentrated in few hands, this has meant a stagnation or even decline in liveability for most people even as the country has become nominally better off.[17] Taxes of stocks of wealth are popular, relatively simple and, if properly administered, hard for people to evade.[18]

The aspiration is to move incrementally from the starter scheme to one that bring all citizens up to around the level of the UK state pension within the space of a single five-year parliament, and then to the MIS within the next five-year period.[19] These changes will not threaten the support given to people with additional needs. In each of the formulations, forms of disability benefit will remain, but conditionality will largely be eliminated in moving from the starter to the intermediary scheme.[20] As we suggest in Chapter 9, we will phase out housing benefit as social housing stocks increase. This means that people with additional needs are protected and will be supported in a co-produced programme of assessment to ensure adequate service and monetary support (see Table 1).

Table 1 Basic income payments under the starter scheme, the intermediate scheme, and the full Minimum Income Standard.

Scheme	Starter		Intermediate		Full MIS	
Period	Week	Year	Week	Year	Week	Year
Under 18	£50	£2,600	£75	£3,900	£100	£5,200
Single adult under 65	£75	£3,900	£185	£9,620	£295	£15,340
Single adult aged 65+	£205	£10,660	£205	£10,660	£295	£15,340
Couple under 65	£150	£7,800	£370	£19,240	£590	£30,680
Couple + one child	£200	£10,400	£445	£23,140	£690	£35,880
Couple + two children	£250	£13,000	£520	£27,040	£790	£41,080

Basic income as a keystone policy

A sufficiently generous basic income scheme would directly realise Sir William Beveridge's central ambition for society: freedom from want. By itself, it does not solve all our problems. Material want is not the only source of misery. Basic income does not make our air cleaner or our parks and hospitals better. It does not make workplaces more democratic or our governance fairer or more representative. Many other policies are needed – policies we will discuss in the rest of the book. But basic income is a keystone: it unlocks the path to improving society in these other ways too.

A great deal of government activity, and of the activity of voluntary organisations, is essentially mopping up a mess that has already been made. Means-tested benefits try to mop up poverty; intensive psychotherapy tries to mop up stress; the criminal justice system mops up crime and incivility; hospitals mop up the sickness brought on by long-term deprivation; food banks mop up hunger. With basic income, we will be intervening upstream, vastly reducing all of these problems and simplifying the solutions. Government and community organisations would have the resources and bandwidth to concentrate on other good things.

Basic income also potentially changes power relations, which relates to the non-domination principle of Chapter 2. People on lower incomes have to accept bad jobs and stay in bad relationships. They can't always pursue the things they value and have reason to believe they could be good at. The uncertainty and difficulty of making ends meet understandably dominate their priorities and choices. Freed from want by a basic income, they will be able to participate more fully – and more equally – in the civic and political life of our communities. This will also transform workplaces: if workers have the added power to walk away from demeaning work, employers have to make the jobs better in order for the work to be done. Basic income is the single biggest tool of workers' empowerment since the rise of unions – indeed, it makes the work of unions, and of organising in general, exponentially more straightforward.

What basic income means for our communities: the case of Jarrow

Jarrow, on the southern bank of the Tyne, is famous for shipbuilding and for the Jarrow March of 1936. It has always been associated both with abject neglect by Westminster and with pioneering social policy. Since the global financial crisis, the need for genuine social security in Jarrow has become ever more evident. Young people are faced with the choice of staying in their communities but with few prospects of achieving the lives they wish to lead in family, work and education, or leaving for lives in London and Manchester, miles from their families and with few guarantees that greater wages will translate into mortgages and the ability to raise children. Communities like Jarrow are rife with diseases of despair that are wholly avoidable and wantonly inflicted on citizens.[21] People have a sense that something must change.

Through several years of engagement,[22] we have mapped out what community members think basic income would do for Jarrow.[23] As long as it is introduced gradually to avoid economic shocks and bingeing,[24] people there believe that basic income could transform lives. It would give young people the secure foundation to develop skills and, crucially, take essential risks in creating the small and medium-sized enterprises that the people of Jarrow desperately need. It is businesses such as this, with assets that remain in the community, which will serve to rebuild the economy from the ground up, complementing the wealth-building activities of an ambitious local authority. Having proper social security will give residents the ability to invest in the long term, engaging in health-promoting behaviour, getting outside, becoming active and contributing to shared activities of importance to the community.[25]

It is this 'prosocial' impact that is, perhaps, overlooked most in discussion of basic income – the phenomenon of people receiving individual benefits coming together to achieve collective ends in ways that are stunted by the current welfare regime. A Jarrow with basic income will be better placed to achieve the promised outcomes of Big Society – people taking responsibility for shared living space precisely because they have the security of resource to do it. It is not a matter of state action crowding out community initiative. Quite the contrary: social security helps us to achieve Big Society.

Basic income is popular

It has become commonplace to say there is no public appetite for raising taxes and increasing spending on schemes that help those in and out of work who are on lower incomes. This is false, and it is important to understand why it continues to be said. Across many developed countries, including the UK, and across decades, most people have wanted the government to spend more on the provision of social welfare than it actually does.[26] This poses the question: if democracy is government that responds to the will of the people, and most people want more welfare spending, how come we don't get it?

The answer is clear. We live in very imperfect democracies. The most affluent people in society, who would be the net payers-in, are more opposed to welfare spending than the typical citizen. This also tends to be true of organised business lobbies. But these groups have an outsized influence on government policy, in the UK as elsewhere. We can tell this because the views of the affluent minority and business groups are a better predictor of which policies government adopts than the views of the majority voters are.[27]

The views of the great bulk of people have almost no impact on the direction of policy: if they did, we would not have the levels of poverty and public services that we have, and people would probably be less disillusioned about liberal democracy to boot. When we hear that there is little appetite for improving welfare by raising tax if necessary, what this really means is that there is little appetite among the wealthiest 1 per cent and organised business groups. These groups own a lot of newspapers and have the ear of political parties. It does not mean there is little appetite among the population at large.

We've conducted extensive research on support for basic income across the UK and in bellwether electoral constituencies in the North and Midlands of England and in Wales.[28] Large majorities of people are in favour of introducing basic income, and of doing more to alleviate poverty in the UK more generally. Moreover, they are quite happy with the idea that more tax will have to be paid.

More recently, in a sample of 800 UK adults, we explored the trade-off between wanting taxes as low as possible and wanting to see poverty reduced.[29] People didn't want taxes to be higher than necessary. On the other hand, they would trade increases in income tax for reductions in poverty. Conservative and Labour voters did not differ as much as you might expect: both would make the trade. For both groups, there was a zone of acceptable policy featuring large income tax increases, as long as poverty was also substantially reduced. The zones for the two groups overlapped (Figure 2). Our starter basic income scheme falls into that overlap zone: it is therefore a policy that can appeal to everyone. In fact, the bulk of the public would want to see us go further.

If you think that basic income is a good idea, then you agree with the vast majority of the UK population. In our survey, we found an average level of support for the policy of 71.4 per cent in the Red Wall, with 61.6 among Conservative and 79.9 per cent among Labour 2019 voters. Nationally, approval was 69.2 per cent, with 55.9 among those intending to vote Conservative, 74.7 per cent among those intending to vote Labour and 65 per cent among those who don't know who they will vote for at present.

The arguments that are most persuasive differ between the two groups. In the Red Wall, 78.3 per cent of voters found an argument based on security most compelling:

Basic income is a living pension for all adult citizens, providing state support for your basic needs. It would be a safety net during short periods of unemployment, giving you some time to support yourself and your family while looking for employment. This helps to stop you slipping into poverty and ensures that you do not face homelessness. As many infamous cases have shown, this is vital for us, as the current system does not keep us secure. There was the case of the diabetic British war veteran whose Universal Credit payment lapsed, leaving him with no money to top up his electricity meter. This meant that he could not keep his medicine refrigerated, meaning that he

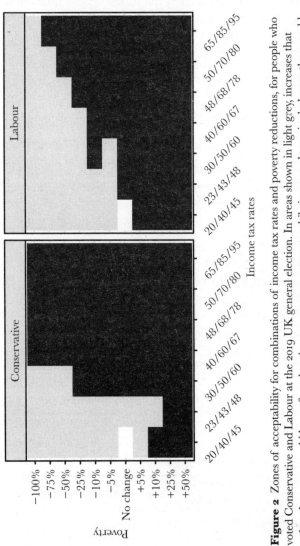

Figure 2 Zones of acceptability for combinations of income tax rates and poverty reductions, for people who voted Conservative and Labour at the 2019 UK general election. In areas shown in light grey, increases that reduced poverty would be preferred to the status quo on average, while in areas shown in dark grey they would not. The status quo is shown in white. The horizontal axis shows combinations of income tax rates (basic/higher/additional).[30]

went into a diabetic coma and died. In our country, you should not have the stress of worrying about meeting your basic needs. You should not have to worry that taking on short-term work will leave you unable to support yourself. [Basic income] secures you from the many unpredictable events in modern society.

Nationally, an argument grounded on absolute gains for the whole country received 75 per cent approval:

The UK welfare system is long overdue for reform. Universal Credit was supposed to replace previous complicated schemes, but has been extremely inefficient. Claiming it requires you to fill in various complicated forms. It takes weeks to receive the first payment and is withdrawn too quickly when people start to earn small amounts of money. This means they stop your benefits when you need them again quite quickly. That puts your entire life on hold, leaving you to rely on Wonga for cash-flow. Basic income guarantees everyone weekly income when you don't earn without fear of it being cancelled when you do. Paying everyone regardless of work status, age and amount of savings may at first seem extravagant and wasteful. However, the cost of administering means-tested schemes far exceeds any payments to those who would be ineligible at present. In 2020/21, there was an estimated loss to the nation of £7.6 billion from fraud or error. Basic income eradicates this and leads to a slimmer, simpler state for us all to navigate.

These are arguments that recur throughout citizen engagement on this policy.[31] Basic income is the clearest multi-purpose policy means of securing the bases of people's lives, and our fellow citizens recognise this across Britain.

Recommendations

This chapter has laid out the case for a single keystone policy of basic income. The starter basic income scheme could be introduced immediately with only modest tax changes and no increase in government borrowing. In time, the basic income should be increased towards a full Minimum Income Standard.

1   Introduce a basic income starter scheme immediately
2   Move towards a basic income payment of around £185 per week within five years, which would remove some conditional benefits
3   Move towards a full Minimum Income Standard basic income scheme of around £295 per week within 10 years, which would remove most conditional benefits, such as housing benefit to private tenants

CHAPTER 4

A GREEN NEW DEAL

Chapter in 30 seconds

Our society needs to transition to a more sustainable mode: lower carbon emissions, less air and water pollution, more liveable cities and regeneration of nature. To achieve these goals requires a linked set of reforms that touch every area of policy discussed in this book. Government investment needs to be reorganised, with improving sustainability as a central criterion. Private investment in green projects must be leveraged through tax incentives. New oil and gas licences must end, with a quadruple lock for workers whose industries are affected. The government needs to invest a minimum of £28 billion annually in decarbonising and expanding the energy supply and reducing energy expenditure and emissions. Progressively higher standards are needed to protect our air and water and make sure developments are planned around walking, cycling and public transport. To facilitate this, social control over energy, water and transport networks needs to be reasserted and devolved to community level, in line with the community wealth principle. Public investment in the countryside needs to be directed to regenerating nature rather than intensifying production, and community nature regeneration projects should be encouraged. Large areas of our seas need to be set aside for nature. These are not issues affecting only other species – we humans cannot survive without these measures.

Introduction: the need for a transition to sustainability

In terms of the global system that sustains us, we are passing tipping points on a near daily basis. The climate receives much attention, but we are also facing the destruction of nature and near ecological collapse. It has often been said that the climate crisis is coming. This is a misstep: the climate crisis is here and has been for a long time. We are already seeing it around the world, and across the UK in our communities. The people who have done the least to cause the climate crisis are often those who face the worst impacts and are the least resilient. In 2023 alone, we have seen wildfires and floods where often the people least likely to be insured or to have the option to move, and most likely to be discriminated against by emergency responders, are global-majority and working-class communities.

We need, urgently, to transition to a greener and more sustainable way of life. This means reducing carbon emissions to the point of net zero, but also fostering cleaner air and water, making our cities more liveable, reversing the decline in wildlife and biodiversity, having healthier food, and allowing the countryside and seas to regenerate.

The reasons we need this transition are so evident at this point that we will not rehearse them here. What we want to stress is that in the long term, there is no fundamental trade-off between greenness and individual wellbeing. People live better where they can move around their communities without the need for cars, where their homes are well insulated, where their air is less polluted, where they have efficient public transport and where they have access to nature. The jobs they could have in green industries could be better paid and more fulfilling than those they might have in the oil and gas industries. And, if we fail to make the transition, then our future wellbeing will be unimaginably worse than that of the present.

Though there is no long-term trade-off between wellbeing and sustainability, moving to sustainability does nonetheless require very deep change. Such deep change will be unsettling to some, and some groups will be at risk of losing out in the immediate term. Some of these groups are powerful corporations, who will lobby hard to resist change but must in the end be stood up to for the greater social good. Others, however, are ordinary workers and families, and the disruption and loss from the transition must be mitigated if we are to bring everyone with us. The equality principle advanced in Chapter 2 must apply to the sustainability transition. This is something only government can do. In the long term, everyone, without exception, will be better off from making a transition to greater sustainability.

What is the Green New Deal?

The goal state for the sustainability transition is one where:

- The country's carbon emissions have reached net zero, through a combination of:
  - a total decarbonisation and expansion of the energy supply, with generation moved to non-fossil-fuel-based alternatives

- ○ a substantial reduction in energy use by homes, public institutions, agriculture, transportation and workplaces
- Biodiversity is allowed to regenerate, through rewilding and deintensification of parts of the countryside
- Pollution of our air, water and land by transport emissions, sewage and pesticides is greatly reduced
- Less waste is created and released into our environment

Making this transition is a society-wide challenge that requires solutions on the scale of the 1933–38 New Deal that reconstructed the United States after the Great Depression. This is why the programme required to take it on has come to be known as the Green New Deal. Like the original New Deal, the reforms required touch every institution of government and the economy, every sector from finance to agriculture, every policy from housing to transport. In short, the Green New Deal is a remobilisation of society's resources and energies towards rather different goals than those that have been pursued in recent decades. The need to do this is widely recognised, although in some quarters more enthusiastically than in others. The time has come, though, to stop nodding at the Green New Deal and start making it happen.

New electricity generation, better insulated homes and new transport links all cost money. However, the Green New Deal requires no more money than the government and the private sector already spend. It merely requires that the investment be redirected. For example, it means diverting public expenditure from building unnecessary new trunk roads to making Total Transport Networks of the sort we outline in Chapter 10, and from subsidies for intensive agriculture to support for natural regeneration; and diverting private investment from extractive industries to constructive ones in forms such as that in Chapter 5, and from speculation to improving the housing stock as in Chapter 9. In that regard, it is not an isolated policy initiative – it is intimately connected with the policies we discuss in Chapters 12, 9, 10 and 3, on the economy, housing, transport and the social safety net. Moreover, the government needs to introduce and gradually increase a tax on carbon emissions at source. This will naturally incentivise the shift towards lower carbon intensity, while generating funds for investment.

Most importantly, the Green New Deal is not about finding *more* money but rather about redirecting the resources we have. This requires new tax incentives, democratisation and devolution of power to regulate and plan, new financial institutions that direct investment in the desired way, and new public utility companies. And given that the resources that we need are being expended, the value of redirecting that money increases daily. Indeed, producing a national surplus of electricity through renewables is one of the key means we have at our disposal of reducing costs and ensuring the security of our energy sources. This is a reallocation of resources that we cannot afford not to make.

The transition must be led by workers

Before turning to the policy elements of the Green New Deal, we note that the programme is impossible without the support of workers. All too often, policies to protect our future have been presented in opposition to workers' interests. In the 2016 US presidential election, Hillary Clinton's commitment to climate change mitigation was articulated in such a way as to

71

suggest that they would attack the livelihoods of the most vulnerable workers in left-behind parts of the United States. Our future depends on protecting workers.

We propose a fully costed and funded quadruple lock to protect the interests of those 260,000 workers[1] in carbon-intensive industries who will lead our transition.

The transition job guarantee. We will ensure that all those whose jobs are lost to decarbonisation are employed at the same or higher salary, at the same or higher level of seniority, within 50 miles of their current place of work. This means that those who work on fossil fuel extraction in the North Sea will face no substantive disruption to their career development or to their community stability. In the absence of alternatives and the need for house-building, other high-carbon-producing industries need to be protected via state investment to reduce carbon emissions.[2] There is an overwhelming sustainability and security argument for ensuring that we manufacture steel, iron and cement in the UK rather than importing.[3] The transition will protect these workers.

Strategic investment in sites of transition. We will ensure that the publicly owned energy generation and infrastructure that we outline in Chapters 4 and 5 is located in places that currently hold significant numbers of jobs threatened by decarbonisation. This means that, for example, Aberdeenshire would remain a key hub of energy production and distribution, revitalising communities that currently face a cliff-edge induced by climate change.

Education and skills guarantee. In further and higher education, we will develop bespoke co-produced vocational training and higher apprenticeships to meet the need of the expanded sector and retrain workers during transition. Only skills development can

72

equip our workforce to meet the challenges of tomorrow, and only public education can deliver that effectively and efficiently.

An enterprise safety net. Our workers in sectors affected by transition have highly transferrable skills and abilities that can be deployed in any number of different roles and professions and can be the basis for new enterprises that transform our communities. Our social safety net gives workers the ability to take advantage of opportunities that are currently available only to the wealthy, by giving us the ability to take good risks. This redresses the unfairness of the current system that grants socialism to the rich.

The quadruple lock ought to provide reassurance to trade unions not only that workers' interests are prioritised, but that the transition can be the basis for worker-led control of our new and revitalised industry. This plan places production and generation at the heart of policy in ways that have been lost during the neoliberal settlement. Britain will again be a manufacturing and industrial hub, leading the world in protecting human life while organising our activities democratically and collectively.

As an increasingly publicly owned and controlled sector, energy will be directed in the interests of workers by placing trade union representation at the heart of governing boards, providing a direct incentive for trade union membership. The enhanced status of workers within the public sector will provide a direct comparison with workers in the private sector, granting additional power in collective bargaining for the introduction of, for example, pay ratios and worker representation on boards.

Without coupling public investment and ownership to democratic, worker-led control, we will continue to trundle towards catastrophe. By acting now, we will ensure that the immediate interests of workers in vulnerable sectors are no longer at odds with the longer-term interests of us all.

Financing the Green New Deal

The Westminster government directs investment in the economy in several ways. First, it invests money directly. Second, it disburses money to local authorities and other agencies. Third, it directs investment from other sources. It does this, for example, by setting tax incentives, deciding which activities to license and making regulations to govern entities such as pension funds. The government can rapidly direct finance towards the Green New Deal through all three of these routes.

In terms of its own investment, the government should make the effects on sustainable living goals the primary basis for cost–benefit analysis of its direct investments, instead of, as present, GDP growth or maintenance of the value of financial assets. The Office for Budget Responsibility should be required to incorporate sustainability impacts into its forecasts. Investment should be coordinated through a National Investment Bank reformed from the UK Infrastructure Bank, as we outline in Chapter 12, with cooperation between the Treasury, the Office for Budget Responsibility, the Bank of England and the National Infrastructure Commission to ensure that investment is coherent, forward looking and compliant with long-term sustainability goals. This would rapidly lead to the reallocation of government direct investment, away from the trunk road building programmes of recent years and towards improving public transport connectivity and facilities for walking and cycling. It should accelerate the transition from subsidising landowning to investing in nature generation (see the section 'Regenerating nature' below).

It should lead to the elimination of non-productive subsidies like quantitative easing, where the Bank of England buys financial assets, in favour of productive investment.

Second, we should devolve much of government investment in transport and housing to local authorities and elected mayors (as we outline in Chapters 10 and 11). Local authorities and mayors have a clear incentive to pursue sustainability: their electoral survival depends on making people's lives more liveable at the local scale. In Chapter 11 we deal with government corruption through the receipt of party political donations from environmentally destructive special interest groups, but it is important to emphasise that devolving budgets produces an additional check on central government corruption in procurement and investment. Investment budgets devolved to localities are more likely to be turned into cycling and walking facilities, electric buses, trams and local trains, and less likely to be directed to unsustainable and expensive national projects that benefit few people.

Third, the UK government should set the regulatory and licensing framework in such a way as to direct investment towards sustainability. As we emphasise in Chapter 5, this means ending new licences for oil and gas exploration and banning extraction within a short period. The government should also change the regulations surrounding pension funds. It effectively – and rightly – subsidises pension saving through income tax, corporation tax and national insurance. But it could add requirements on pension funds in order for them to enjoy these reliefs. For example, pension funds should be required to place at least 25 per cent of their investments into bonds or funds that finance the Green New Deal. These bonds or funds could come either from the private sector, appropriately approved, or else from local and regional governments. Investment should be coordinated both by our National Investment Bank and investment funds at the combined mayoral authority level. This policy could raise at least £20 billion a year for the Green New Deal, based on the estimated level of current contributions.[4] It is a clear example of redirecting investment that is happening anyway by virtue of the attractiveness of green assets, rather than creating novel costs.

Decarbonising the energy supply

Fossil-fuel-based energy sources need to be phased out, which means that alternatives such as wind, solar and tidal energy need to continue to be expanded to the point where they can produce a national surplus. In Chapter 5, we assert the Labour Party's 2021 commitment, now dropped, to £28 billion in annual investment as the baseline for public investment in energy production;[5] this is a minimum, but it is an amount that is wholly feasible. Incentives for micro-generation (solar panels on houses and farm-scale turbines) need to be increased and made easy to access.

The ability to use and distribute renewable energy depends on the electricity grid being improved, and this can only be achieved through nationalisation. The decarbonisation of the energy supply requires taking back social control of energy generation and supply, and we set out a plan for this in Chapter 5. This does not mean the creation of a single state monopoly. Rather, there should be a national energy company that coordinates the activity of regional, community and municipal suppliers and distributers. The money made through generating and distributing energy will be ploughed back into the system rather than distributed as rent. These are basic but transformative changes to the way in which we make use of energy as an essential good.

Improving housing and transport

Reducing the carbon intensiveness, and increasing the size, of energy supply is one half of the equation, but reducing unnecessary energy use is the other. This can be done by a combination of incentives and improved regulatory standards. It is a win-win strategy: better incentives and regulation stimulate the private sector to supply expertise in improving housing insulation, replacing boilers, and building bike lanes and electric buses. This creates good jobs, and makes everyone's lives more pleasant.

Let us take the example of retrofitting houses to modern energy efficiency standards. Millions of people in this country are living in cold, damp and mouldy homes. The unsuitability of housing contributes to waste on an enormous scale. London's homes and workplaces are responsible for 68 per cent of the capital's carbon emissions and 72 per cent of its energy use.[6] That is wasted resource – burning money for the want of proper insulation, triple-glazed windows, heat pumps and solar panels. Retrofitting is often a triple win. It reduces emissions, lowers bills and creates good green jobs. Street-to-street insulation programmes massively reduce costs because of the economies of scale.

This is the kind of programme that can be financed by the National Investment Bank, by devolving investment decisions to local authorities, or by the appropriately incentivised private sector.

Thus, the government should provide direct incentives to householders and landowners to improve and retrofit their houses to modern insulation standards. Likewise, support should be given for upgrading existing housing, both via a National Building Service aimed at achieving a UK-wide transformation and via short-term subsidies while that service is developed. This national rebuilding effort is consistent with Labour's pledge to invest £60 billion over 10 years,[7] but the effort needed to achieve these outcomes can only be coordinated in the longer-term through a National Building Service that has collective purchasing power and is specific concerned with the transition to renewables. The service can be organised and implemented through local authorities and drive forward the social housing commitments in Chapter 10. The service should contribute directly to development of a much-needed new generation of green construction qualifications and higher apprenticeships available within further and higher education and provided at no cost to apprentices.

The combination of service, capacity and skilling is essential to replacing gas heating systems that ought to have been prohibited years ago and replaced with electric-based alternatives, such as heat pumps and solar-powered panel heating. It is essential that heat pumps and solar panels be installed as part of all new developments, and this requires legislation to update building codes. Domestic electrical goods made in the UK should be required to have AAA energy efficiency ratings, and we should impose prohibitive levies on imported goods that do not do the same. We cannot continue to contribute to climate catastrophe for lack of a manufacturing sector.

As part of Total Transport Networks based at a combined mayoral authority level as we set out in Chapter 10, planning frameworks should be revised to place provision of walking and cycling facilities and access to public transport as central requirements for all development. Developments should be predicated on the increasing cost and decreasing ease of private car driving in the future, and on the desirability and practicality of having people on foot as the central mode of interaction and space use.

Regenerating nature

We face not only a climate emergency but severe ongoing loss of natural capacity, in terms of a diverse community of plants and animals and the healthy soils upon which our lives and the lives of other species depend. This has arisen in part because the subsidies and transfers inherent in the system of recent decades have favoured intensification and extraction at the expense of stewardship and protection. We should accelerate the replacement of the current system of payments for agriculture with environmental land management schemes that provide public funding only for the public good, where this is understood to involve the restoration and improvement of natural capital. Under such schemes, the total subsidies available to any one individual or corporation should be limited. The UK has one of the most unequal distributions of land ownership of any country.[8] Allowing very large landowners to extract very large public subsidies perpetuates this situation, and presents obstacles to local communities acquiring local land for rewilding and public amenity. Community interest groups ought to be able to acquire unused land and receive public support for rewilding activities.

While we need to plant more trees, our environmental goals are not best served by direct subsidies for, for example, monocultural conifer plantations. These achieve very little in terms of the regeneration of biodiversity, even though they do sequester some carbon. Environmental land management schemes should favour the regeneration of native biodiversity, whether through complete rewilding of areas or more regenerative farmland.

In tandem with changing our subsidies to the countryside, we should introduce ever more stringent standards on the use of pesticides and herbicides, agricultural run-off, and other damaging interventions in the countryside. The goal should be a thriving agricultural sector, but one based on regenerative principles, which prioritise sustainable food production and the production of timber for new buildings.

The nature that needs to be regenerated is not just on our land but also in our seas, which are 27 times the size of the UK's land-mass. As the UN notes,

> The ocean generates 50 percent of the oxygen we need, absorbs 25 percent of all carbon dioxide emissions and captures 90 percent of the excess heat generated by these emissions. It is not just 'the lungs of the planet' but also its largest 'carbon sink' – a vital buffer against the impacts of climate change.[9]

Guy Standing provides a comprehensive overview of the need to protect the seas from pollution, overfishing and exploitation.[10] Here, though, we need to emphasise the need, within fisheries policy, for a comprehensive commitment to creating large marine protected areas.[11] These allow fish stocks to recover and thrive. The existence of substantial no-fishing areas is so beneficial that it can actually improve the profitability of fishing where fishing does take place, because fish disperse from safe source areas. Having large protected areas where no fishing takes place protects the whole ecology of the sea and sea bed, and it is much simpler to enforce than quota systems, which have been ineffective at protecting the marine ecosystem.

Reducing pollution and waste

Our current way of life is based on too much of a linear flow from creation to consumption to waste. The true cost of waste – landfill, incineration, or the dumping of toxins and sewage into rivers and seas – is not paid, so the incentives are skewed and we all end up worse off. The government can change this situation through a combination of incentives and regulations.

We need higher standards, and above all much more proactive enforcement, for emissions into the air and discharges into water. Air pollution standards should be raised at the national level, levelling up the complex patchwork of different emissions requirements that our major cities now have. Scrappage for older vehicles needs to be combined with incentives through vehicle excise duty to switch to zero-emission vehicles.

As for water, the handing of private monopolies to unaccountable and largely unregulated corporations has not worked. As we argue in Chapter 5, we need to bring water companies back into public control.

More generally, the costs of waste materials need to fall on the manufacturers and providers. Extended Producer Responsibility (EPR) ensures that producers are made responsible for the lifetime costs of objects they produce, including costs of disposable or clean-up. By placing a cost on manufacturing products that cannot easily be recycled or repaired, the EPR incentivises recyclable and repairable products. Single-use plastics should be banned, and reuse schemes created for such items as bottles. In public procurement, which accounts for a large fraction of consumption, carbon costs and waste externalities should be monitored and factored into decisions. These innovations would create an incentive for manufacturers to improve the sustainability of what they supply, as is happening in many other countries. It is also a key means of funding recycling.[12]

A Green New Deal is popular

In our Act Now survey, we found an average level of support for the policy of 69.4 per cent in the Red Wall, with 64.9 per cent among Conservative and 83.6 per cent among Labour 2019 voters. Nationally, approval was 74.5 per cent, with 59.7 among those intending to vote Conservative, 80.6 per cent among those intending to vote Labour and 69.6 per cent among those who don't know who they will vote for or who don't intend to vote at present.

An argument based on gains for the whole country received 69.9 per cent approval among voters in the Red Wall and 67.7 per cent among voters nationally:

> A Green New Deal just makes plain sense for all of us. By transitioning to renewable energy sources like solar, wind and hydro and curbing oil and gas extraction, we can safeguard our planet from the devastating impacts of pollution, extreme weather events, and rising sea levels. And going big in investing to build up renewable infrastructure could kickstart an economic renaissance across the country. This is a real chance to commit to an environmentally sustainable future, where we aren't threatening our shared future in Britain. I know change on this scale won't come easy or cheap for that matter. But looking at the shape we're in today, and thinking about the country and world I want my children and grandchildren to inhabit, pushing hard for renewables just feels like the right call. Communities and populations should own the energy companies. The energy created in Britain is our natural resource and should not be a burden on the shoulders of people.

People understand the clear national and global importance of this policy. We need to stop thinking that a Green New Deal is something that only committed environmentalists in urban centres support. There is clear support for the transition across the country, and knowing that it will secure our energy needs is the key argument for change.

Recommendations

The Green New Deal is our response to the great challenge of our age. But the challenge of our age is also the opportunity of our age. The Green New Deal is an exciting, inspirational project for society that people can take pride in, that can improve their wellbeing, that can row back the rise of inequality, and that can reconnect people to the idea that democracy and their state can serve them.

The government should:

1   Reorganise public investment so that improving sustainability is a central goal for all infrastructure projects
2   Invest at least £28 billion a year in decarbonising the energy supply and reducing energy expenditure
3   Create a National Investment Bank out of the UK Infrastructure Bank and use the tax system to incentivise pension funds to invest in green projects
4   Introduce and progressively increase a carbon tax to generate funds for investment, and guide the development of the economy towards lower-carbon solutions
5   End new licences for fossil fuel projects
6   Invest in a National Building Service to advance a programme of retrofitting and improvement of the housing

stock, including by making the installation of heat pumps, solar panels and other sustainable investments mandatory in all new buildings, and by training workers

7   Introduce tougher regulation and enforcement of regulations related to pollution of water and air

8   Divert public support away from intensive agriculture and towards the regeneration of nature in the countryside, and introduce marine protected areas

9   Place the costs of disposal and waste onto the producers of projects, and encourage reuse, repair and recycling by introducing Extended Producer Responsibility (EPR)

CHAPTER 5
PUBLIC UTILITIES

Chapter in 30 seconds

This chapter highlights the decades-long failure of an ideological experiment. The privatisation of public utilities is an aberration that can be sustained only by subsidising profits, paying more in bills, accepting dependence on fossil fuels and receiving poorer services in return. Not only have our assets been stripped, but we are paying for the privilege of bailing out failing companies, many of which are based overseas and represent the interests of other states. There is no good economic justification for this. We present an obvious alternative: ownership of our natural resources and public control over their use. We set out a programme of democratic reform that will prevent our assets from being misappropriated again, ensuring that we can bring our energy and water back into public ownership in a pragmatic programme oriented around removing the subsidies and acceptance of poor performance that sustain private companies. In complementing the Green New Deal in Chapter 4, we show that the sustainable transition is in all of our interests and can be achieved only through a combination of investment in renewables and planned direction of natural resources.

National self-sufficiency is key to tackling the cost-of-living crisis and preventing it from ever reoccurring.

Introduction: public goods as a public good

The UK is an extreme ideological outlier when it comes to our essential assets and public services. Margaret Thatcher's privatisation of energy and water (among other vital goods) in the 1980s has been failing the country for 40 years. As we gear up for new environmental challenges like reaching net zero and cleaning up our rivers and seas, this model is utterly unfit for purpose.

Energy and water networks are both natural monopolies. Indeed, those natural monopolies exist at almost every profitable level of the system, including the National Grid and the major electricity distribution network operators (DNOs) and the gas distribution networks (GDNs), which control the distribution of gas and electricity from the National Grid to end consumers.[1] There is no competition because, by definition, there can't be any real competition in a natural monopoly. Just like in the game Monopoly, we are all paying rent every time we switch on a lightbulb or turn on a tap. Privatisation means we waste money on shareholder dividends and fail to invest in the green infrastructure of the future.

No wonder that 66 per cent of us believe energy should be in public ownership, and 69 per cent, including a majority of Conservative voters,[2] want to see water in public hands. Public ownership can be combined with the transition to net zero, providing both control and increased investment in infrastructure. This would enable long-term planning, more stability and reduced vulnerability to collapsing companies. If it is done right, the public can have real accountability mechanisms rather than relying on a 'market' that does not really work.

Bring energy into public ownership

The most important energy policy is to leave fossil fuels – coal, oil, gas – in the ground. Right now, the government has a historic, once-in-a-lifetime opportunity to make our planet liveable for our grandchildren. Public ownership, along with a ban on extracting fossil fuels, gives us a vital tool to make the transition to net zero more effective and fairer for households, workers and communities.

As Russian gas was cut off because of the war in Ukraine, oil giants Shell and BP made record profits because the price of gas drove up the price of electricity (the two are linked). Our energy bills spiralled out of control. But even before that, energy privatisation had been a huge failure. UK households had been paying far too much, and when crisis hit, other countries were far better able to weather the storm because of their public ownership policies. In France, publicly owned EDF increased prices by only 4 per cent in 2022 and 15 per cent in 2023, while UK household energy bills increased by 54 per cent in April 2022 and 27 per cent in October 2022.[3] And in Norway, the country used its sovereign wealth fund to keep bills manageable.[4]

The UK has actively pursued full privatisation of its entire energy system at every stage – from generation of the energy, to transmission of it across the country, to distribution to homes and offices, to supply within the retail market. This has come at huge cost, provided few benefits to the public and created significant obstacles to achieving net zero. A recent report by Unite shows that every household in the country could have saved £1,800 in the last year had energy been in full public ownership.[5] Tracing the structure of support provided for privatisation enables us to understand how public ownership offers a better alternative.

The waters around the UK include oil and gas reserves and huge potential for wind and hydropower. But so far, we've squandered the opportunities given to us. In Norway, instead companies like BP and Shell being allowed to make astonishing profits, oil wealth was used to create a sovereign wealth fund is now used to pay 80 per cent of people's energy bills above a capped price.[6] Oil and gas companies operating in Norway pay a corporation tax of 22 per cent *and* a special tax of 56 per cent.[7] In other words, there is a permanent windfall tax, as compared with our recently introduced windfall tax, which has actually saved corporations billions.[8] Looking at Norway gives a taste of how the UK could use its natural resources for the benefit of the country, creating options to benefit people and planet, instead of just handing them over to corporations.

Norway first invested in developing its hydropower, so today 98 per cent of the country's energy is renewable.[9] It then used its oil wealth to set up Statoil, now called Equinor, which is 67 per cent owned by the Norwegian state,[10] and to create a sovereign wealth fund for the future worth $1.5 trillion.[11]

Unfortunately, however, Equinor is still investing in fossil fuels, and the British government has given it a licence to drill in the Rosebank oil and gas field off Shetland. While this indicates that public ownership isn't a substitute for good climate policy, it does demonstrate that it gives governments the ability to direct action.

The top priority for the UK government should be to phase out oil, gas and coal on an emergency timescale, with the aim of banning extraction within two or three years. Public owner-ship is essential to ensuring that the transition to renewables can be achieved, including by ensuring the security of workers through our quadruple lock and by taking over legacy assets. As a first step, the government needs to submit written notice of intention to cancel all licences for private operation. These licences give security to private companies that they will hold long-term monopolies over their particular remit within the operation of our public utilities. This means, for example, that the National Grid PLC and electricity distribution companies have a 25-year licence, while gas distribution companies have 10-year licences.[12]

The government then needs, within two to three years, to introduce legislation to cancel those licences with only one- to two-year transition periods. This is likely to reduce the market value of those operations to negligible levels, removing the arti-ficial inflation of value by the licences. The current value does not reflect the standards or forms of service or the failure of those corporations to deliver any meaningful capacity for the transition through, for example, managing renewables or pro-viding for car charging. The estimates of book value provided below are therefore likely significant overestimates. Indeed, a previous example of a failing private infrastructural body is indicative. When the Blair government renationalised Railtrack within National Rail, the compensation was £500 million and shareholder claims for additional compensation were rejected in court as 'ludicrous'.[13] A company without a service to provide cannot hold the value provided by a state guarantee against the impact of poor performance when that guarantee is removed. As a society, we can no longer afford to prop up failing private enterprises that stand in the way of transition.

Alongside this, the UK should immediately set up a new publicly owned renewable generation company to move us faster towards renewable power such as wind and water. Around 50 per cent of UK offshore wind is publicly owned right now, but only 0.07 per cent of it by the UK.[14] Instead, publicly owned companies from Denmark and Norway take the opportunities and make the profit.

Nine out of ten of the countries leading the green transition have a state-owned renewable energy generation company: the UK is lagging behind.[15] Sweden, Norway, Denmark, Switzerland, Austria, Finland, New Zealand, France and Iceland all have one. The Norwegian state owns Statkraft, the largest renewables generator in Europe (which operates in the UK). Meanwhile, Denmark owns 50 per cent of Ørsted (previously DONG Energy), the world's largest developer of offshore wind power.

Research shows that state-owned utilities in general invest more in renewables, and that they also encourage more private sector investment. Evidence from the MIT Center for Energy and Environmental Policy Research shows 'a consistent pattern concerning the role of ownership on renewable energy investment among European utilities: state-owned utilities dedicate higher shares of investments to renewables, particularly in countries with stringent climate policies and when the general quality of regulation is high'.[16]

Globally, the role of the state is crucial to the transition to net zero. The state provides research and development (R&D) funding – for example, Vestas and General Electric, two of the largest manufacturers of utility-scale wind turbines both drew heavily on research funded by the US and Danish governments.[17] Private sector R&D funding sticks to established technologies such as wind and solar, whereas the public sector de-risks new technology such as tidal and wave energy.[18] Private investment depends on public funds such as feed-in tariffs. Cutting these crucial government subsidies has drastically cut the rate of investment in new renewable energy.[19] Research by Deleidi, Mazzucato and Semieniuk shows that 'public investments not only have a positive but also consistently the largest effect on private investment flows relative to feed-in tariffs, taxes and renewable portfolio standards in general'.[20]

The Labour Party has promised to create Great British Energy in public ownership, which is excellent news, although it is not yet clear on what scale this will operate at or what the role of the private sector will be. A publicly owned renewable energy company would skill up workers and create decent jobs locally, regionally and nationally as part of the transition from oil and gas to renewables. Profits would flow back to the public purse as we lead the charge to net zero.

Once energy has been generated, it needs to be transmitted across the country. National Grid is responsible for gas transmission across the UK mainland and electricity transmission in England. You don't have any choice about this as a consumer – it's a private monopoly. Over the past five years, shareholders have received almost £9 billion in dividends and share buyback schemes – money that could have been reinvested into the system to speed up connections.[21] The UK is the only country in Europe, apart from Portugal, which has a completely privatised electricity grid.[22]

A handful of privatised distribution companies also take the energy – gas and electricity – from the power stations to your home.[23] Shareholders from around the world profit from these monopolies. For example, if you're in the North East, your electricity is delivered to your home by Northern Powergrid. This company is owned by American conglomerate Berkshire Hathaway, which is owned by US billionaire Warren Buffett. If you're in London, the South East or the East of England, your electricity is delivered to you by UK Power Networks, owned by Hong Kong billionaire Li Ka-shing.[24]

The UK government is pushing ahead with plans to create a new publicly owned 'future system operator' by 2024 which will take over some of National Grid's responsibilities in planning and overseeing the network.[25] As part of the arrangements, the UK Treasury is passing legislation and compensating National Grid shareholders financially for the transfer of some of its powers. Nationalisation is happening quietly behind the scenes because even this Conservative government understands that it's necessary.

But the government is doing the bare minimum here for planning purposes rather than bringing the whole grid into public ownership. This is a mistake because our privatised grid is making it harder to tackle climate change. The grid upgrades needed for net zero could cost between £40 and £110 billion by 2050.[26] The think tank Common Wealth argues that the ageing network is seriously slowing down progress because of structural underinvestment, which it describes as a feature, not a bug, of the private monopoly model of grid ownership.[27] We need to bring the grid back into public ownership by buying back National Grid PLC and SSE and invest in electrical transmission appropriately to achieve net zero and capacity for a surplus in cheaper electricity. Unite has estimated the cost of renationalisation at £62 billion,[28] and a budget of £4 billion a year needs to be set aside for upgrades to enable us to meet net zero. This will be directed through the National

Investment Bank and evaluated through updated Green Book criteria.

From a household perspective, privatisation was supposed to bring competition and lower prices. Even before the current energy crisis began, domestic energy bills had been increasing in real terms (adjusted for inflation) and people were confused by deliberately complex price structures. In stark contrast to France and Norway, which kept bills low, UK energy bills in July–September 2023 were more than 60 per cent higher than in winter 2021/22. Research shows that prices are 20–30 per cent lower in systems with public ownership.[29] In Germany, France, Italy and the US, most people buy their energy from a publicly owned company.[30] The UK should give people that option.

We need at least one publicly owned energy retail company in the UK. People are relatively slow to switch energy provider, so a large customer base is needed from the beginning. Since 2018, 40 mostly smaller energy supply companies have gone bust, including council-owned Robin Hood Energy and Bristol Energy, which had to start from scratch in gaining market share.[31] The government could easily have created a public retail company when Bulb collapsed, leaving its 1.7 million customers stranded, by bringing it into public ownership. Instead it propped up the company at a cost to the public of £6.5 billion before returning it to the private sector.[32]

Today, in the absence of another big company collapsing, our best option would be to buy one out. British Gas is the obvious choice. It used to belong to all of us, before Thatcher's sell-off in 1986, with the famous 'Tell Sid' advert pushing individuals to buy shares. Buying back British Gas and using it to deliver lower bills and fairer pricing would be hugely popular.

The new publicly owned British Gas could also insulate homes across the UK so that they no longer leak heat.[33]

The cost would be minimal: the TUC (Trades Union Congress) has calculated that it would cost only £2.85 billion to buy back all of the Big Five energy retail companies, and buying back British Gas itself would cost only around £1 billion. This would be both a real and a symbolic triumph, buying back this company that once belonged to us so that it can again work for the benefit of British households and deliver clean, green energy through our now publicly owned system.[34]

This approach needs to be deployed to water as well.

Bring water into public ownership

Nowhere in the world runs its water the way that England does. Margaret Thatcher's privatisation of our regional water companies in 1989 was part of a wave of sell-offs that were supposed to benefit consumers. But water is the ultimate natural monopoly. It should be crystal clear that there is only one set of pipes, and you have no choice about where you get your water from or who deals with your sewage. There is no market.

That's why, for the last 34 years, the public have been ripped off by the people who now own our water – largely shareholders from around the world and asset management funds. The English water companies are more than 70 per cent owned by shareholders abroad. For example, Wessex Water is 100 per cent owned by a Malaysian company, YTL; Northumbrian Water is owned by Hong Kong businessman Li Ka-shing (yes, him again!); and Thames Water is partly owned by investors from the United Arab Emirates, Kuwait, China and Australia.[35]

Since 1989, water company shareholders have had a bonanza at our expense. They started out with zero debt and the government even gave them a 'green dowry' to help tackle pollution. But their control over such a valuable asset meant that it made sense to build up a vast debt mountain of over £60 billion.[36] This debt was used to finance excessive shareholder dividends amounting to £72 billion and counting. Meanwhile, all of the infrastructure investment since 1989 has been funded by customer bills. The private sector has brought absolutely nothing to the table.[37] Since the 1990s, the money spent by the privatised English water companies has gone down 15 per cent.[38] CEO pay has been excessive, often topping £2 million a year. These companies hide dividends, dodge tax and lie about their sewage outflows.[39] Water privatisation is a legalised scam.

Water companies want to increase bills by an average of £156 a year to pay for the investment that is needed in the infrastructure.[40] They have sold off reservoirs that could have helped with drought and failed to build a single new one since privatisation.[41] Now they want us, the public, to pay (again) for 10 new ones. Essentially, after 34 years of privatisation, they are doing a whip-round for £96 billion. It's also becoming very clear that these companies are financially as well as environmentally irresponsible. As interest rates rise, the debt they took out in better times is becoming unmanageable. The chartered accountant and tax campaigner Richard Murphy argues that if these companies were required to spend the money needed to fix the problems with sewage that they've failed to fix, they would be 'environmentally insolvent'.[42]

Thames Water, which serves the most customers, is already teetering on the brink of bankruptcy, having loaded itself with £14.7 billion debt. At the time of writing, auditors were warning that it may collapse by April 2024; we know the government has an emergency nationalisation plan but would likely intend to return Thames to the private sector.

In the last few years, campaigners such as Surfers Against Sewage and clean river groups across the country have drawn attention to the scandal of England's privatised water industry, and the public are incensed. People are outraged that water companies receive millions in dividends while releasing sewage thousands of times into our rivers and seas, even in dry weather (which is not supposed to be allowed). They are horrified by the failure of regulator Ofwat and the Environment Agency to hold the water companies to account for their pollution. There is a revolving door between the regulator and the industry – for example, Cathryn Ross, the interim co-CEO of Thames Water previously worked at Ofwat. Sewage was a major issue in the local elections in 2023 and is expected to be a key issue ahead of the next general election.[43]

The Thatcher government's experiment with water privatisation was never popular. In fact, it was so unpopular in Scotland that they rejected it altogether and kept their system in public ownership. But even in England, a majority of people have believed ever since 1989 that water belongs in public ownership. This trend applies across different demographics, old and young, rich and poor, across different regions, ethnicities, and so on.[44] Polling consistently finds that a majority of around seven people in ten support public ownership of water.

Scottish Water is in public ownership, accountable to the Scottish government and working for the Scottish people. It invests 35 per cent more than the privatised English water companies, or £72 extra per household per year. If England had invested at that rate, an extra £28 billion would have gone into the infrastructure.[45] The company isn't perfect, but it is the most trusted utility in the UK, and in Scotland the rivers and seas are cleaner and water bills are lower.[46]

We can also look across the channel to France. France did privatise water but used a different model to ours. England sold off its assets wholesale, the pipes and the infrastructure, whereas France kept the assets but handed out contracts to private companies to run the service. This also failed, so now French cities are taking water back into public hands by not renewing those contracts. In the past 15 years, 106 French cities have remunicipalised their water.[47]

Paris is the most famous example. Water in Paris was brought into public ownership in 2011. Since then, water bills have reduced, there has been more investment, and they've even introduced still and sparkling water fountains across the city![48] The board of Eau de Paris is made up of city councillors, staff representatives, a consumer rights group, an environmental association, a local democracy expert, a water scientist and representatives of the Water Observatory. The Water Observatory represents different water users – housing management agencies, tenants' associations, consumer associations, trade unions and environmental associations. Eau de Paris is innovative in its approach – for example, it buys agricultural land and makes it available to farmers with cheap leases. In exchange, the farmers agree to use organic and sustainable farming methods to improve the quality of water downstream.[49] The company also produces renewable energy directly and works with the City of Paris on greening buildings and boosting biodiversity in urban areas.[50] Water is the stuff of life, and water privatisation is actually illegal in the Netherlands and Uruguay.[51]

England is full of people who want to help clean up our rivers and seas but who have no mechanisms that they can use to hold the water companies to account. River trusts and local campaign groups are producing plans and proposals, but there is no public authority to submit them to or take notice of their concerns. As Professor David Hall from the Public Services International Research Unit (PSIRU) at the University of Greenwich puts it, 'There is by contrast a total democratic deficit in the UK'.[52] He proposes creating new 'shadow' democratic English water authorities in each region, starting now, bringing together councillors of all parties together with consumers, trade union representatives and environmental groups. This will ensure we're ready to take over with a more democratic structure in the case of any collapsing private water companies.

Every household in England is paying extra to service the debt and dividends of unaccountable water monopolies. We can't afford the waste of privatisation, especially as we face climate crisis and water shortages as well as pollution damage to our natural environment. A huge amount of investment is needed to clean up the mess. Public ownership is the most efficient way to deliver this, with every penny invested towards helping households, looking after our rivers and seas, and treating water with the respect it deserves – all in keeping with our Green New Deal policies in Chapter 4.

As with energy, the first step is to trigger the water companies' 25-year notice periods and then introduce legislation within two to three years to cancel those licences with only one- to two-year transition periods. This, along with the huge debt of companies such as Thames Water, is likely to reduce the market value of these operations to negligible levels, removing the artificial inflation of value by the licences. Nationalisation can then proceed along the same lines as with energy, with similarly low compensation paid for failing businesses.

What should public ownership look like?

In the UK and around the world, public ownership is totally normal. We can look at the hundreds of examples of remunicipalisation worldwide and the way that other European countries run their energy and water.[53] Right here in the UK, we often forget that we have lots of examples of publicly owned institutions to learn from. Scottish Water and the NHS of course, but also nine municipal bus companies, rail franchises in public ownership and institutions like the Met Office, Ordnance Survey, the Land Registry, the Royal Mint and Channel 4.[54] These organisations are professionally run and make a profit for the public purse.

As we create new public ownership in water and energy, we have a huge opportunity to learn from best practice and to build on it. Public ownership in itself is an improvement on privatisation but not a panacea. It's vital that we design publicly owned institutions thoughtfully to create success – and to create new accountability mechanisms to involve citizens, consumers, communities, workers and the environment in delivering the outcomes we need.

Public ownership isn't about 'renationalising', which implies centralisation and remoteness from community control. Instead, public ownership will be local, regional and national. Publicly owned organisations will operate at different levels; for example, bus companies are local, water companies regional and the National Grid is national. We need responsiveness and new ideas at every level, alongside an overriding strategy, national standards and best practice to keep improving. Put simply, we need four accountability mechanisms for the public as part of the regulatory system.[55]

First, publicly owned companies need to be managed by professionals day to day, and held accountable by a supervisory board representing broad, long-term public interest. A number of different groups need to be involved in twenty-first-century public ownership. Alongside elected politicians and people appointed for their expertise, let's include the people who use public services, workers and civil society – social, environmental and community groups. This could mean clean river groups getting involved in water companies or community energy projects having a say in our energy system.

Second, we need new public duties for the big challenges we face. In keeping with the Green New Deal, publicly owned organisations should have new duties, for example to decarbonise, to ensure access for all to crucial services, to work with communities, to steward public assets and land.

Third, we need a new, independent, democratic organisation, 'Participate', to represent citizens, the people who use public services (much as trade unions represent workers). It will hold publicly owned companies to account, fight any threat of privatisation and maximise participation. You can get involved by finding out what's going on, because all data is available; voting for Participate representatives; attending board meetings; going to a shopfront on your high street; feeding back with complaints and compliments, problems and proposals; suggesting new ideas online; popular planning; participatory budgeting; joining with workers to improve public services; or voting against any proposals to privatise. Finally, we need an Office for Public Ownership to draw on international best practice and innovation and sunshine regulation trade associations which share data on public meetings and debates to improve services.

With these democratic structures, we can prevent our resources from being misused and misappropriated in future.

Renationalising public utilities is popular

In our Act Now survey, we found an average level of support for the policy of 77.8 per cent in the Red Wall, with 70.4 per cent among Conservative and 84.7 per cent among Labour 2019 voters. Nationally, approval was 78.5 per cent, with 65.3 among those intending to vote Conservative, 80.8 per cent among those intending to vote Labour and 75.6 per cent among those who don't know who they will vote for or who don't intend to vote at present.

The arguments that are most persuasive among the two groups are different. Voters in the Red Wall evaluated at 79.6 per cent approval an argument based on relative gains for those with low–middle incomes funded by removing benefits for the wealthy:

Since privatisation, many of our utilities have been sold to opaque foreign private companies which have loaded them up with debt and pocketed huge dividends for themselves. Renationalising energy and water would stop companies creaming off profits for shareholders and directors who exploit price fluctuations and increase the spending power of ordinary Britons. It would mean that services go back to being run with a cost base that only covered costs and improvements. Bringing them back into public ownership would also ensure revenue from British bill-payers remains in Britain to benefit British people rather than foreign private equity owners. It would also make it easier to plan investment that maximises long-term benefits rather than short-term profits for shareholders. This would increase the spending power of low–middle-income families and provide good, well-paid and secure jobs in less wealthy areas of the country, making money for families go further. Those that can pay more, should pay more – they will survive.

Nationally, an argument grounded in increasing democratic control received 81.6 per cent approval:

> Renationalising key parts of public utilities, such as National Grid, British Gas and water, would bring nationally important infrastructure under government control. By removing the corporate drive to make profit, the government could ensure that a national strategy for the provision of utilities is integrated with other national objectives. For example, this could ensure that the National Grid is upgraded appropriately to handle the renewable electricity that we want to generate, and increased capacity for charging electric vehicles all over the country. Bringing the water companies under the same control will ensure that water can be handled better as a national asset and ensure that everyone can access it as they need. This new strategy will enable governments to plan better for the long-term and ensure that our national infrastructure can keep pace with the need to move to renewables, changes to population and help to level differences between regions.

People understand the clear national importance of this policy. We need to stop thinking that renationalising our resources is unpopular. We find consistently high levels of support, and people understand the relationship between controlling our resources and their affordability.

Recommendations

We have a full list of steps to bring our energy and water back into public ownership, which we detail in Chapter 12. In sum, government should:

1 Immediately begin to create the organisations needed to bring our utilities back under democratic, decentralised public control

2 Trigger notice periods immediately, legislate to cut these down to short transition periods, then buy back the National Grid, regional distribution centres and British Gas and reconstitute them as Great British Energy, a new, publicly owned company that will receive £28 billion of investment a year – the same level as Labour's 2021 commitment – via the National Investment Bank

3 Work towards a national surplus of, and self-sustainability in, electricity generation to make electricity affordable and decouple it from wholesale gas prices, and make decarbonisation actively attractive to the country

4 Ban the extraction of new coal, oil and gas, and plan for a fast (2–3 years) complete transition to renewable energy

5 Trigger the English water companies' 25-year notice period, legislate to cut that timeline down to a short transition periods, take failing water companies into special administration on financial (debt) and service grounds, use steep equity fines to punish other water companies that perform poorly and, under public ownership, invest in infrastructure at large scale to reduce leaks and waste

6 Protect all workers affected by the sustainable transition through the quadruple lock plan outlined in Chapter 4

7 Introduce progressive billing where users get a guaranteed amount of energy paid for and heavy users pay more

CHAPTER 6

HEALTH AND SOCIAL CARE

Chapter in 30 seconds

The NHS is the clearest example of how social solidarity and risk pooling mitigate against the risk of illness and financial ruin due to healthcare bills. However, more than three decades of policies have undermined the founders' vision, contributing to the progressive dismantling of the system. As with education, which we will tackle in Chapter 8, we need to return funding to pre-austerity levels in real terms, end private provision and contracting within the NHS in ways that build community wealth, create a National Pharmaceutical Service to remove the exploitation of the NHS by predatory pharmaceutical bodies, nationalise GP practices into Primary Care Networks and integrate social care into the NHS via Integrated Care Boards. This plan is fundamental to ensuring that our society is secured against avoidable illness and resilient against the threat of further emergencies.

Introduction: a system broken apart

Illness is neither an indulgence for which people have to pay, nor an offence for which they should be penalised, but a misfortune the cost of which should be shared by the community.

Aneurin Bevan

The principles upon which the NHS are founded are public funding through taxation, public ownership, and services free at point of need, not based on ability to pay. But the principles that underpin social solidarity have been eroded over time, with the result that public satisfaction with the NHS is at its lowest since 1983.[1]

There has been an increase of more than 30 per cent in people choosing to self-fund care since 2019, with 'market-beating growth' reported in the self-pay market since the COVID-19 pandemic.[2] Waiting lists in England now stand at 7.5 million.[3] Over twenty thousand people may have died in 2022 because of overwhelmed emergency services, with many ambulance services and hospitals declaring critical status.[4] Yet at the same time, the public still overwhelmingly support the NHS's founding principles as a comprehensive service for everybody freely available at the point of need.[5]

We have reached this point via successive reforms by the Labour government in 2003, the coalition government in 2012 and the Conservative government in 2022, which have created ever greater opportunities for private asset-stripping and provision.[6] What now exists, especially in England as compared with the NHS in Wales and Scotland, is a two-tier service that increasingly resembles healthcare in the United States. After more than 30 years of reducing public capacity, increasing marketisation and promoting private healthcare, the system has now become embedded within the NHS, facilitated by increased reliance on healthcare professionals with often lower levels of qualification, private GPs and entrepreneurial consultants. This, as the tragic Lucy Letby case illustrated, at a time in which NHS-based consultants appear to have diminishing capacity to influence the running of hospitals in light of increased lay managerial power.

Reduced NHS capacity was seen starkly when the pandemic hit: the NHS simply didn't have enough hospital beds. The UK had one of the lowest per capita bed numbers among comparable countries, as their number had more than halved from 299,000 in 1987/88 to 141,000 in 2019/2020.[7] Critical bed shortages and lack of facilities and services in the community have resulted in inappropriate admissions of older people to acute beds and delayed discharges from hospitals.[8] In England alone, the NHS spends £2 billion a year on private hospital care for mental health patients. This adds up to 13.5 per cent of its total mental health spend. As a result, nine out of ten private beds are filled by NHS patients, funded by the taxpayer. Given this publicly funded cash cow, it is no surprise that private investment companies are queuing up to take advantage of the opportunity.

Herein lies just one of the problems. Private corporations are motivated by profit. The NHS is not. It is not in the interest of private healthcare providers to solve the crisis facing the NHS. It is not in their interest to support measures that would prevent mental health problems or even prevent the relapse of current patients. The fact that many leading politicians, both Tory and Labour, have financial ties to private medical companies, merely underlies the conflicts of interest inherent in allowing private interests to profit from public healthcare. The Care Quality Commission's recent finding that 12 of the 80-odd private mental health hospitals in England are providing 'inadequate' care similarly suggests that while the NHS is forced to cut costs due to escalating demands or reduced funding, private hospital providers most likely do so to make more money.

Ultimately, the most powerful path to recovery is to ease the pressure on the NHS through improving population health. We set out means to achieve that in Chapter 3 and elsewhere: better health comes not just from better healthcare but also from a better standard of living and better places to live. At the moment, not enough attention is paid to improving health to stop people becoming so ill in the first place. The lion's share of private and public funding for mental health research, for example, is spent on psychopharmacology, not prevention. This creates a vicious cycle where ever more patients are prescribed ever more drugs, fuelling ever more investment in psychopharmacology, given the profits that can be made. Making matters worse is the fact that pharmaceutical companies not only market their wares aggressively to doctors but also lobby the UK government and individual politicians for funding and other inducements. This is why we need to exercise control over R&D and pharmaceuticals.

Public funding and the shift to private control

NHS expenditure, coming from our taxes, has in practice been increasingly directed to private corporations. For example, contracts valued at £10 billion were awarded in the summer of 2022 to 52 private companies in order to help reduce waiting lists for elective surgery.[9] These contracts were a lifeline for private hospitals, especially for those whose profits were falling before the pandemic.

The two-tier system has also progressed as a result of parliament having legislated in 2012 to permit NHS foundation trusts to obtain up to 49 per cent of their income from private patients and other non-NHS sources.[10] There is no obligation on the trusts to reinvest income from private patients in the NHS: they are required only to give information in their annual report on the impact of that income on NHS services, and there is no data that demonstrates that NHS patients have benefited. And, again, it is NHS staff who treat the private patients. Tens of thousands of staff are working across the public and private sectors on a fee-for-service basis, as the employees of private companies or even under the direction of NHS foundation trusts. Moreover, hundreds of medical consultants, mostly employed by NHS foundation trusts and NHS trusts, have equity shares in 34 joint ventures with private hospitals, such as HCA and other private health companies.[11]

The government claims that use of the private sector is additional to that of the NHS and will increase capacity. However, recent studies for elective surgery for hip and knee replacement and cataract removal show that the private sector has overtaken the NHS in providing these, with a downturn in admissions to the NHS and the private sector now substituting for NHS services rather than bringing in additional capacity, in both England and Scotland.[12] Crucially, since 2008, as outsourcing has increased, inequalities have been driven by the private sector. The government policy of outsourcing NHS care and expanding the number of private providers operates in favour of the rich to the detriment of the poor.

General practice provides another example of private sector penetration of the NHS. The 2003 Health and Social Care (Community Health and Standards) Act introduced four contracting routes for GP services, three of which were restricted to GPs and NHS bodies, but the fourth, Alternative Provider

Medical Services (APMS), allowed the entry of private companies. They have been described by a health industry lawyer as 'the private sector's gateway to providing primary healthcare to NHS patients'.[13] According to NHS Digital, there were 235 APMS practices in England in 2022/23, covering over 1.6 million or 3 per cent of registered patients.[14] There are an estimated 70 GP practices and hubs around England in the hands of Centene Corporation alone, a giant US health company with revenues in 2022 totalling US$144.5 billion.[15] NHS England's total budget for 2022/23 was £157 billion.[16]

GP practices are closing, the number of fully qualified full-time equivalent GPs has fallen, and the number of patients per GP and per practice is rising.[17] This has occurred as major companies awarded APMS contracts are reported to have failed, with Serco pulling out of its out-of-hours contract in Cornwall in 2013 after a damning Select Committee report.[18] When the state hands over control to monopoly providers with shareholders and investors, price gouging, quality shaving and cost inflation result. Shareholders need a return on their investment, and the model of care changes as providers are incentivised to minimise costs by denying care, changing the skill mix of staff, carefully selecting patients or introducing referral mechanisms that reduce the power of GPs to refer to specialists without prior authorisation. Wherever companies cannot make profits under standard levels of care, they divest.[19]

The private sector is expanding into a troubled primary care sector. GPs in the UK report higher levels of stress than in other countries and are very concerned about mounting administrative burdens and briefer consultations with patients.[20] Increasing insecurity in practice finances and a reluctance among newly qualified GPs to enter GP partnerships mean that sale to a private company may be an existing GP partner's only option.[21] Indeed, there are an estimated seven million private GP consultations a year. While these amount to less than 2 per cent of the 370 million NHS GP consultations in England,[22] they take perhaps two to three thousand GPs out of the NHS workforce for at least some of their working time and, more importantly, put pressure on existing NHS GPs through onward referrals, follow-ups, prescriptions and so on.[23]

Continuity is a particular headache for GPs, who in the UK have historically worked not just with NHS services but with social workers and other local authority services such as housing. GPs play an important role in bringing together different parts of the wider health system, for instance sexual health, long-term care and mental health. Local government has had severe cuts in its budgets since 2010, including in its ringfenced public health budgets. When the wider system is weakened, GPs are able to achieve much less.[24]

Social care is an example of where the rest of the NHS is heading. Long-term care was carved out of the NHS in 1990. Today, social care services in the UK are among the most privatised and fragmented in the Western world. They have been underfunded for decades. Between 2010/11 and 2017/18, local authority spending on social care fell by 49 per cent in real terms, reducing from £16.1 billion in 2010/11 to £14.8 billion in 2016/17.[25] According to the Competition and Markets Authority, in 2016 the care homes sector was worth around £15.9 billion a year in the UK, with around 410,000 residents and 5,500 different providers operating 11,300 care homes for older people. For-profit providers owned 83 per cent of care home beds, with a further 13 per cent provided by the voluntary sector.[26]

Although £60 billion flowed into this sector from the state and individuals in 2021 in the UK,[27] care is often tragically poor, with care workers paid very little and treated badly.[28] The sector is 152,000 workers short,[29] which results in inadequate care, while the use of agency staff moving from one home to another increases the risk of disease transmission. Some 32 per cent of care workers are on zero-hours contracts (compared with 3.4 per cent on average), and at least 35 per cent are paid less than the Real Living Wage (as calculated by the Living Wage Foundation).[30] Not only does the system fail those in need and those it employs, it also forces care back onto unpaid family members, disproportionately affecting women, people from ethnic minority backgrounds and those with low incomes, producing negative consequences for us all in terms of health, well-being and activity.[31] All of this further is burdening the NHS.[32]

While there is often concern about the effect of inheritance tax on those unable to avoid it, it is important to remember that private provision of social care has a significant impact on reversing the wealth redistribution brought about by expanded levels of home ownership in the 1960s and 1970s, with high care costs borne directly from the person's estate.

A clear plan to reverse the decline

The pandemic exposed once again the pressing need for a universal integrated health and social care service and highlighted the failure of successive governments to get to grips with our broken system. Although care is a continuum, the split between health and social care has always been used to move the dividing line between what is publicly funded and what is not. Whereas most services for long-term care were once funded and provided by the NHS, the 1990 NHS and Community Care Act cemented the split and shifted responsibility for funding from the NHS to local authorities, with services provided on the basis of means testing. In this way, responsibility for funding has shifted in turn from the state to individuals and their families, until they are too poor to pay. Long-term social care provision in the UK is mostly outsourced. The present system of partial public and partial private provision of care is both expensive and ineffective, consuming individual savings as well as tax revenues. Long-term care and dentistry illustrate the trajectory we are on, towards an NHS with fewer services and more private funding purchasing private provision.

As a first step, legislation is urgently needed to reinstate the duty on the Secretary of State to secure and provide services and in turn to reinstate the NHS and social care as a planned system of publicly funded and provided care. This should be accompanied by ending contracting and by bringing services and staff back in-house, abolishing student fees for training and education, and ending the two-tier system within the NHS, which is resulting in growing inequalities and unfairness.

Reinstate funding in real terms at pre-austerity levels

We spend less on healthcare than comparable countries. Institute of Public Policy Research (IPPR) analysis in 2020 found that the UK would need to increase spending on health by £27.7 billion a year to match the average level of spending as a percentage of GDP across G7 nations. [33] Even excluding the United States as an outlier, the amount would be £7.6 billion. But our system is different to those of most other countries. A better measure of the kind of investment we need is to consider the position we would be in if austerity politics had not undercut funding increases for the NHS since 2010. During the New Labour years, the average real terms increase was 5.5 per cent a year. During the Conservative and Liberal Democrat coalition government from 2010/11 to 2014/15, it was 1.1 per cent. From 2015/16 to 2022/23, it was 2.8 per cent.[34, 35]

Our proposals in other sections seek to address areas currently regarded as public health. For example, issues with housing are examined in Chapter 9, while a full basic income, described in Chapter 3, is designed to ensure that everyone has access to, among other things, good-quality food and opportunities for physical activity. But there are some public health issues that would remain. For example, sexual health services are currently the commissioning responsibility of local authorities, even if they are often delivered by NHS providers. There were reasonable expectations that local government might be better placed to deal with social determinants of health than the NHS, but funding cuts have ensured this has never materialised.

Instead, we propose bringing remaining public health provision into an integrated health and care system, with the NHS responsible for services like sexual health, drug rehabilitation, smoking cessation, obesity prevention and health visitors. As an immediate step, we propose returning public health spending to the level it would have been at without austerity budgeting, which has simply created additional pressures in the form of more expensive, often less effective reactive healthcare, which in turn has added compound pressure on the entire system. Research for the Health Foundation has found that the public health grant paid by the Department of Health and Social Care has reduced by 26 per cent per person in real terms since 2015/16, with time-limited funding for drug and alcohol treatment still only narrowing the gap to 21 per cent.[36] These cuts have been even greater in the most deprived areas, where public health activity is most needed. This is, once again, 'penny wise, pound foolish': the research found that each additional year in good health resulting from public health interventions cost just £3,800, compared with £13,500 when it results from reactive NHS interventions. Excluding the time-limited additional funding, the grant is just £3.5 billion in 2023/24, a tiny proportion of overall health spending.

End private provision within the NHS

Change approaches to treatment. Given the critical shortage of beds and staff, the government should immediately require the NHS to stop treating all private patients and halt all future contracts. It should also ask doctors, nurses and other staff to choose between NHS and private practice and place restrictions on those who choose to work in the NHS. In return, the NHS must deliver greatly improved working conditions. There is both an economic and a pure health argument to this. A recent *Lancet* article using observational data found that changes to for-profit outsourcing since 2014 were associated with an additional 557 treatable deaths across the 173 Clinical Commissioning Groups (CCGs) included in the study.[37]

In 2014, the Centre for Health and the Public Interest (CHPI)[38] estimated (conservatively) that creating and maintaining an internal market in the NHS had resulted in financial and opportunity costs of some £4.5 billion a year. Given the increase in the scale of that market as well as the enormous costs of private provision in the wake of the COVID-19 pandemic, this is likely much higher now.

As the CHPI has also highlighted, it is impossible to tell whether the treatment of private patients in NHS Private Patient Units (PPUs) has a net financial benefit to the NHS, as profits are treated as commercially sensitive, with only income declared.[39] In a time of staffing crisis, NHS consultants are treating private patients without the time used necessarily being backfilled. The CHPI also found that 9 of the 41 NHS trusts that responded to its Freedom of Information (FOI) requests had made a loss on treating private patients in some or all years between 2010/11 and 2015/16. One of these trusts made a loss of £18 million over the six-year period.[40]

In terms of private delivery for NHS money, the Department for Health and Social Care annual report and accounts for 2021/22 recorded spending by NHS Commissioners in England of £10.9 billion, after a spike in 2020/21 to £12.1 billion on independent sector providers.[41] There is likely to be a significant increase in this expenditure, as the government plans to use private providers to reduce waiting lists.[42] Unlike contracts delivered by the NHS, the vast majority of this money is lost to the public purse and the UK economy. By expanding NHS delivery, profits will be retained by NHS trusts for use on further services, any profits will be taxed and, ultimately, costs will be reduced.

End outsourced contracts. All contracts, including Private Finance Initiative (PFI) contracts, should be brought back in-house along with staff. IPPR has found that PFI funding for hospitals brought in just £13 billion of investment but will cost £80 billion in total.[43] In 2019, £55 billion of the debt was still outstanding, and it is being paid at a rate of more than £2 billion a year, set to peak in cash terms at £2.6 billion in 2030.

Phase out all private locum provision within five years. Contracts should be normalised and working conditions improved for all staff. The NHS spends £10 billion on locum and temporary staff each year simply because the government refuses to take adequate measures to ensure appropriate staff levels.[44] While locum cover for certain shifts due to illness or holiday will still be necessary, this should be facilitated solely by NHS organisations, namely NHS Professionals.[45] Private agencies should not be able to profit from registering NHS doctors to do NHS shifts. NHS England's Long Term Workforce Plan already suggests that reliance on temporary staffing should reduce from 9 per cent in 2021/22 to around 5 per cent from 2032/33, but we need to be more ambitious.[46] At the very least, private agencies should be removed from the picture within five years.

End subsidisation of private provision. We should also look to ensure that the state does not simply subsidise private provision, by training medics at public cost. If private providers recruit from NHS-trained staff, they should compensate the public. Similarly, no private provider offers Intensive Care Unit (ICU) facilities. If things go wrong in private practice, the NHS is forced to cover the cost of treatment. Private providers ought to pay the NHS directly for any ICU use, much as sporting organisations are often required to fund policing of events.

Double the number of doctors, nurses and dentists trained, and prioritise domestic places

The government estimates the cost of training each doctor at £230,000, of which £65,000 is paid through student loans.[47] A doubling of places is already in NHS England's Long Term Workforce Plan, with a target of 15,000 by 2031/32.[48] However, the number has increased by only around 2,000 in the decade since 2013.[49] In 2021, the Medical Schools Council used a 2017 estimate of cost per place of around £200,000 to suggest an additional 5,000 places would cost around £1 billion. We suggest that we should be more ambitious, given the scale of shortages and the pace with which doctors are leaving the profession due to poor conditions. The Long Term Workforce Plan also recommends an almost doubling (a 92 per cent increase) of adult nursing training places, a 40 per cent increase in dentistry places and a 29 per cent increase in pharmacy places. However, the plan is dependent on an 'ambitious' assumption of an increase of 1.5 to 2 per cent in labour productivity.[50] Increases in productivity are possible if working and broader social conditions improve and more investment is put into the NHS, as opposed to temporary, *ad hoc*, emergency top-ups whenever it nears collapse.

We endorse the proposals in the Long Term Plan but also suggest that all efforts should be made to accelerate the number of training places towards, and even past, the target at a faster pace than initially planned. The British Medical Association (BMA) reports that there were 8,858 vacancies for doctors in secondary care in England alone as of September 2023, with the workforce ageing and many retiring early.[51] The BMA has also found that England would need an additional 16,700 GPs to meet the OECD (Organisation for Economic Co-operation and Development) average.[52] UCAS (the Universities and Colleges Admissions Service) reports that there were 24,150 applicants in 2024 for medical school places following big spikes in the wake of the COVID-19 pandemic. Even if the target were to be achieved well in advance of the planned timeline, there remains enough space in the number of applicants for medical schools to remain selective and for UK students to be prioritised. The government has already committed the funding requested by the Long Term Plan,[53] but an assessment should be made as to whether further funding could accelerate the planned timescales.

In 2019, even Jeremy Hunt, then chair of the Commons Health and Social Care Committee and subsequently Chancellor of the Exchequer, suggested that the locum doctor bill could be cut by training more doctors.[54] Indeed, he argued that 'Yes, it costs more to train additional doctors, but it costs even more not to train them because we then hire expensive locum doctors and agency nurses'.[55] This is exacerbated by the fact that unlike employed doctors paying tax through PAYE, locum doctors can set up limited companies to take advantage of tax reliefs and avoid the higher rates of income tax.[56] With an annual spend on locum staff (through agencies and NHS trust staff banks) at £8.9 billion in 2021/22 according to Labour Party analysis extrapolating available data from 60 trusts, there is significant room for budget savings through ensuring more effective salaried staffing. Allocating £1 billion now to save on the annual £8.9 billion bill more rapidly is money well spent. Further, we should consider flexible means for those with initial medical training, such as nurses and physiotherapists, to convert degrees to perform other roles within our health and social care service.

National Pharmaceutical Service

There are various ways in which our national investment in research is taken up and patented by large pharmaceutical companies that then impose prohibitive costs on the provision of treatments, restrict access arbitrarily or fail to meet demand for delivery of essential materials.[57] We will create a National Pharmaceutical Service (NPS) that has first call on patent development from publicly funded research by universities conducted in the UK. It will consist of a national centre for treatment development, a production facility, and a procurement and provision stream to secure for the NHS the treatments it requires using the collective bargaining power of the country.

The number of medications of which there were shortages in the UK was at 185 on 5 December 2023, compared with 165 a year earlier and 113 in May 2022.[58] While there are a number of potential supply chain causes, there is some suggestion that an increase in shortages in 2010/11 may have been the result of several generics manufacturers ceasing trading in the wake of the global financial crisis.[59] More recently, Brexit and the COVID-19 pandemic may have resulted in further shortages due to international supply chain systems and 'just-in-time' logistics.[60] Such shortages cause a range of issues, including impacting pharmacist workload and potentially harming patient care.[61]

Mariana Mazzucato and Henry Lishi Li recently argued for a public pharmaceutical option to address the prioritisation of 'blockbuster' medications that make large profits at the expense of others that are essential for public health, pricing that fails to account for the contribution of public funding and is driven by inefficient competition and over-financialisation (an issue we see in Chapters 4, 5, 9 and 10) and offshoring of manufacturing that reduces local capacity.[62] The potential risks of relying on an almost completely overseas supply chain and manufacturing process were played out during the COVID-19 pandemic, as wealthy countries sought to outbid each other to secure vaccine doses – as well as large quantities of medicines and personal protective equipment – produced in developing nations with lower labour costs. The European Investment Bank (EIB) has invested in production of vaccines within the EU.[63] However, this approach does not guarantee supply of medications and vaccines, with companies receiving public investment still acting commercially. China and India, the former a regular foreign policy adversary of the UK, produce 50 per cent of the world's ibuprofen, 60 per cent of paracetamol and 90 per cent of penicillin.[64]

In 2021, the UK government spent almost £3 billion on health R&D, 21 per cent of the total spent on R&D as a whole.[65] Although the model differs between nations, there is evidence that even a majority of drug development may be funded from public sources.[66] There is also good evidence that the idea that innovation is driven by a profit-motivated sector is a fallacy. A large proportion of investment goes not to the areas where it is needed, such as antibiotic development,[67] but instead to copycat 'me too' drugs that target conditions already treated effectively by other medications or alter existing compounds very slightly in order to obtain a new patent and continued monopoly.[68]

The need for a genuine alternative to the domination of large, multinational pharmaceutical corporation in order to address the lack of progress in discovering new antibiotics to fight increasing resistance in bacteria was highlighted even by the former Conservative Commercial Secretary to the Treasury and former Chief Economist of Goldman Sachs, Jim O'Neill.[69] A report commissioned by Global Justice Now and STOPAIDS found that £1 billion was spent by the NHS in 2016 on medicines developed with significant reliance on UK public funding. Such medicines included two of the five on which the NHS spends the most.[70] There has also been an ongoing debate about whether pharmaceutical corporations spend more on R&D or marketing.[71] This focus on a binary good or bad outcome depending on a very fine margin between the two conceals the fact that such companies spend a shockingly large amount of money on marketing that could otherwise be used for new drug discovery and development.

We propose that initially, the NPS is provided with a £1 billion budget in order to recruit a team with backgrounds in public and private pharmaceutical R&D and manufacture. It will then spend an initial period reviewing publicly funded research programmes, and becoming actively involved in development and ownership where possible. Gradually, the approximately £3 billion public budget currently spent on health R&D through a range of partners would be brought within NPS control. Commissioning of university-based teams may remain, but this should be the decision of an NPS with the remit of innovating and manufacturing medicines for the public good. Generation of profit overseas would be permitted, but with partnership with other publicly funded bodies encouraged.

Nationalise GP practices

Existing GP surgeries should be acquired at market value where cost effective, or built where facilities need to be updated or cannot be run as a nationalised service in the current location (i.e. where they are part of a larger dwelling). GPs should be moved onto NHS contracts. This is not without challenges, and there is debate between doctors about the relative merits of the current model versus full nationalisation.[72] The chair of the Royal College of General Practitioners Professor Kamila Hawthorne has been quoted as saying that the 'partnership

121

model of general practice is extremely good value for money for the NHS because it relies on the goodwill of GP partners going above and beyond, and a recent independent review of the partnership model found it to be a viable one when resourced appropriately'.[73] While appropriate resourcing is essential, being dependent on the generosity and goodwill of health workers is neither fair nor sustainable. The NHS is not a charitable endeavour built on volunteering but a public service funded through general taxation and available free at the point of need and use. The dangers of expecting GPs and other health workers to go above and beyond is clear in the 11 per cent decrease in the number of full-time equivalent GP partners between September 2019 and September 2023.[74]

This proposal is not necessarily a left–right issue either. In 2022, while Sajid Javid was health secretary, it was reported that there would be a full review of general practice, with GPs incentivised to be directly employed by 'academy-style' hospitals rather than remaining independent contractors.[75] This system of 'vertical integration' has, in fact, already been implemented, with nine GP surgeries part of the Royal Wolverhampton Trust Primary Care Network.[76] While we believe that Integrated Care Boards might provide a useful means of administering such networks, having hospitals manage surgeries in their area is an alternative, and one that should be explored further, especially as it has already been put into practice in Wolverhampton. This kind of integration could be voluntary and incentivised, as in Wolverhampton, or could be dealt with through a one-off capital investment in nationalising all surgeries.

The *Telegraph* has reported that internal Department of Health and Social Care (DHSC) analysis based on 2019 figures, which was not subject to independent scrutiny or verification, estimated the cost at around £7 billion.[77] This figure, as a capital investment rather than day-to-day spending, is not that great given that a substantial quantity of real estate would be acquired. However, it may not actually be the case that GP premises need to be purchased or retained in the longer term. Instead, premises that include pharmacists, dentists and other allied health workers could be established in areas based on population need, rather than simply where is most profitable. This will have its own costs, so the £7 billion figure can perhaps be used as a guideline. The cost in hospital doctor equivalent salaries compared with the existing system of different pay scales depending on the practice and position within it is more difficult to establish. There were 36,826 fully qualified NHS GPs in England in October 2023, equivalent to 27,368 full time. The internal DHSC analysis estimated a salary cost of £670 million a year to bring 'some' of these onto hospital doctor equivalent salaries.

Level up England by removing charges
for the final 4.9 per cent of prescriptions

England is the only nation in the UK to have any prescription charges. But even within England, over 95 per cent of prescriptions are exempt from charges. Administering payments and penalties on the final 4.9 per cent of prescriptions creates significant costs to society, not only among those who have to pay for prescriptions and in funding teams within NHS Prescription Services and Penalty Charges Services, but also in the considerable time, money and headspace devoted by pharmacists to dealing with a complicated and punitive system in which many of those who are entitled to free prescriptions are unaware of their entitlement or of the need for certification to

access it. This is an excellent example of conditionality producing perverse outcomes in which those in work are forced
to choose between prescriptions at a time when taking the
medication is likely to produce better long-term outcomes and
reduce burdens on the NHS more generally. In 2022/23, the
cost of charged prescription items in community pharmacies in
England was £506 million.[78] Given the likely savings resulting
from improved efficiency health and wellbeing, there is a good
chance of actually having a positive return on investment by
removing the charge.[79]

Integrate social care into the NHS

Rather than creating a new service, care needs to be brought
within NHS ownership and control, since many staff and services will have to be NHS-based and -integrated. Where suitable
care homes exist, these will be purchased at market value. Where
acquisition is not feasible, new facilities will be built. Funding for
private provision will reduce annually until removal at the end
of five years. Responsibility to distribute resources will lie with
Integrated Care Boards. Nationalisation of the care sector is
again not a left–right issue: it was proposed by both Conservative
Baroness Altman and Labour's former Shadow Chancellor John
McDonnell, among others, during the COVID-19.[80]

According to IPPR, personal care that is free at point of use
would cost only 1 per cent of total government expenditure,
around 7 per cent of NHS spending, and only marginally more
than the 2017 Conservative proposal of a floor of £100,000 in
assets above which individuals would be liable for care costs
and a cap on total liability.[81] An integrated, public system would
do away with the debt, tax leverage, overseas ownership and

aggressive offshore tax avoidance that characterise the current private social care system.[82] IPPR suggests that an integrated system would also save the NHS £4.5 billion a year by 2030 as a result of scrapping NHS Continuing Care, reducing hospital admissions and 'bed blocking', and having more care in the community.[83] This pays for a large proportion of the cost of personal care provision. Ensuring that all care staff in the service are paid at least the Real Living Wage would provide secure and remunerated employment for those who perform this vital work. This is not 'pie in the sky' thinking: the London Borough of Tower Hamlets already pays all staff, including care staff, above the London Living Wage.[84]

Nationalising health and social care is popular

In our Act Now survey, we found an average level of support for the policy of 80 per cent in the Red Wall, with 71.7 per cent among Conservative and 87 per cent among Labour 2019 voters. Nationally, approval was 77.1 per cent, with 67 among those intending to vote Conservative, 83.8 per cent among those intending to vote Labour and 76.7 per cent among those who don't know who they will vote for or who don't intend to vote at present.

The arguments that are most persuasive among the two groups are different. Voters in the Red Wall evaluated at 80 per cent approval an argument based on relative gains for those with low to middle incomes funded by removing benefits for the wealthy:

Health and social care should never be privatised. It is time that we end inequality and stop giving wealthy people benefits to skip the queue and buy their way into better health. Privatisation means that people from deprived areas who are on low–middle incomes would not get access to good health and social care. Normal people are often most in need of healthcare because our stressful, demanding working lives and other factors mean that we are more likely to face pressures on our health. By increasing funding and increasing the number of doctors and nurses, we're making sure that hospitals and services can meet the needs of working-class people, not just the select few who have money. We wouldn't have to rely on big, overseas pharmaceutical companies who are only concerned with profits too. Supporting these policies would make health and social care more of a democratic, level playing field rather than something only accessible by those who are rich.

Nationally, an argument grounded in benefits to the whole country received 81.6 per cent approval:

We will deliver a world class service delivered fairly to all. This plan for Health and Social Care means that we all receive essential services. Healthcare shouldn't be for profit – it should be for the wellbeing of the community. Every citizen can access high-end health and social care regardless of wealth. Returning funding to pre-austerity levels, ending private provision and nationalising GP practices will mean that healthcare is no longer a privilege, but a right. Getting rid of private involvement in the NHS means healthcare decisions aren't driven by profit, but by helping people recover. Making pharmaceutical services national and nixing prescription charges makes it fair and secure even on economic downturns. This brings quality and fairness to all. It's about creating a system where everyone can access the care they need when they need it the most. We can have the peace of mind of knowing that we can all benefit from free health and social care whenever it is needed.

People understand the clear national importance of this policy. Our NHS has survived longer than other public services precisely because it is universal and free at the point of use. Governments need to know that providing these universal services, ensuring that they are owned and operated publicly, and integrating complex disparate elements within a single body is extremely popular. Private provision, on the other hand, is extremely unpopular.

Recommendations

The measures we need are common sense. Privatisation has failed, and we need to take control. As the pandemic demonstrated, our health and social care is at the heart of our society. We cannot afford to wait for another national emergency to build national resilience. We need to:

1 Enact legislation to reinstate the duty on the Secretary of State to secure and provide services, and in turn to reinstate the NHS and social care as a planned system of publicly funded and provided care; this should be accompanied by ending contracting and bringing services and staff back in-house
2 Reinstate funding in real terms at pre-austerity levels
3 Double the number of doctors, nurses and dentists trained, and prioritise domestic places
4 Introduce a National Pharmaceutical Service
5 Nationalise GP practices
6 Integrate social care into the NHS

CHAPTER 7

HEALTHY AND FLOURISHING CHILDREN

Chapter in 30 seconds

The common-sense notion that investments in childhood are critical to outcomes in adulthood is all too often dismissed on grounds of cost, or ignored by politicians focused on short-term gains. Whether it be the removal of free milk by the Thatcher government or the continued debate over free school meals, the failure to apply basic cost–benefit analyses to return on investment leaves the UK more dysfunctional, anti-social, unproductive and unequal. As universal early years provision in some US states and comprehensive support for families in many European countries have shown, investment in children pays off – creating healthy, active adult citizens capable of making good on our vision. We argue that this can be achieved only by reversing child poverty through the social safety net set out in Chapter 3, introducing free school meals for all, investing in early childhood services and education consistent with education policies in Chapter 8, and future-proofing choices affecting children by embedding Equity Impact Assessments and levelling up the UK with Wellbeing of Future Generations Bills in England and Northern Ireland. This represents a fundamental

investment in the children who will be responsible for rebuilding our society in future decades.

Introduction: the state of the nation's children

There can be no keener revelation of a society's soul than the way
in which it treats its children.

Nelson Mandela[1]

It would be hard to find anyone, including politicians anywhere on the political spectrum, who wouldn't agree that a
society should look after its children well – giving them a good
start in life, protecting their interests and their health and wellbeing, promoting their development and education. Our children are our future – our long-term societal wellbeing depends
on them. But sadly, we only have to look at the international
comparisons provided by the United Nations Children's Fund
(UNICEF), the agency of the United Nations responsible for
providing humanitarian and developmental aid to children
worldwide, to see how badly we are fulfilling these responsibilities.[2] In its most recent report, out of 38 rich developed
countries, the UK ranked 29th for mental wellbeing, 19th for
physical health and 26th for skills – in spite of the country
being the fifth-richest economy in the world. Let's dig a bit
deeper into those rankings.

The infant mortality rate – deaths among infants under
one year of age – is a widely used indicator of the health of
a population. It is so sensitive to changing conditions that it is
often described as the 'canary in the coalmine' of public health.
The UK used to do quite well in the international rankings: in
1960 we ranked sixth best in Europe.[3] But although our infant
mortality rate continued to improve, it declined faster in other

129

countries, so that by 1990 we had dropped to 10th best and by 2020 to an appalling 27th place (Table 2).

Even worse than our declining performance in relation to other rich, developed countries is the fact that the infant mortality rate shockingly began to *increase* in the UK, starting in 2010 and at first only for the most disadvantaged children but noticeable from 2014 in the trend for all social classes and levels of deprivation.[4] The downward trend has since stalled, but we're clearly not as good at preventing these deaths as our European neighbours, and every year more than 3,000 British families experience the agony of losing a baby or an older child.[5]

Another important indicator of the health of our children is the prevalence of obesity. The UK ranks 28th for child obesity among rich countries.[6] We measure the height and weight of all UK children entering Reception year in primary school (aged 4–5 years) and again in primary school Year 6 (children aged 10–11 years). In 2020/21, 10 per cent of four- to five-year-olds were obese and an additional 12 per cent were overweight; at

Table 2 Infant mortality rate in the UK over recent decades and ranking among OECD countries.[7]

Year	Infant mortality rate (deaths under one year per 1,000 live births)	Ranking among OECD countries (1st is best/lowest rate)
1960	22.5	6th
1970	18.5	8th
1980	12.1	9th
1990	7.9	10th
2000	5.6	15th
2010	4.2	18th
2020	3.6	27th

10–11 years, that rose to almost a quarter who were obese and an additional 14 per cent overweight.[8] Overweight and obesity among children rose noticeably during the COVID-19 pandemic and remains higher than before it. This bodes ill for our future population health and our economy.

If we turn to mental health, the UK ranks 31st for life satisfaction among children aged 15 years: only 64 per cent of our children have high life satisfaction, compared with 90 per cent in the Netherlands.[9] The most recent UK data from 2022 shows close to one in five children have a probable mental disorder, following increases over recent years with a particularly sharp rise for older teenagers (17–19 years old).[10] COVID-19 seems to have made the problems worse particularly for children: in 2021 there was an 11 per cent increase in referrals to mental health services for adults compared with 2019, but an 81 per cent increase for children and young people.[11] Over the same six months, there were 15,000 emergency/crisis care referrals for mental health for children.

Poverty and inequality are the key drivers of child development, health and wellbeing

All of the ways in which children in the UK are worse off than children in other rich countries are strongly associated with the high level of income inequality in the UK.[12] A vast amount of evidence shows that children living in disadvantage and deprivation have worse development, health and life-course trajectories than more advantaged children.[13]

Although the UK made progress in reducing child poverty throughout the years that the New Labour government was in power, the 14 years of austerity that followed under successive

Conservative governments have undermined and reversed all of that progress.[14] Relative poverty increased in the UK in the years leading up to COVID-19, and at the time of the pandemic 4.3 million children, or 31 per cent of all children in the UK, were living in relative poverty (in households earning below 60 per cent of the median income in a given year) after housing costs. That puts us 31st among rich countries.[15] Progress in reducing absolute poverty (households earning below 60 per cent of the 2010/11 median income, held constant in real terms) has also stalled since 2010.

Our social security and welfare systems, which should be protecting our children from the devastating impact of poverty, are failing them.[16] One in ten of our children – 1.5 million children – lives in a household affected by the two-child limit, and 280,000 children are affected by the benefits cap, with affected families losing an average of £50 per week. Some 110,000 children are affected by both the two-child limit and the benefits cap. One in ten households is in fuel poverty, rising to three in ten among lone-parent households with two or more children. The Food Foundation has been tracking food insecurity in the UK since 2020; from its most recent survey, it estimates that nearly a quarter (23.4 per cent) of households with children experienced food insecurity in June 2023 – that's more than four million children.[17]

Beyond the average

All of the grim statistics above are averages for the population, or percentages of the population. If we dig deeper and look at the differences for children in different places or different groups within the UK, the picture is even more distressing.

Inequalities in material resources and power intersect with geographical inequalities and inequalities between groups with different identities (see Figure 3).[18]

Relative child poverty has increased more steeply in the North of England since 2010 than the rest of England; 34 per cent of children are in poverty in the North, compared with 28 per cent in the rest of England – this equates to 160,000 extra poor children.[19] In some parliamentary constituencies, more than 45 per cent of children are in poor households, for example Bradford West (51 per cent), Newcastle Central (48 per cent) and Manchester Gorton (47.5 per cent). More than a quarter of children living in the North East are suffering absolute poverty. In Yorkshire and the Humber, 17.5 per cent of households are in fuel poverty, much higher than the national average of 12 per cent. Food insecurity affects 11 per cent of households in the North East, compared with 8 per cent in England as a whole.

Health inequalities for children in the UK are stark.[20] Infant mortality is more than twice as high in the most deprived parts of England as in the least deprived and higher for babies of non-white ethnicities than White British ethnic groups (much higher for babies of Black and Pakistani ethnicities). Similar inequalities are seen for stillbirths, low birth weight and pre-term babies. Inequalities in child obesity, mental health, oral health and long-term physical health conditions can all be seen across different regions of the UK, by deprivation measured in communities, by poverty and incomes, and by ethnicity.

In the past, we might have expected these inequalities to be mitigated by public services. Instead, the greatest cuts to services supporting children have hit the areas with the highest proportions of poor children. Cuts to local authority spending have been significantly higher in deprived areas and in the

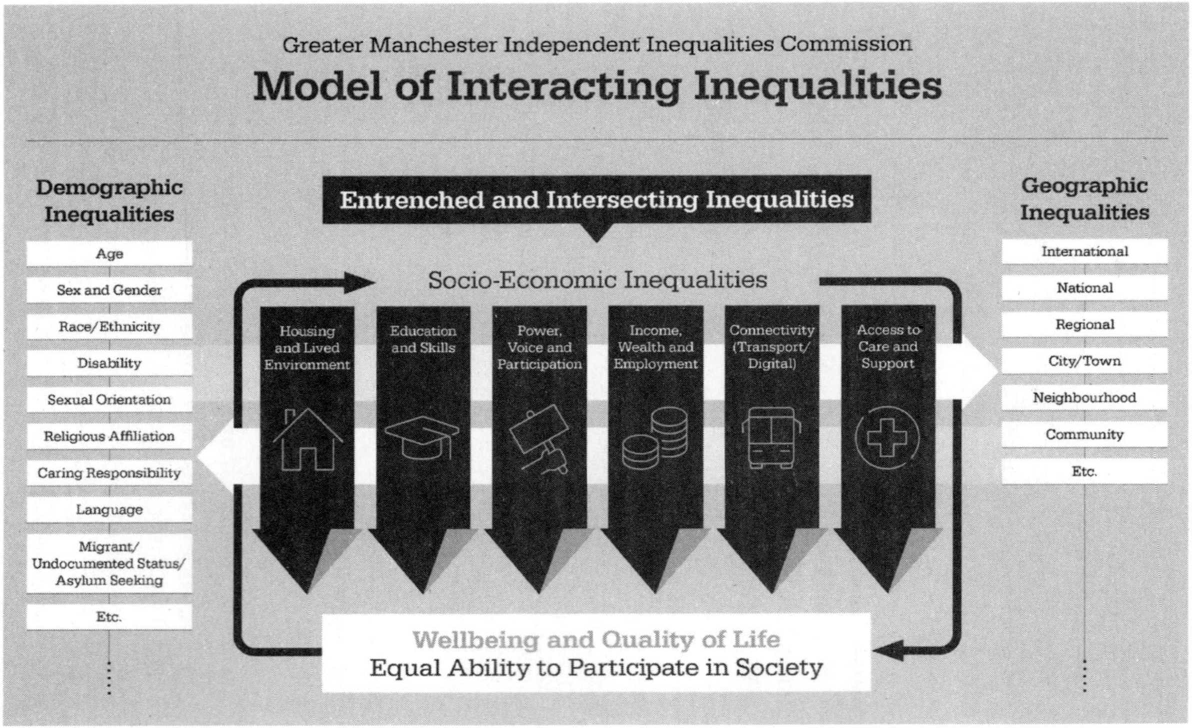

Greater Manchester Independent Inequalities Commission

Model of Interacting Inequalities

Demographic Inequalities

- Age
- Sex and Gender
- Race/Ethnicity
- Disability
- Sexual Orientation
- Religious Affiliation
- Caring Responsibility
- Language
- Migrant/Undocumented Status/Asylum Seeking
- Etc.
- .....

Geographic Inequalities

- International
- National
- Regional
- City/Town
- Neighbourhood
- Community
- Etc.
- .....

Entrenched and Intersecting Inequalities

Socio-Economic Inequalities

- Housing and Lived Environment
- Education and Skills
- Power, Voice and Participation
- Income, Wealth and Employment
- Connectivity (Transport/Digital)
- Access to Care and Support

Wellbeing and Quality of Life
Equal Ability to Participate in Society

Figure 3 Inequalities logic model.[21]

North compared with the South, leading to worsening health outcomes.[22] The North saw larger cuts to Sure Start children's centres, with funding cut by £412 per eligible child compared with £283 in the rest of England.[23] Schools in London receive almost 10 per cent more funding per pupil than schools in the North.[24] In a survey of local government councillors, eight out of ten said that children in their local area are at risk of destitution and seven out of ten said that their health and social care services don't have enough resources to cope with current pressures.[25]

Beyond the human cost

As well as it being an issue of social justice, there are compelling economic reasons for addressing low levels and inequalities in children's mental, physical and skills development.[26] Child wellbeing shapes and influences the future performance of the economy. Any detriments to child cognitive development, social and emotional development, and health will impact on educational attainment, labour market outcomes and adult health.

A single statistic can serve to illustrate the economic benefits of prevention of inequalities in children's development and wellbeing. The mental health conditions that children in the North of England developed during the pandemic will cost an estimated £13.2 billion in lost wages over their lifetime earnings. Think of that loss compounded by all of the losses caused by inequalities in physical health and skills development: the consequences of not investing in children are obvious.

This is why we need formal protection for younger and future generations. The Welsh government has pioneered such legislative work through its Well-being of Future Generations

135

Act (2015), which grants Wales 'the ambition, permission and legal obligation to improve our social, cultural, environmental and economic well-being'. As part of this, Wales has the Welsh Future Generations Commissioner,[27] responsible for upholding this legal obligation, identifying future threats such as the development of automation and developing formal responses. We need this across the UK.

As the Nobel Prize-winning economist Professor James Heckman has shown, investing in early childhood development and education strengthens the economy. It is a cost-effective strategy for reducing social costs like poor health, school dropout, poverty and crime, and for promoting economic growth.

> The highest rate of return in early childhood development comes from investing as early as possible, from birth through age five, in disadvantaged families. Starting at age three or four is too little too late, as it fails to recognise that skills beget skills in a complementary and dynamic way. Efforts should focus on the first years for the greatest efficiency and effectiveness. The best investment is in quality early childhood development from birth to five for disadvantaged children and their families.[28]

What this means for our communities: the case of Bradford

Bradford is a vibrant and diverse district in West Yorkshire in the North of England. Its history is tied to the Industrial Revolution, which transformed it from a rural market town to an international 'wool capital' and trading centre, with growth (and subsequent decline) intimately connected to migration from Europe and South Asia in particular. Bradford is a district of juxtapositions: of urban development, wild moors and rural countryside; a thriving, multi-ethnic place to live and work, yet a district in which one in three children lives in poverty (up from one in four in 2014/15).[29] Disadvantage and inequality are reflected in the infant mortality rate across the district, which, at 6.3 deaths per 1,000 live births, is considerably higher than the English average of 3.7.[30]

The social security policy measures suggested here would provide a stronger economic foundation for family livelihoods, contributing to a reduction in child poverty, and with particular benefits for minoritised ethnic groups and families in which someone lives with a disability, who are among those most at risk of poverty. Nationally backed auto-enrolment on free school meals (FSM) would not only help to address inequalities in access to food and support children's concentration and educational engagement: it would also make a considerable difference to the budgets of families living on the lowest incomes. Local action is being progressed to auto-enrol children for FSM on a location-by-location basis, supported by the Fix Our Food network, and with interest in progressing this in Bradford, national policy on this would remove many of the bureaucratic and legal hurdles that exist when attempting to do this locally. There are considerable potential benefits for children in Bradford.

In other similar local authorities, auto-enrolment has enabled more than 6,000 children to access their FSM entitlement, raising an extra £3.8 million in Pupil Premium funding for local schools.[31] Similarly, national policy on Children's Rights Impact Assessments and devolved citizens' assemblies would strengthen existing local action in Bradford to ensure that children's voices and wellbeing needs are at the forefront of decision-making – with local work in this space including

the reinvigoration of school councils, building of a Youth
Voice network and the co-design new urban green spaces with
young people.

Improving support to young children is popular and can be more popular

In our Act Now survey, we found an average level of support
for the policy of 65.5 per cent in the Red Wall, with 52.9 per
cent among Conservative and 79.2 per cent among Labour 2019
voters. Nationally, approval was 67.3 per cent, with 50.7 among
those intending to vote Conservative, 75.6 per cent among those
intending to vote Labour and 65.4 per cent among those who
don't know who they will vote for or who don't intend to vote
at present.

The arguments that are most persuasive among the two
groups are different. Voters in the Red Wall evaluated at 67.2
per cent approval an argument based on redistribution to ordinary families from taxation on the wealthy:

> No child should be malnourished in a well-off country like the
> UK. Increasing welfare payments to families with children will
> give the families more resources to raise their children with a
> decent quality of life. It will help protect ordinary families from
> economic shocks, such as the cost-of-living crisis, and sudden
> job losses for parents and caregivers. These measures could be
> financed by taxing the wealth of the richest in society who have
> been given special tax breaks for decades. This will allow ordi-
> nary parents to raise children in a more secure and stable home
> environment. In turn, this should help the children to grow and
> be nurtured into healthy, well-adapted, resilient and produc-
> tive members of society. Giving England a Future Generations
> Commissioner as they have in Scotland and Wales will ensure

efficient implementation and monitoring of the outcomes. This will allow hard-working taxpayers to see that their money is being used for the benefit of ordinary people in society.

Nationally, an argument grounded in security received 69.2 per cent approval:

Adopting these policies would help empower the country as a whole to be more caring and more socially inclusive, rather than the dog-eat-dog world we have at the moment. Guaranteeing all children a healthy meal every day should be seen as a right in a first-world country such as ours, and showing families and children in particular that they are worthy and secure could have all sorts of future benefits, including reduced child abuse and neglect, better educational achievements and therefore better job prospects, more social mobility and less poverty and crime. This can secure us from the shoplifting and thefts caused by people struggling to get by. Yes, it will be expensive to introduce these policies, but spending on children, the adults of tomorrow, is the most important thing we can do to reduce child abuse and neglect and resulting social problems, such as anti-social behaviour, homelessness and drug and alcohol addiction.

One of the key concerns that people raise in opposition to support for children is that removing the two-child cap will incentivise people to have larger families. Once it is made clear that that policy has had no positive impact on reducing child births, some of the opposition is removed. Despite what we might think about the popularity of reducing child poverty, it is clear that in an ultra-insecure society, the longer-term impacts of support for children need to be spelled out: this is a policy that will reduce anti-social behaviour and myriad public health problems over time.

139

Recommendations

The policy recommendations in this section are drawn from the work of the Child of the North group and the York Cost of Living Research Group.[32] They come from a series of recent reports and are based on research evidence and the lived-experience testimony of the low-income families who have participated in the Changing Realties and Larger Families research projects and young people who have engaged with the Child of the North All-Party Parliamentary Group.[33] The overarching policy aim for children should be to invest in welfare, health, education and social security systems that support children, particularly in deprived areas and for those experiencing the greatest inequalities in outcomes. The government should:

1   Introduce the social safety net laid out in Chapter 3 and remove the two-child limit and benefit cap; or, *at the least*, increase child benefit by £20 per child per week, removing the two-child limit on Universal Credit and legacy benefits and ending the benefit cap[34]

2   Tie rates of social security support to the cost of living and immediately pause the five-week minimum wait for Universal Credit

3   Introduce free school meals for all and auto-enrol all eligible children; make the Holiday Activities and Food Programme scheme permanent and extend support to all low-income families

4   Allocate additional funding to secondary and post-16 providers to address the lag before the new (fairer) alternat (NFF) takes effect, and implement the National Audit

Office's recommendation to evaluate the impact of the NFF

5 Adjust the NFF to include the child health burden borne by schools

6 Expand the Health Improvement Fund to support Family Hubs, health visiting and children's centres with investment proportional to need and area-level deprivation

7 Embed Equity Impact Assessments in all policy processes at national, regional and local levels; use Children's Rights Impact Assessments to evaluate the specific impact of policies on children and young people; and use devolved citizens' assemblies that include young people to make sure their voices are included when making policy decisions

8 Pass the Wellbeing of Future Generations Bill to bring England and Northern Ireland into line with the progressive Future Generations Act and policies in Wales and Scotland

CHAPTER 8

A FAIRER EDUCATION SYSTEM

Chapter in 30 seconds

Britain's education system frequently fails to produce the outcomes we need. Our children are seldom equipped with the skills necessary for the challenges they will face across their lives. In the state school sector, there is an obsession with a small number of subjects to the detriment of the diversity of experience and knowledge needed to engage with a rapidly developing society. This system is associated with unhappiness and poor health outcomes in both children and teachers, not least because they know that those who can afford to pay for education are likely to leapfrog state school pupils for reasons that have very little to do with merit. In order to have an educational system that facilitates democratic processes and realises the potential of all children, reforms are required at all levels. We need a system that prioritises care, consideration and cooperation across the sector, with a significant increase in educational spending to level the playing field and reduce the segregation that concentrates wealth and opportunity in an ever smaller and more detached part of society. Here, we set out means of broadening and balancing the curriculum to produce healthy, happy children capable of repairing our society in adulthood and creating democratic structures that restore and recognise teachers' professionalism.

Introduction: an underfunded system in need of support

As with health, education has been severely underfunded since 2010 due to austerity measures in England and the related reduction in funding available to the Scottish and Welsh governments and the Northern Ireland Executive.[1] In order to have an educational system that facilitates, rather than gets in the way of, democratic processes and realises the potential of all children, not just the few, policies must target all levels of the system. These will address macro concerns around structure, micro issues of teaching and learning in classrooms, and questions around the purpose of education and the values that underpin it.

Possibilities for developing a much fairer system do exist, and evidence suggests that they are popular. The vast majority of British people still see education as a right that should be made available to all rather than a commodity to be competed for in an educational marketplace. We just want our children to have a good education that allows them to realise their potential.

Prioritise care, consideration and cooperation

While the OECD reports that in 78 per cent of education systems students achieved more highly when they cooperated rather than competed with their peers, it also identifies the UK as one of four countries where competition in schools is the most prevalent.[2] The impact on emotional aspects of the self is evident in terms of fear of failure and reveals a culture of fear and anxiety in English schools.

In UNICEF's recent report on those aspects of children's wellbeing attributable to how well they are served by their national educational systems, the UK languished near the bottom with an overall score well below the average for the 24 countries surveyed. For example, the proportion of young people not looking beyond low-skilled work is more than 35 per cent. Even more concerning, only slightly more than 40 per cent found their peers kind and helpful – in contrast to most other European countries, where over 70 per cent found their peers kind and helpful. Less than 20 per cent of UK pupils like school a lot. Just as concerning, in relation to self-harming and risk behaviours, the UK languishes at the very bottom of the rankings by a considerable distance.

Overall, the report concludes that in terms of both children's subjective sense of wellbeing and objective criteria, the UK is markedly below the average. We are seeing the lowest levels of children's wellbeing in the UK in decades. There is a pressing need to recentre care, collaboration and empathy in our schools. The 'Good Childhood Report' published in 2022 found that England ranked 24th out of 24 countries for life satisfaction and fear of failure.[3] English children were more unhappy with their schooling than with the other nine aspects of life examined in the survey.

It is the values and ethos that underpin the educational system that we have to change. We have allowed a harsh, judgemental ethos to infuse our increasingly performative educational system, one that, in its preoccupation with results and league table position, pays scant attention to the happiness and wellbeing of our children and young people. Too many children experience our education system as one enforcing control and compliance. The 'Good Childhood Report' found that of the seven areas children were asked about, they were least happy with how much they were listened to in school.[4] Love and care are essential ingredients in themselves in a good education system, but forms of love and care appear to be in short supply, particularly for working-class children, who have always been feared as potentially unruly. We seem to have ended up with an educational system that expects the worst of working-class children, rather than nurturing the best.

Increase educational spending and make it fairer

A survey that looked at public opinion across Germany, Italy and the UK found that education was the most popular social investment policy. Around 88 per cent of the respondents agreed that the government should increase spending on education.[5] The survey also found that decreasing education spending is less popular in the UK than in the other two countries. Yet that is exactly what is happening currently in England, with consequences for the state of school buildings, classroom sizes, children's curriculum offer, and teaching expertise and experience. Recent research also shows that countries with greater educational expenditure have less persistence of poverty across generations.[6] We need to increase both our spending on state schools and the allocation of funding to different types of students within those schools.

There is a wide disparity between private school fees and state school spending per pupil, with private fees 90 per cent higher, having more than doubled since 2010, when the gap was 40 per cent.[7] A first step would be to remove the tax concessions that private schools currently enjoy and make that money available to the state schools. The Institute for Fiscal Studies (IFS) estimates that the removal of VAT exemption would release £1.3 to 1.5 billion a year extra to spend on the state sector.[8]

Removing charitable status from private schools is another area where additional monies could be recouped for state schools. The charitable status of private schools is an historical anomaly long in need of reform. However, a further generative way of levelling the current very unequal playing field would be to move towards a policy of merging the private and public sector in a process through which private schools have to offer a significant proportion of places for state school pupils.[9] These places would become, in effect, part of the state school system and would need to be offered to the full range of pupils across ethnic, class and ability differences, with the added bonus of enhancing the social mix in private schools. This is a first step towards prohibiting profit-making in private schools, which follows the Finnish model.[10]

We have seen real-terms cuts in educational funding over the last decade.[11] Overall, state school spending per pupil in England fell by 9 per cent in real terms between 2010 and 2020.[12] This represents the largest cut in over 40 years. But that fall has been greatest in the most deprived schools, which experienced a 13 per cent real-terms fall in spending per pupil between 2015 and 2019, compared with a 7 per cent fall among the least deprived schools. A first step is to increase funding by at least 9 per cent to address the funding shortfall.

The Pupil Premium system is supposed to support the learning of our most deprived learners. But it has never been sufficient to compensate for their much lower levels of family resources and at the time of the coronavirus pandemic, when

146

the extent of that disparity in resources was cruelly exposed, was being stripped back even further. A fairer education system would increase Pupil Premium funding, extend it to 16- to 18-year-olds and ensure it reached the target group.

Fairer funding would also ensure smaller class sizes, particularly in schools with high numbers of Pupil Premium students. Currently, the wealthier you are, the smaller your class size. There is a stark gap between class sizes in private schools, with an average size of 12, and in the state sector, where the average is 27,[13] although some academy schools are introducing 'master-classes' with 60 to 90 pupils to deal with teacher absenteeism. Smaller classes enable teachers to emphasise learning rather than discipline and provide possibilities for teaching to be more varied, less prescriptive and more attentive to pupils' needs.[14] The current preoccupation with discipline and behaviour in state-maintained schools is, in part, because class sizes are too big to enable anything other than teacher-led instruction and heavily controlled pupil groups. Smaller class sizes would allow for more of the investigative, wide-ranging, problem-solving learning that is increasingly becoming the monopoly of the private sector.[15]

Beyond class sizes, there is also the issue of school sizes, in part due to the process of academisation but more generally because of the two-tier school system of primary and secondary schools. Too often, pupils go from small, cosy primary schools to large, impersonal secondary schools. The contrast in scale and the sheer breadth of the age groups can contribute to school disconnectedness, in which children feel that they do not belong to their school and are not cared for by adults within schools, which in turn leads to bullying and serious mental health challenges.[16] This all contributes to absenteeism.

147

It is possible to restructure to address this using the same resource base, including by breaking up large schools into smaller schools[17] and shifting to a three-tier school system of first, middle and high schools.[18] If harnessed to critical pedagogic voice in schools, in which children have genuine agency to shape their institution, there is real potential to alleviate issues such as bullying, pressure, connectedness and wellbeing.[19]

Reduce educational segregation and value social mix

The strong focus on parental choice has further increased educational segregation and polarisation, with children from similar social class and ethnic backgrounds clustered in the same schools.[20] All the major political parties valorise choice without recognising that choices come with resources that remain very unequally distributed. One consequence of a choice-based system is that the working classes have largely ended up with the educational 'choices' that the middle and upper classes do not want to make. Increasingly, research talks in terms of rich and poor schools when it describes the English educational system because that system is increasingly segregated by levels of parental income.

It is vital, therefore, to change the current status quo which gives priority to upper- and middle-class parental choice and produces a grossly unfair system that has become a means of getting ahead of others, of stealing a competitive edge. Educational segregation is damaging for all social groups, it reduces social trust and tolerance of those who are different, but it is particularly damaging for disadvantaged children who end up in schools seen to be undesirable places to learn.[21] We need to promote policies that develop a more inclusive social mix. That entails directing more funding towards schools seen to be 'poor', but it also necessitates a different approach to school admissions. Local authorities would be given control of admissions, with a brief to establish fair admission policies that prioritise social mix over affluent parents' choice. And they would be adequately funded to take on this task.

Ensure all children have a broad and balanced curriculum

OECD statistics show that we are at the top of the international league table for memorisation, drill repetition and routine learning, and bottom of OECD league table for critical thinking skills, deep learning and intrinsic motivation, just above Uruguay. It is our relentless focus on testing and assessment that has enabled this race to the bottom. The teaching-to-the-test mentality should be overturned by getting rid of the nine assessment tests that primary children face from Reception onwards. The current primary school regime, where test practice dominates, distorts the curriculum, preventing the development of a more investigative, creative and exciting primary curriculum. Moderated teacher assessment should replace tests.

An excessive focus on assessment, testing and inspection has resulted in a narrow, prescriptive curriculum in the state sector. Yet Nicholson's research, which compares primary education across state and private schooling, finds that there is a consensus among children, parents and teachers that the early years of schooling should be enjoyable, safe, explorative, collaborative, responsive to children's interests and capabilities, and nurturing of their curiosity and creativity.[22] We should expand the breadth and depth of the curriculum at both primary and secondary levels, reversing the cuts to arts education and restoring the importance of humanities, arts and physical education.

Currently, over half of curriculum time in primary schools is spent on just two subjects – reading and arithmetic. The result is that less than 10 per cent of curriculum time is spent on the arts, while 90 per cent of primary pupils fail to achieve the in-school 30-minute daily threshold of moderate to vigorous physical activity.[23] Ensuring a broad and balanced curriculum requires setting thresholds for PE, arts, humanities and sciences and making sure primary school teachers are sufficiently well trained to feel confident to deliver a wide-ranging curriculum that allows all children to flourish.

The concerning democratic deficit evident in schools, in which students are inadequately prepared for future active citizenship, would be addressed by introducing a compulsory critical thinking skills module from primary school upwards, as well as one similar to the module in the Finnish educational system that enables children to recognise and analyse fake news in both print and digital media. Finland was top of the Media Literacy Index for the sixth year running in 2023; the UK was 13th.[24]

More generally, across all stages of state schooling we need to abandon the 'knowledge-rich' approach, which emphasises learning facts and formulaic procedures, such as synthetic phonics, at the expense of deep understanding and problem solving. The role of education is not just to teach facts but to enable understanding, build connections and ensure learners have the skills they need to thrive in the world. We do not want an educational system where private school students are being taught to think and learn creatively from mistakes while state school students are learning to obey, not to question and to be fearful of failure rather than open to learning from their mistakes.

In addition to critical thinking skills and a much stronger focus on creativity, the curriculum needs to include political, social, environmental and diversity awareness. The emphasis should be on a twenty-first-century curriculum that enables children to become questioning, engaged citizens with the knowledge and skills to respond creatively to a rapidly changing world, but just as importantly with the knowledge and ability to make the world a better, fairer, safer place.

Structures matter, and so does democracy

Academisation is essentially a process of enabling rich private individuals (many of whom are Tory party members or donors, and often both) to run state schooling at the taxpayers' expense. As Sambrook and Mansell conclude, some of Britain's wealthiest businesspeople, who have collectively paid millions to the Conservatives, now find themselves in charge of children's futures, often with no educational expertise.[25] Multi-academy trusts constitute privatisation of education by the back door. Academisation has also largely stripped out local democratic involvement in schooling, with many academy trusts seeing little or no role for parents or the local community in their governance. Education should be public provision overseen by national and local authorities, but fundamentally run in collaboration with local communities.

To this end, we need policies to bring all publicly funded educational services back under democratic control. A fairer educational system will have at its heart a comprehensive policy for devolution which comprises local education boards made up of parents, teachers, students, local councillors and residents as well as regional education boards made up of seconded teachers and academics working alongside civil servants to agree on curriculum and pedagogic approaches that both enable all children to realise their potential and prioritise their happiness and wellbeing.

Restore teachers' professionalism

We need to recognise that what is important is not the quantity of teaching hours but the quality of the teaching provided. Extending the school day to eight or nine hours, as was proposed by the government in the wake of COVID-19, would increase teachers' stress levels and reduce children's wellbeing. Instead, there is a need to transform Initial Teacher Education (ITE) from a focus on developing narrow, practical vocational skills development to a programme of intellectual development grounded in substantive engagement in pedagogical theory. We need to make the case for the intellectual base of teacher education. Short-term, quick-fire programmes that do not involve degree-level study are inadequate in preparing individuals to teach and to understand how children develop, how different approaches foster different outcomes and the ways in which critical thinking lies at the heart of a functioning educational system. Such training should be replaced with university-led programmes of study that provide coherent and comprehensive understanding of pedagogy and curriculum development. Quality and professionalism can best be supported through restoring teaching to a graduate-only profession and promoting undergraduate routes into teaching such as the three-year Bachelor of Education (BEd).

Improving quality also requires a well-trained, well-rewarded teaching force with an entitlement to regular high-quality, university-engaged continuous professional development (CPD). A key component of such professional development is allocated time in the school week to reflect, plan and collaborate with colleagues. Emerging policy shifts to standardise teaching through downloadable lessons, PowerPoints presentation and scripts for teachers is reducing quality and professionalism. Instead, funding needs to be made available for increased preparation time for teachers to work together in their schools and localities to devise and share innovative schemes of work designed for their pupils. Excellence in teaching can only be developed from the classroom up, not imposed from above by politicians who know very little about good educational practice.

Work towards a level playing field in higher education

We now have 'a staggeringly unequal university landscape with more extremes of wealth and poverty than secondary education'.[26] Working-class students are increasingly going to university and accumulating debts of £40,000 or more without accruing anything like the economic returns of their upper- and middle-class peers. Yet their average debt levels are £13,200 more than those of their middle-class counterparts.[27] The latest government research brief on this subject states that 'the forecast average debt among the cohort of borrowers who started their course in 2022/23 is £45,600 when they complete their course'.[28] There also needs to be much more recognition of the troubling downward mobility of working-class graduates who, after being socially mobile into higher education, increasingly end up in poorly paid casualised work with thousands of pounds of debt accrued through going to university.[29] The class ceiling that working-class students face demonstrates that social mobility is a flawed solution.[30] We need to move away from policies that promote social mobility as the answer to educational inequalities without an equivalent focus on social justice.

The aim should be to move towards free universal higher education for all, as is provided in other European countries such as Norway and Austria. A first stage is to reduce university fees to level up students with Scotland gradually, while increasing the higher education budget, alongside generous maintenance grants for students from low-income families that allow them to study without having to undertake paid work. Our social safety net policy in Chapter 3 achieves this, providing substantive financial support to post-16 students through a regular basic income payment that fulfils the role of the Educational Maintenance Allowance and university grant in previous generations.

A second stage is to move towards free higher education across the UK over the course of five years, with higher levels of basic income replacing means-tested maintenance grants, as returns on our investment feed back into tax receipts. Money from wealth and corporation taxes on those who have benefited most from our society should be used to fund fairer higher education as well as fairer schools.

Students who attend private secondary schools are around a hundred times more likely to attend Oxford or Cambridge than students who are eligible for FSM.[31] We need policies that challenges the elitism that taints the UK's higher education sector at the expense of modern universities and the majority of graduates. That elitism is evident in the gulf between rich universities like Cambridge and Oxford and poor universities like Edge Hill and Leeds Beckett, with the former having nine times as much income per student as the latter. It is also evident in staff/ student ratios, with Oxbridge students being taught in seminars and tutorials with just a handful of students while some of the modern universities teach much larger groups of 30 to 40.

In place of a system where we increasingly have rich universities for middle- and upper-class students and poor universities for working-class students, we need a system of redistributing funding more fairly across higher education. We should be offering poorer and first-generation students the same standard of university course, with the same levels of resourcing and staffing, that their more affluent peers receive. Restoring government funding of higher education means that one possible way forward is the equivalent of the Pupil Premium, so that universities which offer places to more low-income students are rewarded financially for doing so. But in view of the 100:1 ratio between former private school students and working-class students at Oxbridge, we need to also consider a quota system that implements a fairer social mix within our universities.

How would these changes benefit working-class children?

Currently, the potential of our children is overlooked and unrealised because of the narrowness of the curriculum, the inadequacy of educational support, and social segregation in schools and classrooms. Replacing narrow teaching-to-the-test regimes in schools with a broader and enriched curriculum will ensure that our children develop the skills to enable them to thrive in a complex, rapidly changing world. They would have increased access to creative arts and physical education and increased teaching on political, social, economic and environmental issues, with a core concern for developing critical thinking skills. This curriculum would couple concern for academic success with the need to prioritise childhood wellbeing and happiness, all with the support of highly qualified, highly recognised teachers who have the capacity to lead. Children would be educated in community-focused schools that valued and enabled their voices and those of their parents and wider community. These schools would have a social mix both across the school and within individual classrooms, enabling mutual learning about difference and promoting tolerance and inclusion. And when they move on to higher education, they would do so with a social safety net that enables them to live away from home without the burden of crippling fees.

Transforming our education system is popular

In our Act Now survey, we found an average level of support for the policy of 72.5 per cent in the Red Wall, with 52.9 per cent among Conservative and 79.2 per cent among Labour 2019 voters. Nationally, approval was 72.6 per cent, with 50.7 among those intending to vote Conservative, 78.6 per cent among those intending to vote Labour and 65.4 per cent among those who don't know who they will vote for or who don't intend to vote at present.

The arguments that are most persuasive among the two groups are different. Voters in the Red Wall evaluated at 70.8 per cent approval an argument based on increasing security through education:

The UK education system is insecure. There are practical issues like defective concrete in schools, falling attendance levels since

156

COVID and low staffing levels, particularly for those who need additional support, such as those with Special Educational Needs. When education spending was at pre-austerity levels, there was more stability within the state education system. We had smaller class sizes and funding for resources. Teachers are now leaving the profession in their droves due to demands of the job. Cost cutting hits those at the chalk face hardest. Local Authorities should have more control, removing destructive competition between schools in the new academy system that forces some schools into closure. These reforms return spending to pre-austerity levels to allow schools to pay for increased salaries, food and energy costs and to remove the normalising effect of students starting their working life with a huge debt to repay. This creates security throughout the whole system, stabilising young people's lives as they enter adulthood.

Nationally, an argument grounded in removing advantages from wealthy people within the education system received 70.6 per cent approval:

Our nepotistic education system is rigged against normal people. In education, ability is evenly spread, but opportunity is not. Currently, too many people's chances of getting on in life are adversely affected by where they live. Rich people are subsidised by taxpayers to buy advantages for their children by paying for tax-free private education, often leapfrogging over more talented working-class children. These reforms would mean that rich parents are no longer be able to buy advantages and that more working-class children would be able to attend university and succeed in life without worrying about high levels of student debt. Attendance at university would be more based on grades and abilities as opposed to ability to pay. Tuition fees can be covered by taxation on the wealthy, as they were for many of us in the past. These policies end the postcode lottery of life and bring our communities up to the level of more prosperous areas.

157

As with policies for children, the focus on long-term collective national interests is highly persuasive.

Recommendations

1 Prioritise care, consideration and cooperation and reduce the cliff-edge implications of assessment that harm pupils' health and wellbeing

2 Increase school spending by at least 9 per cent, sixth form spending by 23 per cent, further education spending by 14 per cent and higher education spending by 18 per cent to return funding to pre-austerity levels

3 Eliminate distortionary forces by removing private school charitable status, prohibiting profit-making in the sector, and merging public and private provision

4 Reduce educational segregation and value social diversity by granting local authorities direct control over admissions policy

5 Ensure all children have a broad and balanced curriculum to enable our children to rebuild our society as adults

6 Introduce democratic structures and remove the arbitrary power of wealthy actors in order to ensure that experts direct education, in consultation with communities

7 Ensure that teachers are graduates with core academic capacities to guide our children through education

8 Take active steps towards removing higher and further education tuition fees to achieve a level playing field after five years, removing the ideological experiment that has burdened our younger generations in ways that are projected to last their lifetimes; while this takes place, sixth

form, further education and higher education students will receive additional support from the basic income element of the social safety net, providing a replacement for the Education Maintenance Allowance discontinued under the coalition government

CHAPTER 9

HOUSING

Chapter in 30 seconds

Britain is marked by gross regional inequalities in housing costs, falling levels of ownership and high levels of homelessness. It has an unresponsive and inflexible private house-building sector that is failing to meet the need for sustainability and affordability. With growing intergenerational inequalities in property ownership and rising interest rates, there is an increasing squeeze on mortgage holders at precisely the point in their lives when they are likely to be raising children. The crisis in social care and the likelihood of having to pay at the point of use for those with property means that not even inheritance offers a means of improving conditions for younger generations. We show how reform can end the housing crisis quickly. We can ensure social stability through a programme that changes regressive council tax bands, eliminates leasehold, discourages empty properties and controls rents, coupled with a social housing building programme. At a time of ultra-insecurity, we can easily protect mortgage holders through 'right to stay', 'right to sell' and 'right to buy back' schemes, where those at risk of repossession can transfer in and out of ownership to stay in their houses while circumstances fluctuate. Finally, we must introduce and enforce criminal sanctions against those landlords and bankers whose actions deprive us of our houses or make them dangerous to live in.

Introduction: the problem in housing

There are some very basic things government can do to mitigate Britain's housing problems. Of these, some can be done extremely quickly. There is no need for anyone to be sleeping rough, as we discovered during the pandemic. But policies aimed only at making our streets look respectable, while hiding away the poor and criminalising the roofless through anti-social behaviour orders, are both cosmetic and callous. There is a more fundamental challenge to be addressed if we are to be well housed in England, Wales, Scotland and Northern Ireland. Since housing policy is devolved, we concentrate here on England, but the importance of devolution is emphasised by the fact that 'Both Wales and Scotland, for example, have abolished the right-to-buy and enjoy relatively higher grant rates than England', while in Northern Ireland a single common waiting list is used for all social housing.[1]

Why is housing so much more of a free-for-all in England? To understand this, we have to focus on how the vested interests of politicians in England promote intergenerational inequalities in property wealth. Politicians in England are unusually likely to be private landlords due to changes made to the regulations governing them when Margaret Thatcher was Prime Minister. The situation is far better across most of Europe and elsewhere in the devolved authorities of the UK, which is one of the reasons why our housing provision is now so broken in England.

The connection between housing wealth and the social care challenge (including inheritance tax) also needs to be addressed, as does the impact of a coming a cliff-edge as boomers die. The generation below them, and even the private landlords now passing on the effects of high interest rates to their tenants, do not have the money needed to buy up this housing at the values many people think their homes are worth.[2]

This is both a challenge and an opportunity. The current system is broken for almost everyone, from the young woman sleeping rough in the bushes to the grandmother living in a home too large for her to heat (believing her grown-up children will be ok when she dies because of what they will inherit) to the man running the housing association, giving excuses as to why the properties are in a poor state of disrepair as he pockets a salary that even he feels guilty about while trying to tell himself that he is doing good. The scale of what is required can feel overwhelming, but it is far less of a challenge than the rebuilding required after the Second World War.

Stop measures that promote house price inflation

Given the crisis of exclusion from secure housing, the most important first step is to stop introducing new policies designed to increase or maintain very high housing prices – such as Help to Buy. As Adam Peggs of Common Wealth has explained: 'A government willing to confront the housing crisis head on, rather than focusing on fostering owner occupation and the numbers game of maximising private house-building, would do better to invest in quality public housing'.[3] Peggs goes on to point out (among much else) how a core series of errors have been made through policies like the Help to Buy scheme, which involved £22 billion of public lending, and stamp duty cuts. The sums lost to these two initiatives alone could have funded the building

more than 400,000 desperately needed new council houses.
A year earlier, Peggs wrote:

> While housing seems to perennially be in crisis, this doesn't mean
> that little can be done. Bold and decisive action, motivated by
> new and better priorities, can achieve significant progress even
> within the confines of the current system. This can include steps
> in the direction of a new society grounded on justice for all,
> democracy and generating social value.[4]

The response to an increasing amount of derelict housing unfit
for human habitation has been a concerted effort to present
socially unfeasible and environmentally destructive alternatives
oriented around the displacement of workforces. Leaflets like
the one shown in Figure 4 simply tell people that the last place
they can afford to live is the place they work.

These are not secure or plausible solutions. Home ownership needs to be stabilised. Prices need to not rise. Indeed, over
time, prices stabilise either through government planning or
through a crash, as in Japan in 1989. They never rise or just
'hold steady and high' forever, and we need to be clear that the
present prices are unsustainable. To suggest otherwise is fantasy. We need to control the correction.[5] Private renting needs
kind and careful regulation. If landlords flee the market, homes
become cheaper to buy. Housing associations have largely failed
and need to be treated like the further education sector was
in 2022, when it was made properly public. There are far too
many wasteful, inefficient, neglectful and complacent housing
associations. Indeed, local authorities are already taking back
control over social housing.[6] Charity is a poor model for deter-
mining provision of housing. Worthies should not be making
the key decisions.

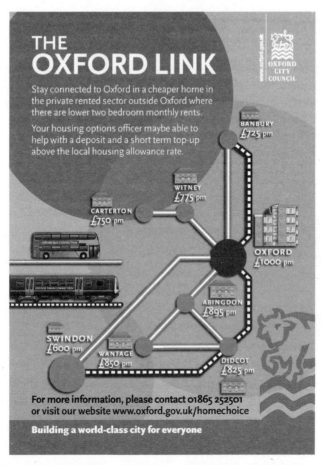

Figure 4 Suggestions for where those working in Oxford might live in 2019. Oxford City Council removed this leaflet from its website when it was pointed out what it implied in light of the strong local rivalry between Oxford United and Swindon Town football clubs. Swindon in 2024 is now an even more expensive a place to live in than it was when the map was produced. Today the map would include Birmingham, and parents-to-be who find themselves homeless are offered homes in Liverpool.[7]

The critical role of social housing

The biggest challenge is rebuilding our social housing system. The rest of this chapter addresses this, drawing on a July 2023 report produced by many hands.[8] The report begins:

> In 2010, the Parliamentary Council Housing Group of MPs and Defend Council Housing (DCH) published 'Council Housing: Time to Invest, fair funding, investment and building council housing'. It was the result of an Inquiry that took evidence from tenants, councillors and others, and combined this in a thoroughly researched analysis of existing government policy, concluding that direct investment in council housing, accountably managed and maintained, was essential to produce and maintain the genuinely affordable and secure homes we have and need.
>
> But the 2012 'self-financing' regime which promised new financial resources for Council housing, has not delivered. Councils have attempted to find alternative sources of much-needed investment, looking to Special Purpose Vehicles, Joint Ventures and Local Housing Companies. These have not brought solutions to the scale of the UK's housing crisis, which continues to deepen.
>
> A lot has changed since 2010, and the pressures on council housing have only increased. Grenfell [Figure 5] is a deadly symptom of what has gone wrong with UK housing policy. And the false economy of current policy is illustrated by the billions of pounds councils are having to spend on temporary accommodation. We are therefore glad to help in updating research to assess the current situation and the different investment strategies offered as an alternative to direct investment.

Countries that fail to provide decent council and other public housing begin to fail in much wider ways, especially in education and health. Extensive international studies have documented how this has occurred over time.[9] Secure public housing serves

Figure 5 Grenfell Tower.[10]

a stabilising function in society; it is the key social determinant in improving life chances for many children, and its widespread provision makes the private housing market more secure and less volatile. When a decent council housing system exists, children are able to stay at the same school for longer as they do not have to move schools when their parents are evicted because of private rent rises. In countries with better housing, teachers and other workers can live nearer work and have lower housing and travel costs. This saves them and the state money and massively reduces unnecessary and environmentally destructive commuting.

A city like Oxford should not have to rely on tens of thousands of people driving across a so-called green belt, emitting huge amounts of pollution, just to keep the city running for the minority of its workers who can afford to live there. The problem of housing is everywhere, from the poorest areas of England to the richest. Even Lord Tebbit has complained of

having to be driven by his chauffeur past row after row of dark-
ened properties in Westminster that he could not afford to live
in and that were clearly not being used.

Health services in countries with a better public housing
system have lower staff costs and far more efficient provision.
People become ill less often as a result of not being forced to live
in unfit homes in the private and housing association sectors.
And poverty is reduced alongside socially destructive inequality, as the rich have fewer incentives to hoard wealth through
property accumulation.

The relationship between our current system and pressures
across our society are becoming clearer by the day. In the UK,
as far as housing is concerned, 2023 is different from 2022 by
virtue of our reaching a crisis point in a long-term trend. In
2023 we were already worrying far more than we had just a
year earlier about mortgage rates, empty (hoarded) rooms and
the collapse of parts of the owner-occupied sector, as well as
record-breaking private rents and falling housing prices.

In October 2023, the long-term 30-year interest rates that
the UK government was able to borrow money at rose to 5
per cent. For Britain, the era of 'cheap money' had ended in
autumn 2022. The inflation of construction costs in recent years
now makes even the most modest new housing scheme less and
less affordable. We compete for iron girders to build homes with
the highly successful social housing schemes of other countries.
A person who builds social housing for students in Norway
knows that he has to compete with the rich of Chelsea for building materials. One such person has described how he wins in
that competition.[11]

The lack of a decent council housing sector in England
is central to this crisis, and housing associations have proven

themselves no substitute. None of the current trends in urban redesign suggests that we are moving towards social stability for our children and grandchildren in terms of how they will be housed. It is clearer than it has been in decades that the state represents our best means of crawling our way out of this mess. But we have repeatedly decimated the local state, akin to cutting off our own legs in case we think of using them as a means of escape. The visceral hatred of social housing that Conservative governments displayed from the 1980s onwards resulted in permanent damage that makes a recovery much harder than it would otherwise have been. But although it is harder, it is far from impossible.

The solution is to redistribute. The UK remains, even after raising its tax take in recently years, the lowest-taxed large state in Europe. International Monetary Fund (IMF) figures demonstrate that public spending as a proportion of GDP is much lower in the UK than in almost all Western European states, including France, Germany, Italy and Spain. Taxes must rise to mainland European norms. Wealth taxes can be introduced that deter people from hoarding housing. You can remain living in your six-bed mansion, should you wish, but you should pay more for the privilege, not less, because you are the sole occupant. Second homes, holiday homes and other largely unused properties should be taxed at a rate that encourages people to think more carefully about their ownership of these assets.

Space is finite. Gwynedd Council's decision to impose 150 per cent council tax rates on second homes is an example of proactivity.[12] Taxes on housing need to be flexible. For example, wealth taxation on homes worth more than £2 million can be slowly raised until such homes begin to fall in value. No home should cost that much, and many of them need to be subdivided in future. The price increases at the top end of the market have been exacerbated by overseas money, often from dubious sources, which has been dumped into UK housing in the belief that it can weather any short-term changes. We need that money to exit the country gradually in order for us to be able to afford our homes.

One person's luxury apartment is another's increased misery. It should be financially advantageous in your old age to move from your three-bed family semi, should you wish, into a modern council-provided apartment, without stairs and where your heating costs will be lower. You should not have to 'think of the children' and stay in that home as long as you can, often freezing, so that they will inherit more, or because 'you need the rooms at Christmas'. As we show in Chapter 12, the money raised through increased tax incentives to do the right thing will contribute significantly to funding a large and popular new council home-building programme. But the greatest effect of such taxation would be the far more efficient distribution of bedrooms within the private sector. We already have more bedrooms per person in England than we have ever had, but more of them than ever are not slept in each night. But although we mostly have the homes we need, we do need to build more.

Councils are pivotal, and the debt settlement needs to be amended

It may come as a surprise to know that council tenants' rents (plus an amount of leaseholder charges) pay for all the management, maintenance and other running costs of homes and estates and also cover the costs of historic borrowing and debt to build council homes. The House of Commons Parliamentary

Council Housing Group report of 2009 showed us that over 25 years, council tenants had paid £91 billion in rent but councils received only £60 billion in 'allowances'.[13] Tenants had paid more in rent than the actual historic debt for building their homes.

Since the 'debt settlement' of 2012, when each council with homes was allocated a proportion of an inflated national debt figure, government changes in the national rent policy (e.g. a four-year rent cut) and increases in the discounts for Right to Buy sales, which increased sales five-fold and vastly increased rent losses, have undermined the basis of councils' 30-year business plans. Individual councils are taking in hundreds of millions of pounds less in rent than was projected in 2012. The debt they were allocated was based on income projections that bear no comparison to what Council Housing Revenue Accounts (HRAs) are actually taking in today.

We should not end Right to Buy in England. There is no need for everywhere in the UK to have identical housing policies. It is wholly understandable that there are people who dearly love being in charge of the home they live in. There are people who want to fix the roof themselves when it fails, organise their own boiler replacement, reorganise the interior walls of a dwelling just how they wish, and that is fine. But the Right to Buy policy (now ended in Scotland and Wales) was not about that. It was about trying as hard as possible to encourage people to buy their home at a huge discount so that social housing could be reduced to a bare minimum, making it stupid not to buy your council house if you could. Many of these homes, especially in South East England, have been sold on to private landlords.

The consequence of a one-way right to buy is that councils are cutting back on necessary work. The starvation of HRAs is resulting in a deterioration in the standard of tenants' homes. Expenditure by all HRAs on debt and service charges is estimated at around 25 per cent of their income. When the Right to Buy was introduced, there should have been no discounts and a complementary right to sell should have accompanied it, allowing a homeowner to sell their home to the local council and remain as a council tenant in that home. People might do this when finding it hard to pay the mortgage, often following divorce, illness or unemployment. At a stroke, the right to sell would end the largest driver of local house prices – how far away a property is from council housing. With a right to sell, at any time the homes next to you could become council houses.

Instead of being visionary, we have been miserly, curtain twitching and nimbyish. The Office for Budget Responsibility predicted many years ago that the rent cap policy would mean that councils would lose an estimated 12 per cent of their expected income by 2020. The Chartered Institute of Housing estimated that councils would lose £2.56 billion over four years and £42.7 billion over the 30-year life of their 'business plan'. The Association of Retained Council Housing (ARCH) had a lower estimate, of £2.1 billion, which would mean, they forecast, a reduction of 21.5 per cent in spending per unit of housing. And all the time we increasingly saw the appalling and wholly avoidable rise in rough sleeping. Indeed, London saw a 9 per cent rise in people sleeping rough in 2023.[14] The reasons for this are not complex and do not require millions of pounds of research to understand: people are unable to afford housing.

David Hall, an independent consultant involved in the creation of the self-financing system – currently most innovative of official housing policies in England – has said that the debt settlement would have been £10 billion lower if the changes to

171

the rent formula had been included in the calculations. There are clear grounds for, at the very least, revisiting the debt settlement. In 2012 the government explicitly gave itself the power to do this in future: the next administration can do it without having to pass any legislation. Thus, there is remedial work that can be done using existing policies and laws alongside thinking about the introduction of new ones.

All of this would also change the tone of the entire housing debate and should help people to begin to understand that in future in England, they will no longer become rich if they spend as much as they can on a home and have parents rich enough to give them the money for a large deposit. That would become a stupid way to act under a government that actually intended to solve our housing crisis, and if it became clear that what we were seeing was a sea change. There will not be another long housing boom like the one leading up to the September 1989 crash or its successor, which began in the mid-1990s, leading up to the 2008 price falls. This time is different. In 2022 and 2023, we did not see a sudden event occurring. Instead, a great readjustment appeared to begin. The value of housing began to slip down and down, faster in some places, slower in others.

It is also notable that ending Right to Buy has not led to any political backlash at all in Scotland or Wales. It has been totally uncontroversial and is reckoned to save around 15,000 homes from sale annually. It has been one powerful way of ensuring that local authority investment is not lost to the private market. But as we say above, we would not extend this to England. We do not think it is necessary. It is possible to maintain a Right to Buy – with no discount – if you also introduce a right to sell. Limited versions of the right to sell have been in operation since the 1970s: we simply need to extend them. We may be forced

172

to do this if house prices fall further. It was house price falls in the past that resulted in limited right-to-sell options being made available. The alternative was growing mortgage arrears and rising evictions by banks and building societies.[15]

Large-scale council house-building is back on the agenda. The scale of our housing crisis and the absence of homes that people can afford, combined with escalating debt and mortgage charges, is refocusing attention on council housing as a solution. Despite the many obstacles that still exist, since the lifting of the borrowing cap in 2018 some councils have begun to build new homes. However, these are a fraction of what is needed. Only a total of 7,310 council homes were built between 2019 and 2022. Many local councils are under pressure and aspire to build far more than current circumstances allow. Some councils without any current council housing (due to wholesale stock transfer to housing associations – previously called large-scale voluntary transfers, or LSVTs) are keen to re-establish local council housing.

Some of the new council homes, as in Goldsmith Street, Norwich, have been built to the highest design and environmental standards. Councils such as Wandsworth have adopted a radical approach to their housing strategy to deliver genuinely affordable houses.[16] Others are considering options to buy up or take over existing under-used private developments. Elsewhere councils are battling to enforce planning conditions for genuinely affordable and council rented homes on new developments involving public land and assets. There remain important questions about types of tenancies, rent levels, and ownership and management of new council homes. But, without doubt, investment via public funds can create a new generation of secure, affordable, first-class, energy-efficient and accountably managed homes. Council homes built in the twentieth century have more than paid for themselves, as a self-financing public investment.

A 10-point plan to address the crisis

Building more council houses is the first step towards addressing our housing crisis. In addition, there are 10 other steps we can take that would transform society.

1   A proportional property tax should be introduced, as outlined in Chapter 12. This would end the current regressive system of council tax that charges those who rent and those who own houses with relatively low values much higher proportions of their income and wealth than it does those who own high-value housing.

2   The existing 'right to stay' should be enhanced into a 'right to sell', giving mortgagors the right to become tenants rather than face eviction. This would support social stability by ensuring that people remain within their communities, rather than being forced to move at the whim of the private rental market. There would be a right to buy back if people's circumstances improve.

3   Second homes, holiday homes and empty commercial property need to be included in a fairer property tax system to discourage waste. This tax policy should be part of a wider wealth tax where the level is set so that second and holiday ownership continually falls until the point where all people in Britain are adequately housed. Finland manages to have second homes too, but they are in areas where people would not want to live all year round. Finland shows

what is possible with regard to second homes when there is adequate provision of first homes. We can imagine a future in England, even with our much denser population, where it is possible to own a second home and not make another family live in overcrowded circumstances.

4   Spare bedrooms should not be taxed. Every family should be able to live in a home with a spare room for visitors. We already have enough rooms. Every single adult who wants their own space should have it. However, homes where there are two or more spare rooms should pay a greater wealth or council tax.

5   An enhanced home-building programme will be needed if more people come into the UK than leave, as has been the case in recent years. It is also needed because so much of our stock has been so poorly looked after that it will have to be demolished, and because we need new housing for our old age – far too many of our homes have stairs, and far too many of us are waiting for hip operations. As we note in Chapter 4, we need a National Building Service with the necessary interest in building social housing in areas of lower land value and with the necessary skills to engage in cutting-edge sustainable construction and retrofitting. We should build as many homes as we can in the time we have. Our housing is in such a dire condition that we do not have to worry about doing too much too soon. But we must plan it well –people in 200 years' time should look back on it and say: 'Something changed in England then'.

6   Benefits are now so low that they must soon rise faster than wages, which must rise faster than home prices. Rents need to stay still, if not fall. All these factors are currently out of balance. Basic income (Chapter 3) is an important tool for

175

making this happen. Housing benefit needs to be slowly tapered out over a 10-year period, as it is simply a transfer of money from government to private landlords and distorts house prices and housing market activity. The basic income plan will make this possible over time.

7   We need to control rents and eliminate feudal payments for which no benefit is provided. Greater income and wealth equality would be achieved by the reintroduction of rent controls, which would also reduce housing benefit bills massively. The already calculated Local Housing Allowances could be used to set the maximum fair rent in an area. We also need to remove leasehold and convert all leaseholders into freeholders or commonholders in the case of multiple dwellings. Compensation for freeholders should be up to maximum of the cost of the initial leasehold purchase, uprated for inflation, minus leaseholder ground rent payments received to date.

8   Squatting and all other acts that are done purely to seek shelter and not to steal items for profit should again be made a civil, not a criminal, offence. Squatting is a symptom of a problem, not the problem. Similarly, anti-social behaviour orders should not be enacted on the roofless, let alone the hosing down with cold water of places in which they might sleep in winter.

9   Illegal actions by landlords and bankers that deprive people of their home and shelter should become criminal, rather than civil, offences. Their actions kill children. We should treat allowing black mould to spread as child abuse.

10 We have to recognise that housing is central to environmental sustainability. When we build, we need to build for the very long term.[17] We need to build new homes that are

planned to last for centuries; that are built assuming that car use in future will fall as it has done in Japan for the last 25 years, every year; and where people can cycle and walk to work during their working lives and to visit their friends in old age.

The need for these reforms is evident in a city like Oxford.

Why only a coordinated, national effort can address our crisis: the case of Oxford

Oxford City Council says that the city needs 26,440 homes over the period 2020–40. This means the people of that city need 1,322 new homes a year. In short, this housing is needed if the city's hospitals are to function in future and if teachers and assistants are to be able to live in or even near the city. The growth of the two universities and numbers of students is also a key issue. Basically, this new housing is needed for the city to function. Figure 6 shows how Oxford almost entirely stopped building housing after the 1970s. By 2011, the city contained 35 per cent of the jobs in Oxfordshire but only 24 per cent of the population.[18] In the absence of a concerted effort of the same scale, nature and motivation as that of the post-war period, action is incapable of matching aspiration.

But the council says that there's only capacity to build 9,612 of these homes – 481 a year – within the city's boundaries. There is not the space to build more and they cannot build upwards, due to the city's spires and views.[19] If houses are not built next to the city, it will increase car use. If the houses are not council owned, they will be unaffordable to those whom the city most needs. It is confounding, then, to know that current

177

1750
population: unknown

In 1750 Oxford consisted largely of the medieval city; outlying villages such as Headington were still separate entities.

1830
population: 24,000

In 1830 there were 24,000 people living inside the modern Oxford boundary. The period saw housing built to the north of the city.

1900
population: 57,000

Between 1830 and 1900 there were major urban extensions into St Clement's and North Oxford.

1939
population: 94,000

The interwar years saw large numbers of houses built in what are now the suburbs of Cowley, Headington and Marston.

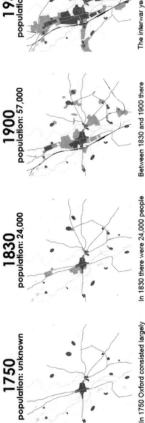

1970
population: 125,000

Council housing estates including Blackbird Leys were built in the postwar period. The green belt was introduced from the 1950s.

2001
population: 134,000

The urban footprint of Oxford has changed little since the 1970s. The most recent urban extension at Greater Leys was built in the 1990s.

2011
population: 152,000

The rapidly growing population since 2001 has been accommodated by increased housing density within the existing urban footprint.

2021
projection: 165,000

With the city still growing but confined by the green belt, developments are planned at Northern Gateway and Barton.

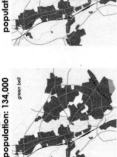

Figure 6 The housing history of Oxford.[20]

plans designate almost all of this housing as private and much of it to be built and operated by employers in near-feudal holdings. We are becoming more and more reliant on solutions that exacerbate the issues the vast majority of us need to be resolved.

How does this compare to the past? In 1927 there was a plan to make Oxford into a decent-sized city – twice the size it is today (Figure 7). This city could be green, could be off the floodplain and could facilitate the sort of Total Transport Network we outline in Chapter 10. But such development can only be done well by the state. In 2027 we celebrate 100 years of not having done this in Oxford. The consequence is that the city has the most expensive housing and the highest or second-highest rate of homeless deaths in England.

This is a case study in how our current system fails the vast majority of us and how the policies we have outlined here can end this. Our housing programme, advanced through a National Building Service building to the highest possible standards, can bring us back to the common-sense ambition of the past and deliver the sustainable, stable and productive communities that our society requires in order to function. If we do this, we can have 15-minute cities that meet the needs of all of us quickly. The greatest failure of the neoliberal era has been to deprive us of the common sense to realise this.

A national public house-building programme is overwhelmingly popular

In our Act Now survey, we found an average level of support for the policy of 71 per cent in the Red Wall, with 63 per cent among Conservative and 79.6 per cent among Labour 2019 voters. Nationally, approval was 76 per cent, with 66 per cent

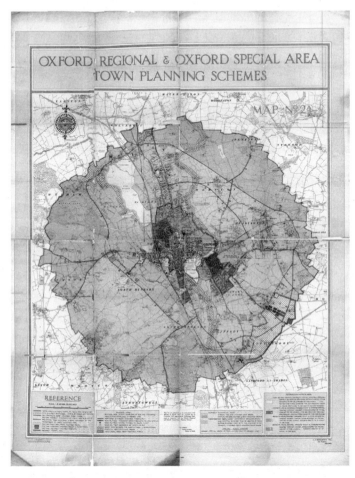

Figure 7 The 1927 plan for the City of Oxford. Taken from an ancient map carefully preserved by Martin Wainwright (former northern correspondent of the *Guardian*) for its potential value in future planning.

among those intending to vote Conservative, 77.9 per cent among those intending to vote Labour and 69.7 per cent among those who don't know who they will vote for or who don't intend to vote at present.

The arguments that are most persuasive among the two groups are different. Voters in the Red Wall evaluated at 71.8 per cent approval an argument based on benefits for the whole country from a national house-building programme

> I feel it is basic human right to be provided with shelter and I believe that we, as a nation, are failing OUR people miserably given the lack of affordable and social housing. Having decent homes that you can afford is crucial in this day and age and there is more than enough wealth to be able to fund this policy. We should be moving towards a world where we are ALL seen as equals and are treated as such. As we are all aware, having good-quality houses contributes to your health, wellbeing, education and so forth. This house-building programme will give us all the opportunity to buy and create a home for ourselves, eventually reducing the need for housing benefit across Britain. With higher-quality houses that are more comfortable and cheaper to heat, we can support the greater good for all Britons and ensure that we are all treated equally.

Nationally, an argument grounded in redistributing from the rich to the vast bulk of us who are struggling to secure housing received 81.6 per cent approval:

> We live in a time when the rich seem to be getting richer and the poor poorer. People who in the past would have been able to comfortably afford a house can no longer get on the ladder. We must do all we can to support workers on low–middle incomes in owning a home that gives the best quality of life and something to be proud of, rather than just lining the pockets of the rich

further with 2nd or 3rd homes that they barely use or rent out. We should increase taxes on owners of empty properties, abolish rip-off leasehold fees and control rents to encourage selfish landlords to sell and to fund a big house-building programme to increase supply to normal people who need it, hopefully ending housing benefit in the longer-term. Ordinary hard-working people need help to get on the property ladder and these policies give us the best means of achieving this.

Throughout all of the narratives produced, there was consensus that housing is a need both specifically for those who cannot afford to buy or even rent and for the nation as a whole. There is clear evidence that we all know that better housing is a national priority.

Conclusion

Decent council housing provision reduces pressure on the private market. Private sector rents reduce. Houses and flats become more affordable to buy. Some argue that this trend dis-incentivises the private sector from building a sufficient number of new homes, but that is hardly well reflected by what has actually occurred in the UK. And we only have to look to Finland, to almost all of the other Nordic countries, to Vienna, to the Netherlands, to so many other examples in mainland Europe, to know that it is possible to have cheap, high-quality housing for everyone. The builders will build – you just need to prevent a few giant firms from buying governments. The consequence of allowing this to happen is that some of the richest people in England are house-builders at a point in time when we have not been as poorly housed in decades. We have a system that rewards rather than punishing failure.

The chief executive of scandal-struck house-builder Persimmon, paid £40 million under the controversial bonus scheme that claimed the scalp of his predecessor, is quitting little over a year into the job. Dave Jenkinson took over from Jeff Fairburn 15 months ago. Fairburn became the poster boy for corporate greed after a scheme paid him a £75 million bonus following a sales bonanza triggered by the taxpayer-funded Help to Buy programme. Jenkinson got £40 million in the same politically toxic deal devised in 2012 but still succeeded Fairburn after he was forced out by the row. He said today he would leave once a replacement is found.[21]

As for Oxford, we could have the 'greenest city in Europe' if we adopted the 1927 plan in 2027. Good plans have features that are timeless in their understanding of human need. We can end our decades'-old aberration.

Recommendations

1 End regressive taxation that punishes those in lower-value housing by introducing a proportional property tax, as outlined in Chapter 12

2 Support social stability by enhance the existing right to stay into a right to sell, giving mortgagors the right to become tenants rather than face eviction

3 Discourage waste by introducing taxes on second homes, holiday homes and empty commercial property

4 End taxes on spare bedrooms to ensure that every family can live in a home with a spare room for visitors

5 Build as many publicly owned houses as building capacity permits to address the housing crisis, with funding designated by the National Investment Bank and construction driven forward by the National Building Service

6 Ensure that the social safety net is sufficient that housing benefit can be withdrawn over time as social housing capacity increases, to remove the direct transfer of wealth from government to landlords

7 Introduce fair rent control and eliminate feudal payments, such as leasehold, for which no benefit is provided and which punish existence

8 Make squatting and all other acts that are done purely to seek shelter and not to steal items for profit once again civil, not criminal, offences

9 Make illegal actions by landlords and bankers that deprive people of their home and shelter criminal, rather than civil, offences, since their actions demonstrably harm life

10 Build new homes that are planned to last for centuries, for both sustainability and value for buyers

CHAPTER 10

TRANSPORT AND INFRASTRUCTURE

Chapter in 30 seconds

Transport affects everyone. Unregulated public transport and dependence on private vehicles has led to colossal market failure and serious environmental damage. Time spent in traffic jams, waiting for delayed trains or finding alternatives to cancelled buses represents an enormous opportunity and financial cost to us all. We spend a fortune on transport, but we spend it inefficiently and reward the wrong actors. A paradigm shift is required, where we think of Mobility as a Service (MaaS) rather than a series of discrete purchases. We should hand regulatory control to devolved authorities to create integrated Total Transport Networks (TTNs) in conurbations and rural hinterlands. With powers to raise and retain income, we can have public transport so good that people will voluntarily leave their cars behind. This chapter focuses on intra-city and intra-regional transportation, where 95 per cent of journeys are made.[1] We outline a transformative programme of democratic control that turns the government obsession with road building on its head. By fully funding – from land value capture, salary sacrifice and

pension investment – a TTN of buses, trams and cycleways, we
can eliminate the traffic jam and all the associated dead time.

Introduction: the scale of the problem

Imagine a situation in which towns in Northern England have
no electricity after 9pm, and cities have intermittent and unreli-
able supply. Imagine that supply is completely unregulated, and
customers seeking full coverage have no choice but to pay different private companies. The transmission system cannot cope
with peak demand, causing residents to waste hours every week
waiting to begin routine tasks. Productivity suffers considerably,
since the lack of electricity hinders business success and prevents people from taking jobs. In response to this market failure,
those who can raise the money buy their own generator, often
becoming heavily indebted in the process. By and large, these
generators stand idle most of the day, but they still cost thousands of pounds a year to own and maintain. The resultant
emissions damage our health and heat our planet.

Nobody would tolerate such a situation. Yet we do have such
a situation with transport. It has been allowed to become the
accepted norm as a result of decades of degradation that has
left us light years away from our neighbours across the North
Sea. Entry costs into public transport provision are prohibitive.
Subsidies are uncertain. Regulations are incoherent. Anyone can
start a bus service, but train services are long-term, central government franchises. There is no compulsion or incentive for different modes to cooperate. The current system is one of severe
market failure. It is suffocating our economy and our cities.

Transport-related social exclusion affects 21.3 per cent of
Northern England.[2] The ultimate result is that poor public

transport excludes 3.3 million northerners from economic and social opportunities. Poor transport is almost the defining feature of a 'left-behind' place. Even in areas well served by public transport, costs and complexity prevent access to work. Foundational economy research shows even in cities, 65 to 70 per cent of journeys to work are made by car.[3] The radial design of public transport is a major contributor. Buses or trains typically go into a city centre and then out again on limited lines. If you live in a suburb and work on an industrial estate, this is not much use.

Even frugal car ownership is prohibitively expensive for low-paid workers. In 2021, owning and running a car cost on average £3,406.80 a year without finance and £5,744.40 with finance.[4] Commuting to work by car is increasingly unaffordable. For those of us under 21, even third-party insurance costs several thousand pounds. Low-paid workers face a Universal Credit taper, but getting a job more than walking distance away from home adds substantial travel costs. In deprived areas, there is a large labour pool of school lunchtime staff and part-time shop assistants but comparatively few people can access better-paid work just a few miles away. Add in collecting kids from school and many millions of us are caught in a poverty trap associated with a transport method that charges consumers insurance even when our mode of transport is sitting idle in the drive most of the time.

Attempting to resolve our transport crisis by building more roads is wholly counterproductive. The speed of car traffic is determined by the journey time of public transport. At first, extra road capacity speeds up traffic, making car driving more appealing. This means that people switch from public transport, fill up the road and remove any benefits that increased road size may produce. This has been tested to destruction. From New York to Los Angeles, there are ten-lane highways choked with traffic.

Simply substituting electric vehicles for petrol or diesel is not viable either. No one has yet proposed a viable method for charging cars in terraced streets. We haven't even got agreement for a universal plug for all electric vehicles. The Jevons paradox states that increasing energy efficiency leads to greater energy usage overall. Jevons developed his model for industrial coal consumption in the nineteenth century. It still holds true. As electric cars become more prevalent, they become more efficient. More people buy them, consuming more rare earth metals and more electricity. Moving big steel boxes around on high-friction rubber tyres is inherently energy intensive. Engineers have made about as much progress as is possible on that. In fact, it's getting worse as more people shift to SUVs. Petrol and diesel for UK road transport used 39 million tonnes of oil in 2019.[5] The combined total of all industrial, commercial and domestic electricity usage was 25 million tonnes of oil equivalent. In other words, if we shift from internal combustion to electric vehicles, we need to increase electricity production by 150 per cent.

Once we consider the environmental cost of replacing Britain's 33 million cars, it gets worse.[6] Scope 3 emissions are the carbon costs of manufacturing. Sometimes called 'embodied carbon', this is the lifecycle cost of vehicle production – mining the ores, smelting the steel, producing the paint.

It is also highly doubtful whether world supply can make enough batteries to replace every vehicle. Nor do electric vehicles guarantee clean air: 50 per cent of lung-damaging particulates come not from the tailpipe of petrol and diesel cars but from the tyres and brakes. Electric vehicles may be better in various regards than petrol or diesel, but we cannot simply replace all cars in this way. We need to offer people a better, and cheaper, alternative to reliance on the private car.

All of this inefficiency is contributing to transport's net contribution of one-third of the total quantity of greenhouse gas emissions. All of this is reversible. Improving public transport speed, comfort, reliability and value for money all reduce car journeys. As soon as we remember what a good transport and infrastructure system looks like, we can radically reduce that impact on climate change while improving people's experience.

What are the principles of good transport infrastructure?

Each conurbation and rural hinterland has unique characteristics. This is not the place for a deep dive into precise designs. The general principles, though, hold true across the country. Great Britain is a highly urbanised island with medieval city plans. Land is an inflexible resource that cannot be increased. Yet vast tracts of this scarce and extremely expensive resource are used inefficiently, and forcing almost all passenger movements into the same corridors is inefficient.

A typical 3.5-metre-wide road can accommodate around 1,500 people per hour (pph) in mixed but mostly car-based traffic.[7] Buses can accommodate 5,000 people in the same space, increasing to 9,000 people on dedicated bus lanes. Dedicated cycle lanes can accommodate 12,000 pph, and pedestrianised walkways another 15,000 pph. We should aim to separate traffic types. Walking should be safe and pleasant, with direct, well-lit routes. Cycling should be safe. Buses should travel at speed along dedicated busways and not be delayed by vans delivering to businesses.

We often hear that 'what business needs above all is certainty'. Correct. It's also true of citizens. Reliability is not just about day-to-day punctuality. Anecdotes abound of people changing to a new job, then finding a few months later that the bus service has been withdrawn.

Henry Ford said, 'If I had asked people what they wanted, they'd have said faster horses'. We're sure that if Mr Ford could have mass-produced faster horses, he would have. This was obviously not viable, but neither is it viable to get more people to increasingly distant locations in shorter times if we insist that each 75kg human take a 1,500kg steel box with them on high-friction rubber tyres. The thermodynamic calculations just do not stack up. We must stop thinking about how we move vehicles and start thinking about how we move people, and we must start collectivising mobility to produce economies of scale as we have in so many areas of infrastructure. We long ago stopped the practice of each household being responsible for its own water supply or sewage disposal.

We need to build conurbation and region-level transport systems that are affordable for everyone, improve public health and save the NHS money – a transport system that is quick, reliable and comfortable and that both eight-year-olds and 80-year-olds feel safe using, where instead of stressing in traffic, you can read your book on the way to work. Alongside a shift in modes of transport, we must stop thinking of public transport as the retail sale of individual journeys and start thinking of it as a form of networked platform provision. The objective should be total network coverage.

If you're the only person with a telephone, it's useless. If only one other person has one, it's an expensive toy. But every additional phone added to the network increases utility, efficiency and value for money. The same holds for transport. The more journeys that can be completed end to end on the same system, without leaving the network, the more attractive the offer. We need to follow examples from other areas of our lives. It's a long time since we paid for telephone calls by the minute or charged more for calls between 9am and 1pm. The solution lies in coordinated, devolved public transport, with Mobility as a Service (MaaS) that focuses on transport as a means of ensuring that our transport needs are met in predictable, secure, affordable forms.

Over decades we've been told that such a vision is a fantasy, but it's the present dystopia that requires mental gymnastics. The only people it benefits are private providers and oil companies whose poor performance is subsidised at enormous public cost. This is not sustainable and should not be sustained.

A Total Transport Network for each region

We need a Total Transport Network (TTN), with complete coverage of an entire conurbation and its rural hinterland. A TTN is a combination of bus, tram, and light and heavy rail offering everyone connectivity, augmented by e-bikes, car clubs and on-demand transport. It provides real-time information about journey times, parking and bike hire. It is the only system capable of supporting precisely targeted policy interventions, such as allowing free travel for specific journeys – including carers travelling to work or apprentices in critical professions travelling to college. Because it is integrated, it enables us to match an end-user app with the smart infrastructure that controls our traffic signals, transponders on buses and sensors on parking bays. Road junction redesign can build a system so well organised that buses are faster than cars. For the travelling public, a single app can allow you to buy your tickets so that buses are faster to use, book your parking space before you get to town, plan your route for walking or cycling, and reserve you an e-bike. If you don't have a phone, you can tap in with a debit card.

Rural areas can have a network of smaller buses, around a revitalised rail network, with on-demand transport via a 'book-a-bus' system – a bit like a big shared taxi. You use your app to book when you want a bus and to where. The system calculates the best route and tells you when it will be near your home. It is only this sort of innovation, along with the provision of functioning broadband, that can make rural life and rural communities viable. Technology means that this is all possible in ways that it wasn't in the past. Indeed, not doing this is massively more expensive for us all than persisting with the same failed system.

Technological change has transformed our understandings of what a functioning day-to-day life looks like. Mobility freedom for the baby boomer generation meant having a car. For younger people, freedom is viewed as continuing life on the go, being able to use your smartphone and not having to worry about parking, the flexibility of not being tied to a vehicle during visits to city centres, with all of the attendant cost and logistical investment, and having the capacity to circumvent traffic jams in finding our way home. Increasingly, that change is accompanied by the realisation that having a car is just not affordable. A properly designed TTN system will make it nonsensical for families to own a second car and open up the possibility of not having the first one. If we can produce a system that allows us to get to work, get our shopping and see our friends without using a car, why would we spend such a massive proportion of our income on something whose value always reduces over time? That's often just wasted money.

We will always need cars for some journeys, but we need to open up the possibility of accessing those cars in ways that are more affordable and targeted at our needs. Where we need to drive away for holidays, we can create cheap hire by simply scaling up the car clubs that exist now. Car clubs have collectively owned cars that can be booked online by the hour or by the day and are kept on public residential streets. We just park them up when we're finished, without any of the hassle associated with private rental.

A single-app payment system, or smart card for the digitally less connected, removes the complexity of all of the individual booking and logistical complication across transport methods, adding in navigation and real-time journey times across the network. While there is an understandable focus on the £2-per-journey cap, this offers much greater scope for innovative charging models that incentivise, rather than punish, use of public systems. For example, we can couple pay-as-you-go, for those without capacity for up-front or direct debit payments, with an upper cap equivalent to £2 per day or £730 a year, beyond which all further travel is unlimited for the rest of the 12-month period. Incentivising use makes it easier to plan and sustain services, with increased use reducing funding gaps; disincentivising it, as at present, makes planning impossible.

Taking people with us (literally)

TTN-MaaS is an argument for freedom, for liberation from enforced car ownership in the absence of feasible alternatives and from the arbitrary whims of private providers who remove crucial services when they aren't profitable. Motoring should become a matter of consumer choice, not a matter of necessity in the absence of a viable alternative. In TTN-MaaS, we have a viable alternative that enhances the freedom we discussed in Chapter 2. We just need to remember that the changes involved are no greater than those we have undertaken before. Going back to Henry Ford, when was the last time you heard someone complain they couldn't find an ostler for their horse? We've made transitions before and we can do it again.

TTN-MaaS is a game-changer insofar as it is in the interests of us all to support it, because it gives us back the two resources we lack most: money and time. The arguments for it do not rest on self-sacrifice for the greater good, and nobody will ever be banned from using cars. However, we need to understand that the state already imposes what are known as 'Pigouvian taxes' (after the British economist Arthur Cecil Pigou) on car users. This refers to a charge on something that the state wants to discourage. The £5.89 excise duty on a packet of cigarettes is a classic example, but the tax of 52.95p per litre on petrol affects a far greater proportion of us.

We can use versions of Pigouvian taxes in more productive and supportive ways. Most local authorities already charge for car parking. This could be extended to a levy on private car parks, including supermarket car parks. With automatic number plate recognition, those of us who drive could be *credited* with a rebate every time we pay a parking charge. We have a choice: use low-cost public transport or drive and pay, say, £5 to park. But every time we pay, we get £2 back in our public transport account. That gives us a growing fund to enable us to use public transport, directly incentivising us to use those facilities we've already paid for. Ultra-low emissions zones (ULEZs) and clean air zones (CAZs) are not unpopular with drivers of newer, expensive vehicles, who are exempt from charges. If the

UK finally ends internal combustion engine cars, the Treasury will lose £24 billion in fuel duty. It is likely they will look to road charging. Again, a rebate system will encourage modal shift.

Popularity is increased when people perceive a social benefit, too. A TTN with personal accounts opens up new areas for public policy. North of Tyne Mayor Jamie Driscoll's plans for free public transport for under-18s in the North East is an example of how we can reduce car usage quickly, but we can go further for targeted interventions. Public services, even private employers, can fund or discount individual journeys with a simplicity that special passes or ticket machines cannot. By linking public services to the transport network needed to get us to our appointments, we can facilitate free transport for patients to visit hospitals without increasing parking facilities in areas with no capacity. We would simply receive a code on appointment letters allowing us to travel for free within an allocated time slot. Salary sacrifice schemes (discussed below) allow participants to receive partially subsidised public transport and would be much easier to organise around a TTN.

Where will the money come from?

In 2022, UK households (not businesses) spent £102.9 billion on private vehicle transport and £5.4 billion on public transport, including rail and taxis but excluding air fares.[8] Diverting even one-tenth of our spending on private vehicles would fund a tripling of public transport fare income. Household expenditure is direct cash spending. If we account for externalities, we see that private transport is even more expensive. The Institute for Fiscal Studies estimates that obesity and weight-related issues costs the UK £98 billion a year.[9] Depending on the methodology, congestion costs the UK between £8 billion and £40 billion a year.

These losses are not easily changed into cash savings, but they need to be accounted for in understanding the broader economic and social costs of our current system. Free travel for under-18s would help to break the habit of children being driven to school and social activities. Habits built in childhood are likely to persist into adulthood. Walking an extra few hundred steps every journey will produce significant long-term health savings.

Clearly there is a strong argument for public subsidy. Every region is different, so we cannot suggest costs without detailed business cases. Conceptually, though, public transport is essentially a fixed-cost model. It costs the same to run a bus carrying five passengers as it does to run one carrying 50. The goal should be to create a TTN for each region and get maximum use out of it.

Much, if not all, of this could be raised by extending salary sacrifice schemes to public transport season tickets. Salary sacrifice is where an employer pays for goods or services and deducts this cost from the employee's salary, and both obtain a tax benefit. Childcare or bike purchases are common examples. Your employer buys you a £1,000 bike, including helmet and lock, and pays you £1,000 less in gross salary. If you are a basic-rate taxpayer, you save 20 per cent income tax and 12 per cent national insurance. So in effect, your £1,000 bike costs you £680. Your employer also saves £138 in employers' national insurance contributions (NICs), providing a strong incentive for employers to sign up. Actual amounts will, of course, vary depending on salary and tax thresholds.

The fact that you can currently get a car on salary sacrifice but not a public transport season ticket is ludicrous. So far, the

Treasury has regarded salary sacrifice for public transport as dead weight. In lay terms, why give season ticket holders a 32 per cent rebate when they'd buy one anyway? We should flip the argument. It's not a 32 per cent subsidy but 150 per cent matched funding.

Actual costs will vary, but let's keep the numbers simple. As an employee, we 'pay' £1,000 gross, which is £680 in take-home pay for a basic rate taxpayer. We get unlimited free travel for a year. Society gets less congested roads, healthier people and lower carbon emissions. It costs the Treasury £453 in lost taxes and NI, but levers in £680 from us as private citizens. In other words, every £1 of subsidy levers in an additional £1.50 of private investment. The TTN network operators could also negotiate with employers to recover some of the 13.8 per cent NICs, in return for a discount.

Unlike most subsidies, the Treasury would not have to pay a penny in advance. The proposal has perfect demand responsiveness – it only pays after the worker has bought their ticket. We could offer all nurses, teachers, postal workers and in fact all working people this deal. A season ticket costing £2 per day (£730 a year), if bought by just half of the UK's 32.8 million employees, would raise £12 billion a year. In 2022 the public transport farebox income was £2.8 billion. These are basic changes with huge benefits to us all.

Land value capture

Where the public builds new transport infrastructure, for example a local rail extension and stations, the value of the surrounding land increases.[10] This is pure windfall – private wealth gain for zero private investment. Placing a charge on real estate or undeveloped land can be worth billions of pounds. The 2013 London Finance Commission calculated that transport schemes costing £36 billion could produce land value uplifts of £91 billion.[11]

For established housing, charging should apply only to house sales. Since sellers are benefiting from public investment by receiving extra capital from the increased equity in the sale, they are not out of pocket. The same would apply to commercial premises. In practice, to maintain public support the charge would be levied at a maximum of 85 per cent of the full uplift, so the homeowner benefits from the land value increase. In other words, no existing homeowner or landowner loses a thing. They get a free uplift in the price of their property, and when they come to sell, they pay back most of what they got for free and keep normal market capital gains. In the meantime, they enjoy the additional amenity of improved infrastructure.

The calculation and collection of the uplift is comparatively simple to administer. It will require legislation and the establishment of a fair valuation system, but beyond that it is easy to implement. It could be introduced as an annexe to any finance paper going through parliament.

Public ownership

As part of any TTN, buses and other municipal transport should be brought back into local authority control. This has been done in London, where the London Bus Service is a wholly owned subsidiary of Transport for London, and more recently in Greater Manchester, where Transport for Greater Manchester runs buses and trams. The government should take control of the national railways too. As Avanti West Coast has itself noted, taxpayers are providing 'free money' in the form of subsidies and providing bonuses for meeting the most basic of standards.[12] Privatisation in franchising has demonstrably failed and, as happened with LNER, failing franchises should return to public ownership and the convoluted, time-consuming and expensive ticketing system replaced by simpler, more consistent fares.[13] Investment for decarbonising transport can be leveraged both through the direct investment of the National Investment Bank and through incentivised private investment from pension and other investors. Whenever capital funding is raised from central government, it needs to be assessed using an enhanced Green Book approach that considers value in terms of better health, low emissions and long-term economic inclusion, as well as just economic uplift.[14]

Pension investment

In keeping with the aims of our Green New Deal, we want pension funds to divest from fossil fuels. That is easier if we give pension fund managers something else to invest in. As we demonstrate in Chapter 6, the example of PFI shows that as taxpayers we have been vulnerable to exploitative investments with apparently low up-front costs. We must never repeat that mistake. Instead, let's encourage pension funds – our money from deferred income – to invest in productive infrastructure.

It is an established model for pension funds to finance buildings and take a risk on the rents coming in. This can be extended to transport. As part-owners of the TTN, the funds would be taking a risk on the success of the system. Pension funds have already indicated they are willing to explore such models. The barrier is *force majeure*. In the event of a future pandemic-like event, public transport revenues would collapse. We know that government will step in: they would have no alternative. But until that is written as a financial guarantee, the investors have an uninsurable risk. We propose that government develop a simple guarantee confirming that it will provide a baseline of income for any pension investment in TTNs. This then allows pension funds to meet their regulatory duties and frees them to invest our money in sustainable projects in the UK that directly improve the amenity and quality of life of their policyholders.

How should we govern it?

The example of transport and infrastructure cogently makes the case for aspects of the democratic reforms we outline in Chapter 11. Devolution is an essential element of building and maintaining a TTN that meets our needs. Such a system cannot be run from Whitehall.

Our local communities must feel that they have a real say in such significant changes. We have working examples that point us in the direction of mechanisms for overarching democratic control. TTN design should make use of citizens' assemblies, to produce informed, democratic opinion on preferences and the trade-offs citizens want to see. This is essential to ensuring adequate support and direction to such a critical aspect of our lives. Once TTNs are operational, passengers will receive occasional requests to rate different aspects of the experience – comfort, reliability, cleanliness and so on – in effect co-designing operations.

Control over infrastructure itself has been presented in different forms with different strengths and weaknesses. Quangos of elected councillors work well in theory, but in practice, lay councillors have little time to lead and scrutinise officers. Worse still would be outsourcing. Long-term sustainability should not be supplanted by short-term quarterly returns. That democratic deficit is what has got us into this mess in the first place. An obvious solution presents itself. The optimal size of governance is the travel-to-work area. This broadly corresponds with the current combined mayoral authorities in England, which we wish to see rolled out across the UK. Mayoral elections then effectively become a referendum on how well the transport system has been run. There are alternatives, but unless they maintain a direct link between the governors and the passengers, democracy and hence public consent is weakened. Major changes need political will to stay on course. Indirect elections to committees are far removed from the public and subject to political machinations. Direct electoral mandates are much stronger.

A TTN run as MaaS opens up possibilities for direct user feedback in a way that is impossible in traditional models. Users who choose to participate can be anonymously tracked across their journey, giving us near perfect data on demand and travel patterns, enabling fine tuning.

This is a transformative policy that gives us our time and money back. At a time in which both are scarce, we cannot keep thinking of transport and infrastructure as an add-on to more important policies. It is at the heart of making our lives liveable again.

Overhauling public transport is popular

In our Act Now survey, we found an average level of support for the policy of 73.8 per cent in the Red Wall, with 70.8 per cent among Conservative and 83 per cent among Labour 2019 voters. Nationally, approval was 76.9 per cent, with 65.1 per cent among those intending to vote Conservative, 80.2 per cent among those intending to vote Labour and 73.6 per cent among those who don't know who they will vote for or who don't intend to vote at present.

The arguments that are most persuasive among the two groups are different. Voters in the Red Wall evaluated at 76.9 per cent approval an argument based on benefits for the whole country of transforming public transport:

> Our current transport system is broken and increasingly unaffordable to Britons. Since deregulation, the number of services has reduced as operators chase profitable routes and there has been a gradual loss of coordination, with buses and trains out of sync, leaving commuters stuck waiting for connections. By bringing the transport infrastructure back into public ownership, this will allow the return of transport coordination, subsidised services that are currently unprofitable and capping of fares, so that we can all travel. Publicly controlled and owned transport networks give us all the ability to get to where we need to get to efficiently and affordably. By making public transport affordable, especially to get to work, more people will use it as it will be cheaper than paying for petrol, helping families that are currently struggling with tax, insurance and car costs. This will help us to access public services and work in ways that we can't at present.

Nationally, an argument grounded in redistributing from the rich to the vast bulk of us who are poorly served by existing transport arrangements received 81.4 per cent approval:

> The transport system in this country is in a mess and requires a radical overhaul. The price of travel in the UK has now reached

such high levels that people on even middle incomes find it diffi-cult to afford to get about. Nationalisation of transport will allow those of us who live far away from London, such as the North or in rural areas, to receive the same levels of service that are currently reserved for the capital. We need to remember that London has a nationalised service and we have been left behind by privatisation elsewhere in Britain. By building publicly owned transport networks funded by taxing wealthy companies and individuals who have benefited most from public investment, we will be able to ensure that those of us who need to get to work can get to work affordably. There is a great potential for this to cause great investment in the infrastructure of left-behind regions like the North East.

Throughout all of the narratives produced, there was consensus that our transport system is failing us all and that only nation-alisation and removing the profit motive can improve our lives. Reducing commuting and congestion is central to the lived experience that drives support for the policy. With devolution advancing, this is a key area in which progress can be made rapidly.

Recommendations

1   Develop Total Transport Networks, running Mobility as a Service, on a regional level
2   Devolve transport regulation to combined mayoral author-ities, with powers extended across the UK
3   Provide seed funding for system design and development
4   Run citizens' assemblies to gain public consent and valu-able information on system design
5   Give devolved authorities land value capture powers

6 Rework Green Book calculations for transport projects to include a broader scope, including long-term health benefits and reduced social exclusion
7 Underwrite pension fund investment in public transport in the event of *force majeure*
8 Extend salary sacrifice to cover public transport season tickets that meet a MaaS standard

CHAPTER 11

DEMOCRACY, POWER AND SECURITY

Chapter in 30 seconds

As the handling of the COVID-19 pandemic and many other issues examined in this report demonstrates, our political system produces unhelpful and wholly avoidable outcomes. The current system channels politicians towards unpopular ideological experiments that entrench and exacerbate crisis. We need to understand that the transformation of society requires systematic democratic reform. In this chapter, we outline a set of reforms that enhance the capacity of our political system to produce the outcomes that the vast majority of our society requires. Building on policy development by the Jenkins Commission (1998) and the Brown Commission (2022), we set out forms of electoral and parliamentary reform that increase competition and the ethos of public service and reduce in-built incentives for careerism and unwillingness to take risks for the public good. We argue that increasing consistency of administrative bodies across the UK while devolving greater powers to nations and regions is essential to making policy that is responsive. The reforms call for bravery among politicians in upholding the public good against opportunities for corruption and the power of unsustainable special interests.

Introduction: an intentional democratic deficit

The kind of secure and thriving society this book outlines has public support and ought, in a democratic system, to be implemented as an expression of the will of citizens. However, the very policies that would enable us to move past our era of multiple overlapping crises have been rejected by political parties for reasons that have uneven relationships with public opinion and economic feasibility. There is a belief that memories of fossil-fuel-driven inflation in the 1970s mean that the case for state intervention can never be won. But there is a more persuasive fear that negative media coverage of policies that, for example, require tax on wealth is likely to have a damaging impact on politicians' capacity for election and re-election.

The policy ideas and proposals in this book are eminently practical and achievable. The problem is that the shape and nature of our political discourse simply excludes such common-sense proposals from even being discussed. This is in turn due to the structures and culture of our democratic system. In general, much of our democratic architecture is unfit for purpose. Britain has an antiquated form of democratic governance in a post-industrial age. We have engagement with the world at our smartphone fingertips, can connect with, talk to and organise people around multiple issues across the globe. Yet our ability to influence our lives through government is extremely limited.

As we have suggested in previous chapters, the process of neoliberal reform strips the capacity of the state to intervene and thereby the capacity of democracy to address critical social challenges. We have to understand that the intellectual figureheads of that process have always viewed democracy as antagonistic to freedom. Key works, such as Friedrich Hayek's *Road to Serfdom*,[1] were motivated by the 1945 settlement's commitment to redistribution as a means of securing all of society for all of its members. For Hayek, as for Milton Friedman, taxation was coercion and therefore unjust: as soon as the state begins to redistribute to promote the interests of those who do not live by wealth, it starts society on the slippery road to Soviet-style communism.

In this view, the only taxation that can ever be justified is that which prevents coercion – physically or through threat of physical harm forcing someone to do something they do not wish to do. This means that there is an ethical reason for stripping the state of the capacity to intervene and rendering it a 'nightwatchman', providing policing to prevent theft and assault but doing little else. Democracy is a genuine threat to that insofar as it provides pathways by which the majority can advance their interests at the expense of the minority – the rich who live by wealth. The post-war creation of a welfare state and nationalised health system was therefore equated with communism and any attempt to sustain it totalitarian, regardless of, and often precisely because of, its democratic basis.

The justification for this constraint on democracy was the claim that freed from social democratic intervention, individuals would be able to pursue an unlimited number of lives that they themselves found meaningful. In this regard, the state was seen to uphold equality between citizens by remaining neutral between conceptions of the good. This is genuinely the liberal tradition of neutrality as equality that is found not just in Hayek and Friedman but also in Rawls, Kant and, in much more limited form, Locke. The point, however, is that a nightwatchman state's upholding of the market's distribution of wealth means that it is never neutral with regard to conceptions of the good.

As the state was rolled back in the 1980s, opportunities receded for pursuing lives that depended on public provision of goods and services. Because those goods and services were unprofitable, they could not naturally be provided by the market. It became increasingly clear that only lives oriented around wealth acquisition were viable, and only lives that bore the signs of that acquisition would be valued. Age-old understandings of the importance of lives being oriented around a rich diversity of activities were cast aside, neglecting J.K. Galbraith's forewarning that though 'there are many versions of the good society, the treadmill is not one of them'.[2]

For enough people for enough of the last few decades, the neoliberal settlement was able to effectively substitute the collective provision of security and a diversity of good lives with an individualised and increasingly narrow alternative. The global financial crisis of 2007/08 and subsequent other crises have made clear the dangers of that trend, and there has been a growing consensus that only the state can deliver the change we need. There is growing recognition that the settlement benefits an ever smaller proportion of the population whose wealth is unchecked by democratic interventions that a majority of us support.

Neoliberalism has been a profoundly anti-democratic project that no longer benefits us. However, in the absence of the ability and willingness of progressive policymakers to deliver change, public support has often been channelled in self-destructive and anti-democratic directions. A democracy that cannot offer basic levels of material wellbeing regardless of the levels of support for such measures, one which actively fosters food banks, is by definition not a democracy.

The reforms that will enable
implementation of this report

Across the country there is a collective need for control. This has been apparent in repeated political events, from the referendums on Scottish independence and Brexit to the decision of voters in traditional Labour constituencies to support the Conservatives in 2019. With the exception of those who live by wealth rather than work, we all understand that we are subject to rather than in control of processes. We feel it in our households, schools and workplaces, when we are waiting for health and social care, and when we are urging the action needed to tackle our climate emergency.

We can only achieve that control through democratic reform. It is no longer sensible to think that democratic reform is a means of making voting fairer or achieving consensus between parties. That was the basis for the 2011 alternative vote referendum, which was advanced by the Liberal Democrats as one element of the agreement that enabled the formation of the 2010–15 coalition government. Arguing on the basis for fairness and inclusivity at a time in which the Coalition Agreement was enabling the introduction of austerity measures that reduced control, and of the increase in student tuition fees that breached one of the key Liberal Democrat manifesto pledges, made no sense. This was a junior partner in a bad government arguing for a system that would produce more bad outcomes.

What is increasingly clear is that we are much more receptive to justification for reform grounded in the outcomes of our lives. IPPR's 'Talking Politics' presents a coherent starting point.[3] The report holds that there is widespread dissatisfaction with democracy and that this feeds into populist movements with regressive ends that highlight the capture of political systems by elites and elite interests. It concludes that democrats need specifically to justify democracy in terms of outcomes. The problem, as the report authors note, is that our representatives fail to deliver.[4] Democracy needs to deliver better outcomes in terms of the principles we identify in Chapter 2, in order to demonstrate its value to citizens.

Part of the reason that politicians have failed to deliver is that the democratic system as it stands promotes bad outcomes. The UK has one of the most centralised political systems on the planet and is bound together with few written rules. The first-past-the-post (FPTP) voting system, combined with incentives for long-term post-holding, mean that parties have internal dynamics and interests that tend towards inertia. The winner-takes-all system locks in a duopoly, in which the worst outcome for either of the two largest parties is finishing second, retaining the public funding that goes with this.[5] This is a gilded system that demonstrably attracts the wrong sort of politicians, with the wrong understanding of public service and the wrong set of interests, and keeps them in post for decades. They know that they merely need to retain the support of their party, which, in turn, knows that it needs only to retain vague engagement with parts of the media in order for its elected members to pursue highly lucrative and secure careers. This is a system that locks out talent, innovation, and both long-term policy thinking and willingness to take short-term electoral risks at the very point when we need these things most.

FPTP locks in the influence of powerful elites, who in such a centralised and narrow two-party system lobby and donate their way to influence, rigging the system to create more wealth and therefore power. Rupert Murdoch doesn't want a tax on his wealth, so politicians do not advance wealth taxes for fear of public destruction of character.

The impasse breeds dysfunction and disruption. People resent the abuse of having to vote for the least bad option. Many refuse to vote, both because they realise that their voting often has little or no impact on their lives and because they do not wish to reward politicians in whom they have little faith.[6] Far from providing secure government, the system increasingly produces unstable and ineffective government that fails to meet people's needs.

The irony is that both of the main political parties preach the benefits of choice and competition everywhere except when it comes to them. There is no other sector that has the ability to regulate itself like our political class, with its capacity to set its own rules and mark its own homework. The notion that the status quo produces strong government is wrong: the last four parliaments have seen one formal coalition, one minority government, the chaos of Brexit and four consecutive Prime Ministers forced out mid-term.

A weak democracy paves the way to even less democracy. Oddly, it's the right wing that seems more alive to this threat. A report for Onward, the right-of-centre think tank, found that 61 per cent of 18–34-year-olds agree that 'having a strong leader who does not have to bother with parliament and elections would be a good way of governing this country' while 46 per cent agree that 'having the army rule would be a good way of governing this country'. Rachel Wolf, former Tory advisor, warns us of 'the spectre of a rise in populism haunting' us, while in *The Spectator* Joel Kotkin argues that:

> The fusion of government with large oligopolistic companies, and the technologically-enhanced collection of private information, allow the new autocracies to monitor our lives in ways that

Mao, Stalin or Hitler would have envied. A rising tide of money and administrative power defines the rising autocracy. If we as citizens, whatever our political orientation, are not vigilant, our democracy will become an increasingly hollow vessel.[7]

Against the backdrop of this structural crisis, even the election of a well-meaning progressive government could accelerate the descent to autocracy if it fails to deliver on the promise of necessary change. The purpose of this report is to give that government the capacity to make that change, and the evidence before us all indicates that doing so requires structural reform.

Those well-meaning progressives need to know that it is in their interests to let go of the apparent certainty of the present in favour of a system with fewer ingrained privileges but which promotes the outcomes we all need.

There are two bodies of reform that our public servants need to enact.

A competitive and responsive democratic structure

FPTP means that the candidate with the most votes in each constituency is elected as an MP, even if they receive far less than 50 per cent of the vote. This means that governments can be formed that reflect the preferences of a small proportion of those who vote and an even smaller proportion of society, given that turnout is often low in the UK. In 2015, the Conservatives gained a majority with 36.1 per cent of the vote on a turnout of 66.45 per cent, meaning that less than a quarter of the electorate gave the government its express consent.[8] This is particularly damaging insofar as the people most likely to be excluded are those whose interests have been least well served by politicians.

These people then become apathetic and are further excluded as parties focus on appealing to those more likely to vote.

Proportional representation, which aims to ensure that the proportion of votes more closely matches the proportion of seats held by parties, has generally been promoted by parties that are disadvantaged by FPTP, notably the Liberal Democrats, the Green Party and UKIP.[9] That promotion has often been ineffective, since those who prefer either of the two main parties or who feel that their interests are adequately advanced feel no reason for change. It is only the delivery case for proportional representation that has a chance of success. We need to build on more proportional examples in Scotland, Wales and Northern Ireland to improve outcomes in England and Westminster.

The Jenkins Commission (1998) set out plans for a system of proportional representation that maintains the link between constituencies and the interests of constituents and their representatives and ensures greater proportionality in allocation of representatives.[10] Alternative vote+ combines two elements. The 'alternative vote' system in each constituency means that voters list candidates in order of preference, having the choice to allocate a preference to any or none of the candidates. All first preferences are allocated to candidates. If a candidate has over 50 per cent of the vote, they are elected. If not, the candidate with the fewest first preferences is eliminated and their second preferences allocated, and so on until a candidate reaches 50 per cent.

This system ensures that more votes count. While there is evidence in different contexts that systems involving ranking benefit centrist candidates,[11] presenting a sufficiently broad policy platform offers genuine capacity to appeal to the majority of us and hence to be electorally successful under such a system.

The policies in this report do that. In the top-up element, voters choose from a list of candidates to represent, in our case, their region, electing several representatives allocated according to the number of people within their combined authority. Again, the need to appeal to a broad section of society increases the likelihood of political parties endorsing popular policies such as those we outline, while also being forced by smaller parties to consider more radical interventions. We believe that there should be 500 seats allocated to enlarged constituencies, with 150 top-up seats allocated proportionally to enlarged combined mayoral authorities.

There is a body of evidence to suggest that while more complex systems are associated with larger numbers of ballots being rejected and a need for guidance to enable participation,[12] more proportional systems are associated with more stable and more diverse government than our own.[13]

Alongside reforming voting systems, we need to end the conscious suppression of voting. On turning 18 or obtaining citizenship, all eligible voters ought to be registered automatically to vote and have a legal requirement to remain registered to vote at each subsequent residence.[14] We should move towards online voting in order to counter cynical exploitation of weather conditions and other environmental factors in order to suppress the vote.[15]

We also believe that no long-term political change can be possible without the elimination of the House of Lords and the introduction of an Assembly of the Nations and Regions as the second chamber.[16] This would feature 200 members, allocated proportionally according to combined authorities, with mayors each represented by a delegate and an electoral cycle that begins in the middle of the House of Commons cycle. Elections would be by single transferable vote to ensure greater proportionality while leaving room for independent candidates to succeed.[17] The primary role of the second chamber would be to formally interrogate and consult on legislation, and it would retain the power to delay legislation for up to one year. It would complement the Commons.

In both houses, only those who have lived in a constituency for a qualifying period of two years would be permitted to stand for election within the constituency. This radically limits the capacity for political parties to place politicians with no understanding of local people's needs in safe seats. It does not change eligibility for office in any other clear respect that would contravene the Equality Act (2010). Moreover, there ought to be consideration, in the longer term, of the possibility of term limits on service in parliament overall, in order to reduce the view of politics as a career rather than public service, and to check vested interests overall.

There is widespread recognition, not least in the government's own Levelling Up White Paper, that British politics is Westminster-oriented to the detriment of Britain as a whole. Centralisation of power has meant massive investment in London at the expense of the regions. There is also recognition that the cost of renovating Westminster is great and that facilities there are often inappropriate for a fully functioning parliament, with office space, internet access and other key infrastructure inadequate. Put simply, Westminster is neither the right environment nor in the right location to enable Britain to recover.

We believe that there is good reason for parliament to move out of Westminster to enable its renovation and that this can be done at far lower cost than through relocation within London.

Parliament can be relocated on a rolling basis to York, Glasgow and Cardiff to sit in specially designed facilities, moved on a minimum five-yearly and maximum ten-yearly basis to coincide with House of Commons parliaments. Building purpose-built facilities not only creates a public asset that brings wealth to each of these regions, it also enables us to save an estimated £12 billion by facilitating safer, easier, swifter renovation of Westminster. Most importantly, as with relocation of Civil Service offices, it forces politicians into areas of the country that are not London, removing the distortionary experience of working in a city that often has little in common with life elsewhere.

The UK-wide reforms above require the restriction of councils and their funding. To ensure effective devolution and administration, the Scottish model of local authorities should be adopted across the rest of the UK, with combined authorities created on a regional basis to ensure regional coordination and representation to the second chamber.[18] We cannot sustain the current incoherence of five types of council in England, with all of the additional bureaucratic malaise this produces. The reforms provide the basis for a much more robust and integrated set of relationships between layers of government.

De-corruption

Our system is fundamentally corrupt. The process of procurement of personal protective equipment (PPE) during the pandemic merely made visible to the public the long-standing practice of government contracting to donors and partners. Politicians' opposition to public ownership stands at odds with the way in which state contracts are given to a small number of large businesses that act as state agents without providing public service to the nation and employment security to employees. Neoliberalism merely subcontracts the big state to a small number of profit-making partners. De-corrupting it can be achieved only by emphasising the return to public service.

The Labour Party has already suggested some good means of achieving change.[19] Banning second jobs for the entire duration of service and introducing legislation to create exemptions from service requirements in professions such as barristers and GPs makes clear that, like jury duty, public servants are required fundamentally to focus on public duties. Banning politicians from taking on paid work relating to previous political roles for five years after leaving office is also sensible. However, there needs to be a total ban on paid lobbying and all lobbying by foreign citizens and entities. We cannot be beholden to the interests of hostile countries who buy access to our representatives. In that regard, we ought to ban membership by politicians of any group affiliated with an overseas country. Dual nationals would be able to retain their non-British citizenship but would not be able to be affiliated with any advocacy group affiliated with overseas interests. Moreover, we ought to ban all gifts and in-kind benefits rather than having MPs declare those gifts. While the thought of politicians paying for refreshments at events sounds administratively onerous, it is far less onerous than having to track the influence of pernicious entities through reciprocal relationships.

To address the scandal of expenses, there ought to be a total ban on allowances for second homes, with overnight accommodation provided in the vicinity of parliament during parliamentary sessions. There ought to be formalised and designated offices with centrally funded and approved office staff, both in constituencies and around parliament. There should be no need for expenses beyond travel and refreshments during visits, which should be booked and reimbursed by a central office.

Labour is right to introduce the independent Integrity and Ethics Commission to scrutinise any ministerial appointment, open investigations into misconduct and breaches of ministerial code, and set binding sanctions for breaches of the ministerial code. These are basic oversights that exist in almost every profession. Finally, politicians' and public servants' pay ought to be tied directly to the UK median salary. Pay ought to be capped at a maximum of 200 per cent of the median salary, which stands in 2023 at £34,963 across the UK.[20] Tying pay to the median provides politicians with an incentive to advance the interests of the vast majority of workers whose pay is currently inadequate by engaging in redistributive measures. This is consistent with incrementalism in the equality principle, with pay at the upper end of the income distribution addressed through progressive taxation.

Beyond individual politicians, the way in which political parties are funded needs to be reformed. Our two main parties are returning to a position in which they are funded by the same group of extremely wealthy donors who use their donations to extract political influence. We need to ban all donations to political parties by individuals and private companies. All individual funding should come from individual membership fees of a maximum of £6 per month, which is affordable to the vast majority of society. Trade union members would automatically become members of parties to which their unions are affiliated, with their political fund donations being available as membership contributions. Beyond this, there ought to be partial public funding for policy development within parties through an expansion of Policy Development Grants to £5 million, since it is policy development, rather than party political campaigning and messaging, that is in the interest of the general public.

These are reforms that prioritise the interests of citizens over the interests of outlying wealth.

Democratic reform is popular

The IPPR has rightly concluded that arguments for democratic reform need to be made on the basis of outcomes, not values. When the latter are deployed, more often than not they are associated with the fringe interests of losing parties within the political system that are assumed, by their very nature, to be outliers either socially or ideologically. There is a compelling body of evidence to suggest that proportional representation is associated with governments that are to the left of those produced by systems like our own.[21] Explanations for this include the notion that, in systems such as Britain, those in the middle of the wealth distribution vote for right-wing parties out of the belief that they will protect wealth and promote their interests, even if they disagree with other aspects of their policies,[22] while left-wing parties are disadvantaged by having their voters clustered in urban centres with higher rates of poverty, winning seats by large margins but not benefiting on a proportional basis.[23]

The problem in Britain is that such a large proportion of society are now exposed to insecurity as to mean that where the Conservatives have been successful recently, they have adopted a commitment to redistribution, as in 2019 and in their pandemic policies regarding furlough.[24] Recent work has suggested that this support is directed most clearly to addressing dysfunction in the House of Commons through electoral reform,[25] but the strongest levels of support come when people see political reform as being directly related to production of better outcomes in policy.

In our Act Now survey, we found an average level of support for the policy of 74.7 per cent in the Red Wall, with 69.2 per cent among Conservative and 81.1 per cent among Labour 2019 voters. Nationally, approval was 77.9 per cent, with 58.1 among those intending to vote Conservative, 78.9 per cent among those intending to vote Labour and 70.8 per cent among those who don't know who they will vote for or who don't intend to vote at present.

The arguments that are most persuasive among the two groups are different. Voters in the Red Wall evaluated at 77.4 per cent approval an argument based on the role of democratic reform in producing a politics that redistributes wealth and resources from the rich to us as ordinary citizens:

The current system favours incumbents committed to the same old lousy policies. Voters are being screwed by a pro-corporation centre who have massive, unchecked influence in both major parties. Most voters are left to struggle with cost-of-living-crisis and austerity cuts, while MPs are being funded to get extra mortgages on second homes and to put family members in jobs as researchers. A lot of MPs are corrupt. We need to force MPs to represent ordinary people, rather than the 1% they currently represent, in order to get out of the stagnation we have been stuck in from two parties that have got fat and lazy on corporate money supported by a friendly media. We need to take this power away from them by removing a voting system that keeps them in place regardless of performance. Making votes count would give power to voters and parties that put the interests of ordinary people first, increasing the wealth of ordinary people in the process.

Nationally, an argument grounded in improving outcomes for all members of society received 80.2 per cent approval:

> As everyone knows there are always plenty of improvements that can be made across Britain to help all have a better life regardless of location. We need a system that holds MPs to account for their actions to focus them on doing what is best for Britain as a whole. Electoral reform to a more proportional system is important to make a real change in the political system. First-past-the-post has driven the UK to a 'middle of the road' system that leaves no chance for parties who want to make a real change on either side of the political spectrum. Proportional representation seems to work well in many other countries across the world and adopting it would mean we could vote for our preferred party rather than 'wasting' a vote to keep certain parties out. This would mean that all politicians would have to improve our country to be elected.

It is not surprising that people are disaffected with politics and politicians. Reforming democracy and emphasising the clear impacts on policymaking are key to demonstrating the material value of prioritising reform.

Recommendations

The recommendations we advance require the traditional view of politics as public service to be enacted. Politicians need to embody the ethos of public service that got Britain through the Second World War, built the post-war consensus and enabled us to survive a pandemic in the absence of competent government. The reforms we recommend call for an end to politics as a lucrative career and for public service to resemble the sombre duty of those who serve on juries or in the Civil Service. Without that public service, serious government is impossible.

Parliament

1 Proportional representation: adopt alternative vote+ for House of Commons and single transferable vote for the second chamber
2 500 constituencies with 150 top-up seats allocated proportionally by combined mayoral authorities across the UK
3 Adopt the Assembly of the Nations and Regions as second chamber
4 Consider term limits if performance does not improve
5 Move parliament out of London to other parts of the UK on a five-yearly basis in each location
6 Require political candidates to live in a constituency for two years before becoming eligible for election
7 Introduce a uniform structure of Scottish-style local authorities and English-style combined authorities across the UK

De-corruption

8 End graft by banning second jobs, paid lobbying, and all lobbying by foreign citizens and entities
9 Fund political party work in the public interest through expanded Policy Development Grants
10 Ban donations to political parties by profit-making organisations and individuals
11 Make parliament a normal work environment: normal offices, normal expenses arrangements and sitting-time accommodation in the immediate vicinity of the parliament for those who cannot commute
12 Tie politicians' pay to the national median wage via a wage ratio of a maximum of two to one
13 Introduce an independent Integrity and Ethics Commission

PART III

MAKING IT HAPPEN

CHAPTER 12

A NEW ECONOMY WITH A FULLY COSTED AND FULLY FUNDED PLAN

Chapter in 30 seconds

Years of reducing tax rates on business have failed to deal with regional inequality and poor productivity. We need a new economy that directs investment to where it is needed most and funds public services adequately. This requires a complete overhaul of fiscal and monetary policy. Since the global financial crisis, wages have shrunk in real terms but wealth has grown. This continues a long-term trend towards reduced remuneration for work and increased returns on unearned income, which contributes to inequality, injustice and tax-base erosion. Since the highpoint in personal taxation in the 1970s, reductions in income, corporation and other taxes have coincided with an increased focus on using income tax as the key means of funding government spending. The policies we outline throughout this report require significant funding, and we show that providing it through responsible capital investments and taxation on passive wealth, carbon production and corporation income advances a new economy that serves the interests of the vast majority of us and stimulates inward investment. The taxes we outline reflect public preferences and point towards viable means of making the economy work for us. We use cutting-edge microsimulation modelling to show the impacts of these reforms, providing an overwhelming economic argument for the policies we set out above.

Introduction: an economy failing on its own neoliberal terms

We argue, throughout this report, that commonplace measures of economic performance are inaccurate and bear little relationship to our day-to-day experience of the economy. Growth, for example, seems only tangentially related to economic outcomes in many of our communities and regions and is largely unconnected with levels of poverty. The same is true of productivity. Increases in productivity, just as with increases in growth, aren't passed on to workers. We are decades away from the future envisioned on *Tomorrow's World* in the 1960s and 1970s of workers benefiting from automation in the form of increased pay and decreased hours. Those benefits are felt overwhelmingly in executive pay and profits. But even on neoliberalism's own terms, our economy is failing disastrously. As the *Financial Times* recently noted, the UK is increasingly a poor country with a few rich residents.[1]

The figures are stark. The UK's performance on productivity in recent decades is, like its performance on inequality and child poverty, poor and declining compared with its own recent history and with other countries. Figure 8 shows that real-terms GDP growth in the UK declined from 3.4 per cent in the 1960s to 1.9 per cent in the 2010s; performance so far in the 2020s

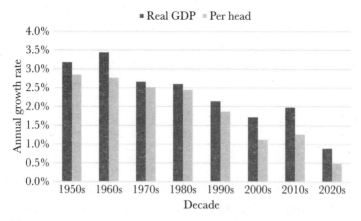

Figure 8 Annual UK GDP growth rate by decade, 1960s to 2020s (so far).[2]

has been even worse, at 0.9 per cent. Correcting for population growth (using GDP per head of the population), the long-term decline is even more pronounced, from 2.8 per cent per year in the 1950s to just 0.5 per cent per year in the 2020s. As Figure 9 illustrates, an analysis of productivity growth (measured as output per worker) produces similar results, with productivity growth declining from 2.9 per cent per year in the 1960s to 1.9 per cent per year in the 1980s and then down to just 0.7 per cent per year in the 2010s.

International comparisons show that the UK's productivity performance vis-à-vis other leading industrialised countries is mediocre at best. Estimates from the National Institute for Economic and Social Research show that between 2008 and 2019, UK productivity (measured in US dollars per hours worked at purchasing power parity) grew by less than 0.3 per

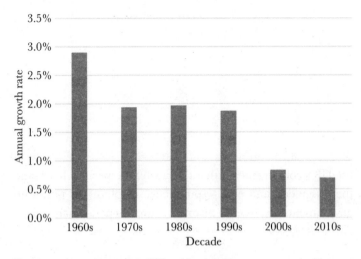

Figure 9 Annual growth in UK productivity (output per worker) by decade, 1960s to 2010s.[3]

cent per year, compared with 1 per cent growth per year in the US and 0.7 per cent per year in France and Germany.[4]

The Resolution Foundation reports that the UK's productivity growth rate in the 12 years following the global financial crisis of 2007/08 was half the rate of that of the 25 richest OECD economies.[5] It also points out that the UK's recent performance on average living standards is even worse than the productivity statistics would suggest, because the UK's high level of inequality by European standards means that the gap between median household incomes in the UK and those in Germany in France is around 10 to 12 points larger than the gap between mean household incomes between the UK and the other two countries. In other words, high inequality reinforces the adverse impact of poor productivity growth.

Addressing the weaknesses

Explanations for the UK's poor economic performance include chronic underinvestment in the public and business sectors,[6] inadequate transport infrastructure,[7] a relatively low-skilled workforce,[8] an inadequate policy framework for encouraging innovation,[9] and relatively high inequality.[10] In the specific context of the period leading up to and following the financial crisis of 2007/08, the growing dominance of the finance sector in the UK economy meant that the crash hit especially hard, and the misguided and counterproductive emphasis by post-2010 governments on austerity meant that growth performance since 2010 has been abysmal even compared with the UK's mediocre pre-2008 trajectory.[11]

Furthermore, a factor which has been known of since the mid-twentieth century but which is now urgent is the need to limit global heating to no more than 1.5 degrees Celsius relative to pre-industrial temperatures.[12] This complicates matters considerably, since to achieve net zero – an economy where the UK's total annual greenhouse gas emissions are equal to or less than the emissions the country removes from the environment each year – the UK needs specific kinds of decarbonising development. High-carbon, non-green economic growth invites a global heating catastrophe, in the UK as in other countries. Even on neoliberalism's own terms, that is a catastrophic cost that has to be mitigated. There is no good economic argument for inaction.

To deliver increased productivity – and the right kind of (net-zero) increased productivity – we need to address all the UK's economic weaknesses simultaneously with a programme of reforms that are radical and transformative but also feasible and carefully costed. We lay out those reforms below. To model their impact on UK households, areas and regions, we have used microsimulation combined with an innovative new model of the relationship between infrastructure investments and productivity (measured as gross value added). The package of reforms is designed to address several of the reasons cited above for the UK's poor economic performance, on the grounds that, while it's impossible to know which explanation is quantitatively the most important, it seems very likely that some – and perhaps all – of them have a part to play. This is a 'belt-and-braces' approach to boosting economic performance.

Proposed reforms

National Investment Bank

There have long been calls for the creation of a National Investment Bank.[13] The UK Infrastructure Bank was a good first step towards this. However, its scope is too limited, capital too low and relationship with public sector too diffuse.[14] Put simply, it needs to have a much larger capacity to fund and manage wealth creation from a much broader variety of activities, including the National Pharmaceutical Service, and needs to play a much more concentrated role in guiding publicly funded activities with clear scope for commercial exploitation.

We need a National Investment Bank, rather than UK Research and Innovation (UKRI), to manage those R&D activities with clear capacity for returns on investment, with scope for retention of stakes in any subsequent spin-off enterprises. Our holding a public interest in enterprises formed by our innovation is absolutely central to recognising the role of government in creating wealth via research funding and to ensuring that our private sector invests in our country. Likewise, only a National Investment Bank financed by the state can channel resources effectively to the wholesale programme of building and transition to renewables that we require to secure our society. These programmes require investment in land, materials and workforces with scope for longer-term and more socially diverse returns than those generally funded by commercial banking.

Re-establishing control over the Bank of England

We also need to revoke the independence of the Bank of England and place its control back in the hands of the Treasury. The notion that independence means objectivity has been shown to be false over the course of 15 years of Bank-led policymaking. The Bank has used quantitative easing in ways that have failed to address the fundamental crises across and between our regions and it has actively contributed to a cost-of-living crisis that could not possibly be addressed by raising interest rates.[15] The key causes of this particular crisis have been the increase in global energy costs due to geopolitical conflict and climate change. The consequence has been to exacerbate the cost-of-living crisis among those on low to middle incomes who do not own their own home outright.[16]

We should be clear that the Bank of England has always acted and will always act as a policymaker driven by a narrow and fundamentally problematic understanding of how economies work. Governors have made repeated policymaking interventions, with Andrew Bailey, paid £575,000 a year, calling for workers facing the choice of heating or eating to exercise wage restraint.[17] Politically, the Bank played a role in ensuring Liz

Truss's resignation as Prime Minister by deploying monetary policy in opposition to fiscal policy.[18] Our era of ultra-insecurity is one that can only be addressed in ways that resemble the post-war economic environment:[19] monetary and fiscal policy need to be deployed in tandem, rather than in opposition to one another, and that requires recognition that both are political and should be governed by elected representatives.

Only the Treasury can direct those two economic measures towards ending our crises by deploying 'people's quantitative easing' in the form of our social safety net and investing in the critical infrastructure around our Green New Deal transition to enable us to control energy prices over time.[20] This is why we need a Bank of England that serves as a direct instrument of government, with the capacity to directly fund the National Investment Bank through quantitative easing and bond production.

The tax system

Britain needs an expanded tax base in order to address our crises of poverty and inequality, which impose huge burdens on society. We recommend a range of reforms to the tax system to help fund the productivity-enhancing policy interventions detailed below while also reducing inequalities. While income inequality remains important, unequal distribution of illiquid assets is of far greater importance and lies at the heart of many aspects of the cost-of-living crisis, with those who own homes outright protected from rapidly rising mortgage costs due to rising interest rates. Indeed, in historical terms, income tax in the UK is a relative aberration, permanently introduced only in 1842 and applied only to the very highest earners until the early to middle part of the twentieth century. We should no longer believe that revision to marginal income tax rates associated with paid employment is the key means of funding reform. It isn't, and can't be, because the relative value of pay from work has been reduced so significantly in recent decades.

While progressive income tax rates can close some of the inequality gap, increases in all but the highest marginal rates are unpopular and, as a consequence, politically unfeasible. However, the relatively recent focus on income tax as the core of our tax base means that financially fairer alternatives are overlooked. Our recent conjoint experiments, adversarial co-production and microsimulation modelling suggest that while many of us feel that we cannot bear increases in income tax rates of more than 3p,[21] there are high levels of support for redistribution through wealth, carbon, corporation and land taxes.

Equalisation of income tax rates and abolition of employee national insurance contributions

We recommend changes to the income tax system associated with previous work on the introduction of a starter basic income scheme. This consists of converting the existing personal allowance into a cash payment, reducing the tax-free allowance to £800 a year to ensure that small payments do not require declaration, and raising by 3 per cent the basic, higher and top rates in England, with equivalent changes in Scotland and Wales. This will raise £106 billion a year to fund the 'starter' basic income scheme discussed earlier. In future years we recommend extending the basic income scheme towards Minimum Income Standard levels. Alongside this, employee

NICs ought to be bundled into income tax rates, producing the following rates: basic 35 per cent; higher 45 per cent; additional 50 per cent. This simplifies the system and reduces administrative costs.

We also believe that income tax rates have to be equalised for income from dividends and other passive forms of activity. This closes the gap in the current system in which those in active work are charged a much higher rate than those who live from wealth.[22]

Together, the abolition of employee NICs and their replacement with income tax and the equalisation of income tax rates for income from dividends raises £58.1 billion in additional revenue per year.

Wealth tax

We recommend introducing a tax on household wealth levels above £2 million – essentially a more progressive version of the scheme recommended by Reed for the Scottish TUC.[23] The tax would be an annual levy at marginal rates of 2 per cent per year for wealth between £2 million and £5 million, 3 per cent for wealth between £5 million and £10 million, and 4 per cent for wealth between £10 million and £15 million, with progressively higher rates for wealth above £15 million. Allowing for avoidance, we estimate that this tax would raise around £43 billion a year. The £2 million threshold sits above any possible context in which someone depends on that level of wealth simply to live. To deal with the possibility of capital flight, we recommend imposition of a tax on large financial transactions to tax money on the way out commensurate with the wealth rates above. This would mean that £20 million sent overseas across a 12-month period would incur a 6 per cent tax. The offshoring of wealth has had a distortionary and damaging impact on our economy and it needs to be disincentivised. Introducing the tax would reduce the assumed avoidance rates of 5 per cent for property wealth, 20 per cent for pension wealth, and 40 per cent for financial assets and physical wealth.[24]

Taxing carbon and fossil fuels

We recommend introducing a tax on carbon, as recommended by researchers from the Grantham Research Institute on Climate Change in the Environment in 2020.[25] To be consistent with net-zero emissions by 2050, the carbon tax needs to be set at around £55 to £60 per tonne in 2024, rising to £75 per tonne in 2030, and it should raise around £6 billion a year in current prices.

In addition to this, we recommend the following taxes on fossil fuel companies as set out in recent research by Oxfam: (1) a permanent excess tax on fossil fuel companies and (2) a redirection of current subsidies to fossil fuel producers.[26] Combined, these measures would raise just under £7 billion a year.

Luxury consumption taxes

We recommend introducing a tax on frequent flyers, as suggested by the New Economics Foundation, which they estimate would raise up to £4 billion annually.[27] In addition to this, a tax on private jets departing from the UK set at £780 per passenger per flight (10 times the current highest rate of Air Passenger Duty for domestic flights), as recommended by Oxfam, could raise up to £500 million annually.[28] This is intended not just to raise revenue but to disincentivise socially and environmentally damaging activity.

Reversing freezes in fuel duty

Since 2010, successive governments have repeatedly frozen fuel duty on petrol and diesel in nominal terms, with the result that by the 2023/24 tax year, revenue from excise duty on motor fuels was almost £20 billion a year lower than it would have been if fuel duty rates had risen in line with Retail Price Index (RPI) inflation for the past 13 years (according to estimates from the Office for Budget Responsibility).[29] We recommend reversing the fuel duty freezes, which would raise almost £20 billion a year of additional revenue.

Corporation tax

In the year 2000, the headline rate of corporation tax in the UK for larger companies was 30 per cent. This was reduced to 19 per cent by 2017 before being increased to 25 per cent in April 2023. We recommend increasing the headline rate of corporation tax up to 30 per cent – the rate which applied in the early 2000s and which applies in Germany today[30] – with a lower rate for small businesses and enhanced tax reliefs for R&D. Corporation tax is fundamentally affordable since it is charged on profits, not turnover. It can be avoided by inward investment – that is, directing would-be profits towards increasing productivity and activity within businesses – which is a means of ensuring sustainability of business and reducing inequality within organisations. Allowing for increased avoidance, we estimate that the increase in corporation tax will raise around £12 billion a year.

Local tax

Reform of local tax in Britain is long overdue. In England, Wales and Scotland the main domestic local tax is council tax, which has two serious weaknesses. First, the system is regressive, with households living in high-value houses paying far less as a proportion of their property wealth than those living in low-value houses. Second, council tax in England and Scotland is based on house price valuations from 1991 that are now more than three decades out of date.

We recommend replacing council tax with a proportional property tax (PPT), as suggested by the campaigning group Fairer Share for England and by Reed for Scotland.[31] Setting the PPT at a rate of 0.7 per cent for primary residences in Scotland, 0.9 per cent in Wales and 0.95 per cent in England would increase overall yield by approximately the same percentage in each of the three countries.[32] Combined with a double rate for second homes and empty properties (i.e. 1.4 per cent in Scotland, 1.8 per cent in Wales and 1.9 per cent in England), the PPT would raise approximately £9 billion a year across the three countries and is substantially more progressive with respect to both household wealth and household income than council tax. This, in effect, levels the other nations up to the situation in Northern Ireland, which has a domestic ratings system that resembles PPT. We recommend that around 20 per cent of the gross yield from the tax be used to fund an enhanced compensation package so that low to middle-income households do not lose out from the reform.[33] This additional yield, combined with the additional funding for integrating social care into the NHS, will be critical to addressing the crisis in local authority funding. We also recommend land value capture taxation powers be granted to combined authorities to fund further infrastructural development, as in Chapter 10.

Removing unnecessary or badly targeted reliefs and allowances in the tax system

The UK tax system includes a large number of reliefs and allowances. Indeed, over 1,000 are listed in a recent report by the House of Commons Treasury Committee.[34] Each of these reliefs and allowances has a cost to the Exchequer in terms of the tax revenue foregone. We have identified around 40 of the largest reliefs and allowances which are unnecessary or badly targeted. According to HMRC statistics, abolishing these reliefs and allowances would result in a gain of just under £74 billion to the Exchequer.[35]

Overall, the tax increases set out in this report would result in increased tax revenues of just under £340 billion – which is more than enough to afford the starter basic income scheme plus the other increases in current public expenditure that we recommend, with the increases in capital expenditure financed by people's quantitative easing.

The combination of basic income and universal basic services

The policies we have set out within this report are ambitious and carry a high up-front cost. The point, however, is that just in 1945, there are no cheap means of addressing our era of crisis and ultra-insecurity. Over decades, we have gone, as a society, from owning our assets to renting and being at the whim of service providers whose service levels have consistently failed. Household economic models have been invoked to jus-tify the asset-stripping: that we need to sell off assets and reduce spending to get out of debt. The more accurate analogy is that we've sold our houses, our cars and our tools, and we are now constantly incapable of getting out of debt as a result of being incapable of building up our wealth while spending all of our resources on renting.

Age-old assumptions that education and hard work lead to property, family and success no longer hold true. Those under 40 are likely to be poorer, less happy, less healthy and live shorter lives than their parents.[36] Many of those exposed to poverty and the most extreme levels of insecurity are, in fact, currently in full-time, insecure and low-paid employment or nominal 'self-employment', with many others in previously comfortable jobs exposed to fuel poverty.[37]

The cost to society will only be fully known in years or decades to come, since today's pressures will contribute to increases in the number and complexity of short-, medium- and long-term health conditions.[38] This is creating a planning and budgeting crisis that will exacerbate challenges for population health over many years, with healthcare expenditure across the UK in 2022 estimated at £230 billion,[39] adult social care in England alone at £26.9 billion,[40] and costs to society across the whole UK asso-ciated with poor mental health at £117.9 billion.[41] We cannot afford to persist with the same failed ideological experiment.

The cost of living has risen considerably, and it has become clear to many of us that the threat to our standard of living is no longer unavoidable tax increases but unavoidable costs for essentials in energy, food and housing. The only way we can become secure as a society is through investment in our produc-tive capacity to control our essentials. If we do this, just as if we take on mortgages for our houses, our wealth increases over time and we have an asset that is ours to control. This creates trans-generational wealth that provides stability and security to our communities.

It is in this longer-term context that our programme of fiscal and monetary reform has to be understood. As we note in Chapter 10, an updated Green Book approach is required within the Treasury and a clear set of criteria regarding impact on climate change, health and social outcomes are required within the National Investment Bank to evaluate the investments we need. The policy programme as a whole reflects a combination of basic income with free-at-point-of-use health, educational, housing and infrastructural universal basic services (UBS), alongside significant investments in manufacturing and renewables.[42]

This is the approach we have adopted in this report, and we not only cost the investments, we provide a projection on their impact across 10 years. This represents cutting-edge microsimulation of our tax and benefit system and sets out a comprehensive, but conservative, projection of what our economy will look like if we take this coordinated approach to investment.

The microsimulation does not account for the significant impacts of economic democracy. Recent research by the think tank Demos shows that increased economic democracy in 'purpose-led' businesses can deliver clear benefits in enhanced productivity.[43] There is substantial evidence for this from a number of countries across the world and we advance democratic reforms throughout each of the policies outlined in this report. As such, the economic impacts of this programme for government are likely to be much higher than we indicate here.

Costing our reforms

In costing our reforms, where costs are below £100 million and cannot accurately be established, we have attributed a figure of 'negligible' on the basis that they fall within existing departmental budgetary allocations.

Chapter 3: A social safety net

1 Introduce a basic income starter scheme immediately.
   Cost = £182.8 billion
2 Move towards a basic income payment of around £190 per week within five years.
   Cost at year 5 = £393.6 billion (i.e. an additional £210.8 billion compared with option 1)
3 Move towards a full Minimum Income Standard basic income scheme of around £295 per week within 10 years.
   Cost at year 10 = £669.7 billion (i.e. an additional £276.1 billion compared with option 2)

Chapter 4: Green New Deal

1 Reorganise public investment so that improving sustainability is a central goal for all infrastructure projects.
   Cost = negligible
2 Invest at least £28 billion a year in decarbonising the energy supply and reducing energy expenditure. This is consistent with Labour's now dropped 2021 pledge for transition.
   Cost = £28 billion a year until 2030[44]
3 Create a National Investment Bank and use the tax system to incentivise pension funds to invest in green projects.

This represents an administrative overhaul within existing Treasury budgets.

Cost = negligible

4 Introduce and progressively increase a carbon tax to generate funds for investment and guide the development of economy towards lower-carbon solutions (see Chapter 12).

5 End new licences for fossil fuel projects. This will lower short-term tax receipts but provide long-term cost savings on climate change and will be funded from increased taxes on carbon production. Costs are included within reform 5, Chapter 5, below.

Cost = see reform 5, Chapter 5, below.

6 Provide a quadruple lock for workers in high-carbon industries whose occupations will change. There are 260,000 workers affected[45] and we will provide an £80,000 retraining and relocation allowance for each worker.

Cost = £2.1 billion a year over 10 years

7 Progressively take back social control of energy, water and transport facilities (see Chapter 5).

8 Invest in a National Building Service to advance a programme of retrofit and improvement of the housing stock, including by making installation of heat pumps, solar panels and other sustainable investments mandatory in all new buildings. The cost is consistent with Labour's 10 year pledge to invest £60 billion[46] in this area.

Cost = £6 billion a year over 10 years

9 Support new training programmes, including higher apprenticeships, developed with the National Building Service to skill our workforce. This fits within existing Department of Education budget.

Cost = negligible

10 Introduce tougher regulation and enforcement of regulations related to pollution of water and air.
Cost = negligible

11 Divert public funding away from intensive agriculture and towards the regeneration of nature in countryside. There is a £56 billion shortfall in spending on regeneration.[47] We propose to spread this investment annually over 10 years.
Cost = £5.6 billion a year

12 Introduce a network of marine protected areas. The estimated cost of each protected area is £1 million per protected area.[48] We propose to invest £100 million in creating a network of protected areas.
Cost = £100 million

13 Place the costs of disposal and waste onto the producers of projects and encourage reuse, repair and recycling by introducing Extended Producer Responsibility (EPR). This will raise tax revenue.
Savings = up to £1 billion a year[49]

Chapter 5: Public utilities

Structural reforms to manage our utilities

1 Day-to-day management of our utilities by professionals, held accountable by a supervisory board representing broad, long-term public interest. Costs would be covered by removing profits withdrawn in current private regimes.
Cost = negligible

2 Formal commitment to decarbonisation and cooperation in utilities.
Cost = negligible

3 Creation of Participate to represent citizens whose lives depend on protecting our resources from misappropriation. Costs would be covered by converting profits withdrawn in dividends from current private regimes into increased operational costs.

Cost = negligible

4 A new Office for Public Ownership to improve services.

Cost = negligible

Energy

5 Ban the extraction of new coal, oil and gas and plan for a speedy (two to three years) complete transition to renewable energy. While National Statistics data shows that in the 2022/23 tax year, total UK government revenues from oil and gas production were £9.0 billion, this was exceptionally high in historical terms due to increased energy prices: in the previous tax year, equivalent revenues were £1.4 billion.[50] Against this, a recent report by Oxfam has identified that taxing polluters fairly could generate an extra £23.1 billion of revenue a year.[51]

Cost = net tax revenue of £14–21 billion a year

6 Start the clock ticking on existing notice periods – let energy companies know they will be losing their licence to operate.

Cost = negligible

7 Introduce legislation to reduce the notice periods to two years.

Cost = negligible

8 Create a new publicly owned energy generation company and invest in it at Labour's previous £28 billion annual

level via the National Investment Bank so it can rival its equivalents across Europe (see reform 2, Chapter 4, above).

9 Work towards a national surplus of, and self-sustainability in, electricity generation to make electricity affordable, decouple it from wholesale gas prices and make decarbonisation actively attractive to the country (see reform 2, Chapter 4, above).

10 Protect all workers through a quadruple lock plan (see reform 6, Chapter 4, above).

11 Set up democratic structures for the public to have a say in our energy system. Costs included in reform 6, Chapter 4, above.

12 Buy back the rest of the National Grid and regional distribution centres.

Cost = £34 billion[52] one-off capital investment and £4 billion a year for upgrades

13 Set up public–community partnerships between publicly owned grid companies and community energy producers to encourage the growth of local renewable energy. Cost included in capital investment in reform 10 above.

14 Buy back British Gas and rename Great British Energy to create a new publicly owned energy retail company that serves the interests of UK households.

Cost = £1 billion one-off capital investment[53]

15 Take over the remaining retail companies as they fail and incorporate workers and estates into Great British Energy within the remit of the Transition Job Guarantee. Cost included in reforms 7 and 8 above.

16 Look at introducing progressive billing, where users get a guaranteed amount of energy paid for and heavy users pay

more. This is revenue neutral, since savings among lower earners are paid for by higher earners.

Cost = negligible

Water

17 Start the clock ticking on the English water companies' 25-year notice periods – let them know they will be losing their licence to operate.

Cost = negligible

18 Introduce legislation to reduce the notice periods to two years.

Cost = negligible

19 Set up shadow regional public authorities in every region. These would be funded from energy and water payments.

Cost = negligible

20 Assess which of the English water companies can be brought into special administration on financial grounds. This would have little up-front cost.

Cost = negligible

21 Assess which of the English water companies can be brought into special administration on service quality grounds. This would have little up-front cost.

Cost = negligible

22 Use equity fines to replace existing fines on water companies when they mess up (taking shares from companies, rather than imposing fines).

Cost = negligible

23 Recognise the scale of investment needed and wherever there is no other way, buy back the water companies at a price negotiated with shareholders – public ownership will

be a better deal for the long-term public interest even if shareholders have to receive significant compensation. The cost of buying out water companies has been estimated at £14.7 billion, but it is likely that companies will merely fail first, and they should be allowed to do so. The value of companies will also reduce once the 25-year licences run down and penalties for poor performance increase. As such, this is a cost that is difficult to predict and is likely not to come to pass.

24 Under public ownership, invest in the infrastructure at scale. Offer savings accounts to the public to help fund this investment. Explore innovative solutions to clean up our rivers and seas as quickly and efficiently as possible. Costs included in budgets for reforms 8 and 11, Chapter 4, above.

25 Look at introducing progressive billing where you get a guaranteed amount of water paid for and heavy users pay more. This is revenue neutral, since savings among lower earners are paid for by higher earners.
Cost = negligible

Chapter 6: Health and social care

1 Reinstate NHS funding in real terms at pre-austerity levels. This does not include integration of social care into the NHS, which is covered in reform 8 below. This requires an increase at the same real-terms rate post-2010 as pre-2010 (3.6 per cent per year) rather than at the post-2010 rate of 1.6 per cent per year, which implies an increase in spending of £68 billion (at the UK level) in 2023/24.
Cost = £68 billion

2   End private provision within the NHS. Cost included in reform 1.

3   Double the number of doctors, nurses and dentists trained and prioritise domestic places. Cost included in reform 1.

4   Establish the National Pharmaceutical Service. Cost included in reform 1.

5   Remove the final NHS prescription charges in England to level up with Scotland, Wales and Northern Ireland. Cost = £700 million[54]

6   Nationalise GP practices. The £7 billion cost is included in the first year's allocation of reform 1.[55]

7   Integrate social care into the NHS. The cost of this is difficult to calculate because of the combination of capital investment and ongoing public expenditure. The cost of buying facilities can be relatively low.[56] Our calculation is based on National Audit Office (NAO) figures for the amount of expenditure on user charges for local-authority-provided care and privately purchased care, assuming that integrating social care into the NHS would convert these to public expenditure, plus an adjustment to go from England to UK figures, suggesting a figure of £19 billion a year for creating a fully publicly funded social care service across the UK. This budget would not indicate subsequent spending, which may reduce as the profit element in care provision is removed. In addition, we reserve a £10 billion (one-off) budget for purchasing estates. Given that many care homes are owned by private equity investors, removal of public funding for private care would lead to a diminution in the cost of buying existing care facilities, meaning that the budget will be reviewed after five years.

Cost = £19 billion a year + £10 billion estates budget

Chapter 7: Policies to ensure that all of our children are healthy and flourishing

Reverse the rise in child poverty

1 Introduce our social safety net in Chapter 3, which will radically reduce child poverty,[57] and remove the two-child limit and benefit cap or, *at the least*, increase child benefit by £20 per child per week, removing the two-child limit on Universal Credit and legacy benefits and ending the benefit cap,[58] which affects 900,000 people and would lift a total of 1.2 million people from poverty at a cost of £12.9 billion.[59] Cost included in option 1, Chapter 3, above.

2 Tie rates of social security support to the cost of living; immediately pausing the five-week minimum wait for Universal Credit. See costs of starter scheme included in Chapter 3 and option 1, Chapter 3, above.

3 Introduce free school meals for all, and in the meantime auto-enrol all eligible children. The cost for rolling out to Universal Credit recipients is £6.4 billion but with £16.2 billion in returns, and to all children £24.2 billion but with £58.2 billion in returns.[60] Making the Holiday Activities and Food Programme scheme permanent and extending support to all low-income families will cost £200 million a year.[61] Cost = £24.4 billion, but with at least £58.2 billion in returns

Invest in early childhood services and education

4 Allocate additional funding to secondary and post-16 providers to address the lag before the new (fairer) National Funding Formula takes effect and implement the National

Audit Office's recommendation to evaluate the impact of the NFF. Cost included in reform 2, Chapter 8, below.

5   Adjust the NFF to include the child health burden borne by schools. This constitutes redistributing the funding to schools after the 9 per cent increase in education funding in reform 2, Chapter 8, so it bears no additional cost.

6   Expanding the Health Improvement Fund to support Family Hubs, health visiting and children's centres with investment proportional to need and area-level deprivation. We have used the reversal of cuts to Sure Start funding since 2010 as a proxy for this. In 2021, a House of Lords Select Committee report found that funding for Sure Start had reduced by £1.8 billion since 2010, meaning that a £2 billion real-terms investment would be required now to restore 2010 levels of funding.[62] However, the report also found that 'During the same period, the money spent on later, costlier, and higher-intensity interventions – such as children going into care, youth justice services or safeguarding – increased by more than a third to £7.6 billion'. This suggests that investment in the Health Improvement Fund is effectively self-financing because it reduces the extent of more costly and higher-intensity interventions later on.
Cost = £2 billion but with £7.6 billion in savings

Future-proof policy choices affecting children

1   Embed Equity Impact Assessments into all policy processes at national, regional and local levels.
Cost = negligible

2   Use Children's Rights Impact Assessments to evaluate the specific impact of policies on children and young people.

Use devolved citizens' assemblies that include young people to make sure their voices are included when making policy decisions.

Cost = negligible

3   Pass the Wellbeing of Future Generations Bill in England, to bring England into line with progressive future generations law and policies in Wales and Scotland.

Cost = negligible

Chapter 8: A fairer education system

1   Prioritise care, consideration and cooperation and reduce the cliff-edge implications of assessment that harm pupils' health and wellbeing.

Cost = negligible

2   Increase school spending by at least 9 per cent, further education spending by 14 per cent and higher education spending by 18 per cent to return to pre-austerity levels .[63]

Cost = (pre-primary and primary (£33.769 billion) + secondary (£54.265 billion) = £88.034 billion × 9 per cent = £7.923 billion + further education £7.2 billion[64] × 14 per cent = £1.008 billion + higher education £4.552 billion × 18 per cent = £819.36 million) = £9.77 billion

3   Reduce educational segregation and value social diversity by granting local authorities direct control over admissions policy. This represents a democratic reform to administration.

Cost = negligible

4   Ensure all children have a broad and balanced curriculum to enable our children to rebuild our society as adults. This has few cost implications.

Cost = negligible

5   Introduce democratic structures and remove the arbitrary power of wealthy actors in order to ensure that experts direct education in consultation with communities
     Cost = negligible
6   Ensure that teachers are graduates with core academic capacities to guide our children through education. This is included in updated the education budget and reflects redirecting non-higher-education privately delivered funding to higher education providers.
     Cost = negligible
7   Take active steps towards removing tuition fees to achieve a level playing field, removing the ideological experiment that has burdened our younger generations in ways that are projected to last their lifetimes. In advance of removing tuition fees, maintenance support for higher education students would be provided via the basic income element of the social safety net in option 1, Chapter 3, above. This would also provide a replacement for the Education Maintenance Allowance for sixth formers and further education students.
     Cost = £9 billion a year in five years' time[65]

Chapter 9: Housing

1   End regressive taxation that punishes those in lower-value housing by introducing a proportional property tax, which is outlined in Chapter 12. The tax yield is outlined in Chapter 12.
2   Support social stability by enhance the existing 'right to stay' into a 'right to sell', giving mortgagors the right to become tenants rather than face eviction. This would likely be

revenue neutral in the first instance. It might impact property prices and hence PPT revenues, but this is difficult to model. Cost = negligible

3   Discourage waste by introducing taxes on second homes, holiday homes and empty commercial property. The tax yield is outlined in Chapter 12.

4   End taxes on spare bedrooms to ensure that every family can live in a home with a spare room for visitors
    Cost = £470 million (cost uprated to 2023 figures)[66]

5   Build as many publicly owned houses as building capacity permits to address the housing crisis, with funding designated by the National Investment Bank. We need to return to levels of building between 1946–80, during which time an average of 126,000 social homes were built each year.[67] Allowing for population growth, this suggests that we should be aiming for between 150,000 and 200,000 social dwellings a year. Shelter has calculated that the up-front cost would be £10.7 billion a year, but the savings in housing benefit would bring this cost down to £3.8 billion, meaning that it would be cost neutral over 39 years.[68] Further social benefits in terms of social cohesion and education, health and employment outcomes suggest the returns to be significantly higher.
    Cost = £3.8 billion a year

6   Ensure that the social safety net and availability of social housing is sufficient that housing benefit for private tenants can be withdrawn over time as social housing capacity increases, to remove the direct transfer of wealth from government to landlords. The house-building programme means that local authorities will have the capacity to offer highly subsidised housing directly to those in need. This policy is centrally concerned with removing the need for

private sector housing benefit because households on low incomes would transfer into the social sector. The costs are included in options 2 and 3, Chapter 3, above, and reform 5, this chapter, below.

7 Control rents and eliminate feudal payments, such as lease-hold, from which no benefit is provided and which punish existence.

Cost = negligible

8 Squatting and all other acts that are done purely to seek shelter and not to steal items for profit should again be a civil, not a criminal, offence. This may reduce burden on policing and criminal justice.

Cost = negligible

9 Illegal actions by landlords and bankers that deprive people of their home and shelter should become criminal, rather than civil, offences, since they demonstrably harm life. The costs of this may be cancelled out by any savings in reform 8.

Cost = negligible

10 Build new homes that are planned to last for centuries, both for sustainability and value for buyers. This is a cost-neutral policy insofar as the increased cost of building dwellings in the social sector results in increased net wealth of the public estate due to higher-quality housing, and costs will be borne by home buyers and/or shareholders of construc-tion companies in the private sector.

Cost = negligible

Chapter 10: Transport and infrastructure

1 Develop a Total Transport Network (TTM), running Mobility as a Service (MaaS) on a regional level. The

long-term underinvestment in public transport outside of London means that there is a significant up-front cost in terms of infrastructure. Locating TTMs within combined authorities presents a funding mechanism and formula for public finance. The North East Combined Authority has been granted £900 million in its devolution deal,[69] while the government has redistributed £7 billion in HS2 savings to the existing £1.2 billion City Regional Sustainable Transport Settlements (CRSTS) budget.[70] These are good starting points. Our proposals include additional financing from pension funds. We believe that the CRSTS budgets ought to be expanded to ensure the creation of TTMs across the country, with a funding formula of each combined mayoral authority receiving £1 billion per million citizens across five years to transform the system annually, with a total budget of £67 billion over five years. This will produce significant returns on investment in terms of climate change mitigation, health, productivity and quality of life.

Cost = £13.4 billion a year

2   Devolve transport regulation to combined mayoral authorities, with powers extended across the UK.

Cost = negligible

3   Provide seed funding for system design and development. Cost included within reform 1 above.

4   Run citizens' assemblies to gain public consent and valuable information on system design. Within existing combined authority budgets.

Cost = negligible

5   Give devolved authorities land value capture powers. This tax is distinct from the PPT in Chapter 12, since it

represents an additional capital gains tax. The tax yield is indicated in Chapter 12.

6   Rework Green Book calculations for transport projects to include a broader scope, including long-term health benefits and reduced social exclusion. This is noted in Chapter 12 and builds on the principles of the Green New Deal in Chapter 4.
Cost = negligible

7   Underwrite pension fund investment in public transport in the event of *force majeure*. Were this to occur, the costs would be met by the Treasury through quantitative easing.

8   Extend salary sacrifice to cover public transport season tickets that meet a MaaS standard. There are small potential changes to tax yields from income tax and national insurance contributions, but these are likely to produce significant reductions to public burdens from congestion, climate change impacts and reduced productivity.
Cost = negligible

Chapter 11: Democratic reform

Parliament

1   Proportional representation: adopt alternative vote+ for House of Commons and single transferable vote for the second chamber.[71] The cost of holding the 2010 general election was £113 million,[72] with overall costs estimated for a more complex electoral system in the 2011 alternative vote referendum uprated to 2023 figures reaching £250–353 million. Our budget presents a worst-case scenario of costs above existing budgets for general elections.
Cost = £200 million

2   500 constituencies with 150 top-up seats to be allocated proportionally by combined mayoral authorities across the UK. Cost of reform included in costs in reform 1.

3   Adoption of Assembly of the Nations and Regions as second chamber, with 200 elected members. This would be integrated into the estates costs of reform 4 below. There are significant expenses costs that would be replaced by a smaller number of salaried members.[73] The policy is therefore likely to be cost neutral.

    Cost = negligible

4   Consider introducing term limits if performance does not improve. There are 440 MPs who have served three or more terms in the current parliament.[74] Were employment law regarding redundancy entitlements applied, the cost of making those 440 MPs redundant after the next term would be $440 \times £40,000 = £17.6$ million redundancy immediately + 50 per cent of $650 \times £40,000 = £14.3$ million per parliament thereafter.[75] This is a possible cost for future consideration.

    Cost = £30.9 million over a five-year period

5   Move parliament out of London to parts of the UK on a five-yearly basis in each location. Estimates for repairs to Westminster with parliament in situ amount to £22 billion. The clearest estimates for repairs without parliament in situ amount to £10 billion, as the mid-point cost in £7–13 billion estimates.[76] A worst-case scenario suggests that the cost of building a purpose-built facility is around £750 million on the basis of the Scottish parliament case.[77] The budget for running parliament would be unchanged, but the costs of working within effectively designed parliamentary spaces and a normal working environment

while parliament is in session would likely reduce. The
£750 million budget per site of new parliaments in York,
Glasgow and Cardiff, would produce £12 billion in savings by virtue of easier repairs to Westminster.[78] The new
parliaments are likely to produce increased-yield proportional property tax and land value capture, while the
repair costs also result in an increase in the net worth of
the public estate.

Cost = £12 billion savings

6 Political candidates must live in a constituency for two years
before becoming eligible for election.

Cost = negligible

7 Introduce a uniform structure of Scottish-style local
authorities and English-style combined authorities across
the UK. Costs included in existing budgets.

De-corruption

8 End graft by banning second jobs, paid lobbying and all
lobbying by foreign citizens and entities.

Cost = negligible

9 Fund political party work in the public interest through
expanded Policy Development Grants. The current cost is
£2 million a year and we suggest increasing this budget to
£5 million a year.[79]

Cost = £3 million

10 Ban donations to political parties by profit-making organisations and individuals.

Cost = negligible

11 Make parliament a normal work environment: normal
offices, normal expenses arrangements and sitting-time

accommodation in the immediate vicinity of the parliament for those who cannot commute.[80] Current MPs' expenses and prospective estates costs are outlined in budget in reform 4 above.

12 Tie politicians' pay to the national median wage via a wage ratio of a maximum of two to one. This may produce small savings.

13 Introduce an independent Integrity and Ethics Commission. This will be included within the existing £1 million a year budget.[81]

Estimating the productivity impacts of spending commitments

The reforms outlined in this chapter have been analysed using a model of the relationship between gross value added (a measure of economic output) and public and private spending on services and investment at the regional and local levels in the UK and constituent countries.

We assume that the capital spending commitments in our recommendations will have positive impacts on productivity via multiplier effects. We use multipliers estimated by researchers at the Institute for Innovation and Public Purpose (IIPP) at University College London using data for a set of European countries between 1970 and 2016.[82] The IIPP estimates suggest that the multiplier for public investment in infrastructure after 5 years is between 2.43 and 3.12 (depending on the precise model used). We use the IIPP central estimate of 2.74 for the estimates in this book. A multiplier of 2.74 implies that an increase of £1 million a year in public spending on infrastructure produces an increase of £2.74 million in GDP.

The initial spending commitments in this book total approximately £377 billion a year, of which just over 80 per cent is current spending rather than capital spending. However, current spending also has multiplier effects. For example, additional spending on the NHS contributes to a healthier workforce with lower levels of premature mortality and morbidity and better mental health. Basic income also has positive multiplier effects on health as shown in 'Treating Causes not Symptoms'.[83] We assume that the multiplier impact of current spending is equal to one-third that of capital spending, i.e. a multiplier of 0.91.

The estimated increase in GDP due to higher capital and current spending generates additional tax receipts from taxes on earnings and corporate profits, as well as receipts from consumption taxes due to higher spending. In line with the current share of tax receipts in UK GDP, we assume that tax receipts increase by an amount equal to 40 per cent of the increase in GDP.

According to our modelling, taking second-round productivity impacts into account results in an increase of just over £206 billion in tax receipts. This increases the total amount raised in tax from around £339 billion to £545 billion. This £339 billion in tax receipts is enough to fund the £308 billion of current spending commitments in our plans – including the starter basic income scheme – with £31 billion left over. With an additional £206 billion of tax receipts after taking second-round impacts into account, it is possible to fund basic income scheme 2 (i.e. the 'halfway to MIS' scheme) with almost £26 billion to spare. Given longer-term positive productivity effects of this basic income scheme and the other spending plans in this report, there is every reason to think that the UK would be able to afford basic income scheme 3 – payments to all individuals in the UK at the Minimum Income Standard level – at some point in the not-too-distant future. This would be a huge and welcome achievement.

It also demonstrates the fundamental importance of running Britain like a business. If we invest in the right areas, we generate wealth that cannot otherwise be generated. When we distribute that wealth effectively, we not only produce gains in those regions and among those communities and individuals that need it most: we grow radically as a nation. If we want Britain to survive and thrive, we must invest.

A new economy is popular

In our Act Now survey, we found an average level of support for the policy of 69.2 per cent in the Red Wall, with 60.2 per cent among Conservative and 80.5 per cent among Labour 2019 voters. Nationally, approval was 72.6 per cent, with 48.6 per cent among those intending to vote Conservative, 76 per cent among those intending to vote Labour and 66 per cent among those who don't know who they will vote for or who don't intend to vote at present.

The arguments that are most persuasive among the two groups are different. Voters in the Red Wall evaluated at 73.5 per cent approval an argument based on direct redistribution from the wealthiest to normal citizens:

> The current tax system disproportionately benefits the wealthiest. They can avoid taxes by paying themselves through dividends, they pay a lower proportion of council tax on their properties and they pay less tax on passive wealth than those of us who go out to work do on our income. The reforms will ensure that the richest pay more to close the gap for workers

and cannot hide their money overseas without being taxed, removing the benefits they currently have. There's only so much money anyone needs to live a comfortable life and we now have a small number of people who have endless luxury while the rest of us who work hard struggle. Imagine the impact of a billionaire for once being forced to pay a fair share of wealth into tax. It would make a difference where it matters: taxing the wealthy more will close the gap, bringing workers towards a good quality of life.

Nationally, an argument grounded in securing us as a society received 73.5 per cent approval:

> As the COVID pandemic and impact of the war in Ukraine showed, Britain is exposed to global insecurity. We need to increase taxation on the highest earners and reduce the burden on low- to middle-income workers in order to secure our society and the resilience of our public funds. Having more money in the government pot will secure us against another shock to the country like COVID and the impacts it had on our economy. We need a reliable source of funding by increasing tax on corporations that currently don't pay their way. These reforms bring multinational companies like Amazon into line with UK companies by stopping them using offshore tax havens like Luxembourg. Introducing tax on large financial transactions also removes the insecurity of big corporations threatening to move their businesses overseas and sending money abroad without paying tax on transfers. Taxing businesses that contribute to climate change will also reduce floods, heatwaves and rising sea levels that are an increasing threat to Britain.

Throughout all of the narratives produced, there was consensus that reducing inequality and funding through taxation on wealth is key to our new settlement. Given that we have

demonstrated the changes outlined in this report are affordable, knowing that Britons support taxation if targeted effectively ought to give us all confidence that change is possible.

Recommendations

The reforms identified in this chapter enable us to run Britain
as a business. By this we do not mean a country based on
unsustainable pay ratios and the offshoring of labour, which
leave most of us in a perpetual state of personal indebtedness and zero-sum competition for work. Rather, we mean a
collective endeavour in wealth creation in which investments
lead to an overall increase in resources and a distribution of
those resources to those parts of our society that need them
most in order to function. By addressing the historical anomaly
of viewing income tax on work as the sole means of funding
Britain, we set out a fairer and popular means of advancing
each of our five principles of reform through our new economy.
Government should:

1 Stop perpetuating the myth that rolling back the state produces growth – it doesn't
2 Invest in the structure of Britain in the same way as every
  business has to invest in order to generate wealth
3 Simplify and limit tax increases on income from work given
  the declining value of that income, tax passive wealth,
  and close the fairness gap by ensuring that income from
  work is no longer taxed at a higher rate than income from
  dividends
4 Increase fundamentally affordable taxes, such as corporation tax, which is paid on profits, not overheads

5   Disincentivise through new taxes carbon-producing corpo-
    rate activities that cost us more in the long term than leav-
    ing the resources in the ground

6   Remove the enormous number of badly targeted or dam-
    aging tax reliefs

CHAPTER 13

CONCLUSION AND A CALL TO ACTION

Chapter in 30 seconds

This report has presented a comprehensive set of policies that would be feasible and popular and would make life in Britain better for almost all inhabitants. The policies are well known and should be common-sensical. It is remarkable that they seem controversial and that neither of the two main political parties currently has the courage to endorse the programme in its entirety. This fact goes a long way to explaining the high level of disillusionment with all of the political parties on offer. However, there are grounds for hope. In times of social change, political parties have in the past shown themselves responsive to an upswell of public opinion. The Labour Party adopted nearly all of the Beveridge Report prior to the 1945 UK general election. It won in a landslide. It did not create the Beveridge Report, but it saw that the population wanted it and were prepared to vote for whoever would offer to make it real. We urge readers to advocate for the policies we have discussed here, or better versions of them, in their councils, churches, workplaces, trade unions, clubs and households. We challenge political parties to respond to that demand, where possible by forming cross-party consensus. The time for change is now. The time to act is now.

Introduction: a common-sense alternative

In this report, we have presented a series of interlinked policies, including a basic income scheme; a Green New Deal; taking control of energy, water, housing and transport; and reforming and decentralising our democracy. Behind these policies – which will no doubt evolve in their detail and implementation – we have identified a set of important principles that should guide policymaking for contemporary Britain: increasing equality, freeing people from domination, tackling the social determinants of health, building community wealth and levelling up between places.

Given the well-documented rise in precarity, insecurity, scarcity and ill health, the decline in the liveability and civility of our towns, and the frustrations of deteriorating services, as well as the obvious failures of our government, the remarkable thing is that these policies and principles will be considered dangerously risky, even extreme, when compared with the usual fare on offer from Labour, the Conservatives and the Liberal Democrats.

They ought not to be. They represent common-sense views shared by most of us. Many others have proposed versions of them. All of the above parties should sign up to them, perhaps with differences of priority. They are not ideological or extreme, and their proponents lie across the political spectrum. They simply reflect the reasonable aspiration that in a democratic country that is wealthier than it was in the past and wealthier than almost all other places in human history, most people should have lives that are materially and psychologically better than the lives of their parents and grandparents. They are concrete, common-sense solutions that are well within the range that other open democracies have successfully explored in terms of public expenditure, taxation and intervention in the economy.

Correcting a basic error we all make

It is worth reflecting for a moment on how we have got to a situation where even self-proclaimed progressive parties do not dare propose easily available policies that would bring about actual progress. We could present a conspiratorial analysis. We could argue that powerful interest groups (who would, let us be honest, be negatively affected by some of the proposals presented here) have used their resources to form political parties that respond uniquely to their interests and fund a media that manufactures a dysfunctional status quo, presenting all alternatives as reckless or extreme. We could describe a Labour Party so bent on winning the game under its existing rules that it forgets what it is there for. There would be some justice in this analysis.

However, we would prefer to conclude with some more positive points. The first is that many people do not understand how many other people agree with the policies proposed here. We often think:

> I would personally like to see basic income introduced, or the water companies brought back into community control, but I will keep quiet about it because others are not talking about it, so it seems beyond the bounds of sane and polite discussion.

The irony is that most of us think like this about policies, going along with something because we believe that others want to go along with it. But public opinion research shows that the vast bulk of the population are more progressive and ambitious than what political parties present as being in the centre. We need to come to recognise in one another the appetite for change and demand of all our political parties that they adopt the reforms proposed in this report.

Our second point is that political institutions have very considerable inertia, but they do ultimately change as society changes. It seems impossible to see the change coming that, once underway, feels completely right and inevitable. Once a set of institutional possibilities has become embedded, it seems hard to even imagine alternatives. They can become unthinkable. This is the famous 'Overton window', the range of reforms that seems serious and feasible at any given moment in time. But in fact, within high-income countries over time, there is a very large range of institutional possibilities available. What we have proposed in this report falls squarely within the bounds of what is historically and institutionally possible. Alternatives to our era of ultra-insecurity *are* possible.

Capturing opportunity for a secure future

The Overton window moves, and at times it even moves fast.[1] The neoliberal reforms illustrate this: in 2008, the former Conservative Health Minister Kenneth Clarke wrote, of privatising NHS provision, that 'In the late 1980s I would have said it is politically impossible to do what we are now doing'.[2] That reform is now accepted. This is especially true in times of crisis.[3] We saw this during the pandemic: when the government needs to do something, it has the scope to do it.[4] Then, public opinion can rapidly coalesce around solutions that seemed impossible to imagine even a few years earlier.[5] In an open society, political institutions either respond to that demand or fail. As one of the key architects of the neoliberal settlement, Milton Friedman, once said:

> Only a crisis – actual or perceived – produces real change. When that crisis occurs, the actions that are taken depend on the ideas that are lying around. That, I believe, is our basic function: to develop alternatives to existing policies, to keep them alive and available until the politically impossible becomes the politically inevitable.[6]

This is what happened with the Beveridge Report in 1942. A dry, fairly technical report proposing detailed institutional reforms that had seemed unthinkable in the 1930s made for an unlikely bestseller. Yet, as we documented in Chapter 1, it had an astonishing impact on the general public and, indirectly through its effect on the public, on political parties. In particular, the Labour Party, in its manifesto for the 1945 UK general election, committed to implementing Beveridge almost in full, as well as other reform proposals that had been generated during the war years. They won in a landslide.

Act now: change is possible when we demand it

Beveridge made it necessary for political parties to say where they stood on specific reforms to how the country worked, rather than just talking about their broad values or personal attributes. Beveridge made public and popular a coordination point for the things people felt they wanted from their country. We hope that the sections of this report could play a similar role for the Britain of 2024. In effect, we have made available a set of concrete ideas. Debate them, revise them, refine them, but above all, talk about them and how they affect you and your interests directly. That is what politics is about. Demand of the people who want your vote that they say whether they will implement these reforms or not. If they say they won't, ask why they want to sustain the failed, extreme ideological experiment that is making your life avoidably insecure.

It is not because these policies are unpopular. As we have shown throughout, each of the policies is popular. Our Act Now survey of public opinion demonstrates that the policy programme overall is popular. In the Red Wall, we found an average level of support for the whole programme of 70.8 per cent, with 61.7 per cent among Conservative and 82.8 per cent among Labour 2019 voters. Nationally, approval was 73.9 per cent, with 51.3 per cent among those intending to vote Conservative, 78.5 per cent among those intending to vote Labour and 68.3 per cent among those who don't know who they will vote for or who don't intend to vote at present. Parties who back the policies in this book will achieve electoral success because as a society we recognise that only a programme such as this has the capacity to make a meaningful difference to our lives.

In effect, after four decades of failed ideological experiment, what we have tried to do in *Act now* is to add to and coordinate the stock of good ideas that are lying around and to present policymakers with readymade solutions to problems that they have struggled to address. These common-sense responses, regularly derided as politically impossible, are, in some form, politically inevitable. We cannot go on as before, with homeopathic solutions to real problems and no arc leading to a better future for the great majority of people. We hope to have contributed to the stock of ideas that are lying around, so that real change can begin.

Recommendations

We urge readers to discuss the policies we have presented here with their families, friends and colleagues. You may like some better than others, or think they can be improved. But, whatever you think, talk about them. Talk about them in workplaces, schools and colleges, trade unions, clubs and pubs, households and places of worship. You will find a surprising degree of agreement about the need for change. Don't assume that you're the odd one out – you aren't. Those of us who want our lives to be secure are in the vast majority and we often agree on solutions. We need to be brave in expressing those opinions.

Challenge political parties to respond to the ideas presented here: will they rule them out or will they commit to implementing them if elected? They should not be mealy-mouthed about this. If they want your vote, they should say where they stand. And if they won't give you the answers you need, take your vote elsewhere. Even the media is ultimately responsive to public sentiment: they will begin to take these ideas more seriously if they can see that most of the people do. Together, we can cause change to propagate through our communities into the media, political parties and eventually government.

The time for change is now. The time to act is now.

NOTES

Introduction

1 This study has been approved by the Faculty of Health and Life Sciences ethics committee, Northumbria University (5814). This committee contains members who are internal to the Faculty. This study was reviewed by members of the committee, who must provide impartial advice and avoid significant conflicts of interests.

What did Beveridge do for us?

1 Leo McKinstry, *Attlee and Churchill: Allies in War, Adversaries in Peace* (London: Atlantic Books, 2019); John Bew, *Citizen Clem: A Biography of Attlee* (London: Quercus, 2016).
2 Taylor Downing, *1942: Britain at the Brink* (London: Little, Brown, 2022), 356.
3 Nicholas Timmins, *The Five Giants: A Biography of the Welfare State*, third edition (London: William Collins, 2017), 33.
4 Georgina Brewis, Angela Ellis Paine, Irene Hardill, Rose Lindsey and Rob Macmillan, *Transformational Moments in Social Welfare: What Role for Voluntary Action?* (Bristol: Policy Press, 2021), https://doi.org/10.51952/9781447357230.
5 Bernard Harris, *The Origins of the British Welfare State: Society, State and Social Welfare in England and Wales, 1800–1945* (Basingstoke: Palgrave Macmillan, 2004).
6 Bob Holman, "Fifty Years Ago: The Curtis and Clyde Reports", *Children & Society* 10, no. 3 (18 December 2007): 197–209, https://doi.org/10.1111/j.1099-0860.1996.tb00469.x; Pat Thane, *Divided Kingdom: A*

History of Britain, 1900 to the Present (Cambridge: Cambridge University Press, 2018).

7 Richard M. Titmuss, *Problems of Social Policy* (London: HMSO, 1950), 516, www.ibiblio.org/hyperwar/UN/UK/UK-Civil-Social/index.html.

8 Marjory Allen, "Children in Homes", *The Times*, 15 July 1944, Letters to the Editor.

9 Philip Alston, "Report of the Special Rapporteur on Extreme Poverty and Human Rights on His Visit to the United Kingdom of Great Britain and Northern Ireland" (Geneva: United Nations, 23 April 2019), https://digitallibrary.un.org/record/3806308; British Academy, "The COVID Decade: Understanding the Long-Term Societal Impacts of COVID-19" (London: British Academy, 2021), www.thebritishacademy.ac.uk/publications/covid-decade-understanding-the-long-term-societal-impacts-of-covid-19.

10 Irene Hardill, Jurgen Grotz and Laura Crawford, eds, *Mobilising Voluntary Action in the UK: Learning from the Pandemic* (Bristol: Policy Press, 2022), https://doi.org/10.51952/9781447367246; Jonathan Calvert and George Arbuthnott, *Failures of State: The inside Story of Britain's Battle with Coronavirus* (London: Mudlark, 2021).

11 UK Covid-19 Enquiry, "Documents", UK Covid-19 Inquiry, 2023, https://covid19.public-inquiry.uk/documents.

12 Downing, *1942*, 359.

13 Timmins, *The Five Giants*.

14 Downing, *1942*, 361.

15 Brewis et al., *Transformational Moments*.

16 Brewis et al., *Transformational Moments*; Harris, *The Origins of the British Welfare State*; Irene Hardill, Georgina Brewis and Rose Lindsey, "An End to 'Want, Disease, Ignorance, Squalor and Idleness': Why the Beveridge Report Flew Off the Shelves in 1942", *The Conversation*, 30 November 2017, http://theconversation.com/an-end-to-want-disease-ignorance-squalor-and-idleness-why-the-beveridge-report-flew-off-the-shelves-in-1942-88097.

17 Timmins, *The Five Giants*, 19.

18 William Beveridge, "Social Insurance and Allied Services (The Beveridge Report) " (London: HMSO, November 1942), 31, http://news.bbc.co.uk/1/shared/bsp/hi/pdfs/19_07_05_beveridge.pdf.

19 William H. Beveridge, *The Pillars of Security: And Other War-Time Essays and Addresses* (London: George Allen and Unwin, 1943), 59.

20 Hardill, Brewis and Lindsey, "An End to Want".

21 Hardill, Brewis and Lindsey, "An End to Want".

22 Pete Alcock, "Poverty and Social Security", in *British Social Welfare in the Twentieth Century*, ed. Robert M. Page and Richard Silburn (London: Macmillan Education UK, 1999), 204, https://doi.org/10.1007/978-1-349-27398-0_10.

23 Lord Beveridge, *Power and Influence: An Autobiography by Lord Beveridge* (London: Hodder & Stoughton, 1953), 319.

24 Hardill, Brewis and Lindsey, "An End to Want".

25 Downing, *1942*, 361.

26 Lord Beveridge, *Power and Influence*.

27 Beveridge, "Social Insurance and Allied Services", 6.

28 Beveridge, *The Pillars of Security*, 11.

29 Thane, *Divided Kingdom*, 187.

30 Thane, *Divided Kingdom*.

31 Bew, *Citizen Clem*, 340.

32 José Harris, *William Beveridge: A Biography*, second edition (Oxford: Clarendon Press, 1997).

33 Anne Digby, *British Welfare Policy: Workhouse to Workforce*, Historical Handbooks 8 (London: Faber, 1989).

34 David Kynaston, *Austerity Britain, 1945–51* (London: Bloomsbury, 2007), 145, 148.

35 Jim Tomlinson, "Welfare and the Economy: The Economic Impact of the Welfare State, 1945–1951", *Twentieth Century British History* 6, no. 2 (1995): 212, https://doi.org/10.1093/tcbh/6.2.194.

36 Aaron O'Neill, "Life Expectancy (from Birth) in the United Kingdom from 1765 to 2020", Statista, 21 June 2022, www.statista.com/statistics/1040159/life-expectancy-united-kingdom-all-time.

37 Paul Addison, *The Road to 1945: British Politics and the Second World War*, revised edition, Pimlico (Series) 117 (London: Pimlico, 1994).

38 Guy Standing, *Battling Eight Giants: Basic Income Now* (London: I.B. Tauris, 2020).

39 G.C. Peden, "The 1944 White Paper on Employment Policy", in *Keynes, The Treasury and British Economic Policy* (London: Macmillan Education UK, 1988), 44–49, https://doi.org/10.1007/978-1-349-07019-0_6.

40 Office for National Statistics, "Unemployment Rate (Aged 16 and Over, Seasonally Adjusted): %", Office for National Statistics, 12 September 2023, www.ons.gov.uk/employmentandlabourmarket/peoplenotinwork/unemployment/timeseries/mgsx/lms.

41 Guy Standing, *The Corruption of Capitalism: Why Rentiers Thrive and Work Does Not Pay* (London: Biteback Publishing, 2016).

42 Christina Beatty and Steve Fothergill, "Hitting the Poorest Places Hardest: The Local and Regional Impact of Welfare Reform" (Sheffield: Sheffield Hallam University, 10 April 2013), https://doi.org/10.7190/cresr.2017.6378897426; Christina Beatty and Steve Fothergill, "The Uneven Impact of Welfare Reform" (Sheffield: Sheffield Hallam University, 9 March 2016), https://doi.org/10.7190/cresr.2017.5563239352.

43 Anne West, "Education and Ignorance in the 80 Years after Beveridge: The Role of Government and Equality of Opportunity", *Social Policy & Administration* 56, no. 2 (March 2022): 299–314, https://doi.org/10.1111/spol.12781.

44 West, "Education and Ignorance"; James Foreman-Peck, "Spontaneous Disorder? A Very Short History of British Vocational Education and Training, 1563–1973", *Policy Futures in Education* 2, no. 1 (March 2004): 72–101, https://doi.org/10.2304/pfie.2004.2.1.10.

45 Harry Lambert, "The Great University Con: How the British Degree Lost Its Value", *New Statesman*, 21 August 2019, www.newstatesman.com/politics/2019/08/the-great-university-con-how-the-british-degree-lost-its-value.

46 Peter Wilby, "Margaret Thatcher's Education Legacy Is Still with Us – Driven on by Gove", *Guardian*, 15 April 2013, Education, www.theguardian.com/education/2013/apr/15/margaret-thatcher-education-legacy-gove.

47 Howard F. Gospel, "Whatever Happened to Apprenticeship Training? A British, American, Australian Comparison", Discussion Paper (London: Centre for Economic Performance, March 1994), https://core.ac.uk/download/pdf/6389044.pdf.

48 IPPR Commission on the Future of Higher Education, "A Critical Path: Securing the Future of Higher Education in England" (London: IPPR, 2013), www.ippr.org/files/images/media/files/publication/2013/06/critical-path-securing-future-higher-education_June2013_10847.pdf.

49 West, "Education and Ignorance".

50 Martin Wheatley, "Student Loans Were an Accounting Wheeze – Now They Are a Fiscal Headache", Institute for Government (blog), 18 December 2018, www.instituteforgovernment.org.uk/article/comment/student-loans-were-accounting-wheeze-now-they-are-fiscal-headache.

51 Alex Matthews-King, "Applications to Study Nursing Fall for Second Year after Removal of Training Bursary", *Independent*, 5 February 2018, News, www.independent.co.uk/news/health/nursing-applications-ucas-course-drop-nhs-grants-funding-debt-tuition-fees-costs-a8191546.html.

52 Office for National Statistics, "How Has Life Expectancy Changed over Time?", Office for National Statistics, 9 September 2015, www.ons.gov.uk/peoplepopulationandcommunity/birthsdeathsandmarriages/lifeexpectancies/articles/howhaslifeexpectancychangedovertime/2015-09-09.

53 Secretary to the Cabinet, "Aneurin Bevan Resigns", The National Archives, 22 March 1951, www.nationalarchives.gov.uk/education/resources/fifties-britain/aneurin-bevan-resigns.

54 Nick Davies, Lucy Campbell and Chris McNulty, "How to Fix the Funding of Health and Social Care" (London: Institute for Government, June 2018), https://nonprofit.report/Resources/Whitepapers/1d7ae026-4af4-453b-8335-155e1e36dc64_Funding_health_and_social_care_web.pdf.

55 King's Fund, "The NHS Budget and How It Has Changed", The King's Fund, 20 September 2023, www.kingsfund.org.uk/projects/nhs-in-a-nutshell/nhs-budget.

56 King's Fund, "The NHS Budget".

57 John Appleby, "Making Sense of PFI", Nuffield Trust, 6 October 2017, www.nuffieldtrust.org.uk/resource/making-sense-of-pfi.

58 King's Fund, "The NHS Budget".

59 Department of Health and Social Care, "Department of Health and Social Care Annual Report and Accounts: 2021–2022" (London: Department of Health and Social Care, 26 January 2023), https://assets.publishing.service.gov.uk/media/63e50dc0d3bf7f05c8e947a8/dhsc-annual-report-and-accounts-2021-2022_web-accessible.pdf.

60 Matthews-King, "Applications to Study Nursing Fall".

61 King's Fund, "The King's Fund Responds the Latest NHS Performance Stats", The King's Fund, 12 October 2023, www.kingsfund.org.uk/press/press-releases/kings-fund-responds-latest-nhs-performance-stats-1.

62 Department for Work and Pensions, "Family Resources Survey 2021/22: Disability Data Tables" (London: GOV.UK, 23 March 2023),

www.gov.uk/government/statistics/family-resources-survey-financial-year-2021-to-2022.

63 Department for Work and Pensions, "Family Resources Survey 2021/22".

64 Department for Work and Pensions, "Family Resources Survey 2021/22".

65 Department for Levelling Up, Housing and Communities, "Levelling Up the United Kingdom: White Paper" (London: HMSO, 2022), www.gov.uk/government/publications/levelling-up-the-united-kingdom.

66 House of Commons Housing, Communities and Local Government Committee, "Building More Social Housing" (London: House of Commons Housing, Communities and Local Government Committee, 20 July 2020), https://publications.parliament.uk/pa/cm5801/cmselect/cmcomloc/173/17305.htm.

67 Savia Palate, "Homes for Today and Tomorrow: Britain's Parker Morris Standards and the West Ham Experimental Scheme", *Architecture and Culture* 10, no. 3 (3 July 2022): 457–82, https://doi.org/10.1080/20507828.2022.2198299.

68 Palate, "Homes for Today and Tomorrow".

69 Barry Goodchild and Robert Furbey, "Standards in Housing Design: A Review of the Main Changes since the Parker Morris Report (1961)", *Land Development Studies* 3, no. 2 (May 1986): 79–99, https://doi.org/10.1080/02640828608723903; Pascale Hughes, "Why Have New Houses Been Shrinking since 1980?", inews.co.uk, 14 September 2018, https://inews.co.uk/news/long-reads/honey-i-shrunk-the-house-homes-been-getting-smaller-since-the-1970s-197594.

70 Palate, "Homes for Today and Tomorrow; Alan Murie, "A Policy History of the Right to Buy, 1980–2015", in *The Right to Buy? Selling off Public and Social Housing* (Bristol, UK: Policy Press, 2016), 31–64.

71 Palate, "Homes for Today and Tomorrow"; Murie, "A Policy History of the Right to Buy", 36–37.

72 Hughes, "Why Have New Houses Been Shrinking?"; House of Commons Housing, Communities and Local Government Committee, "Building More Social Housing".

73 Kiran Stacey, "Plans to Abolish 'Feudal' Leasehold System in England and Wales Dropped", *Guardian*, 10 May 2023, Money, www.theguardian.com/money/2023/may/10/plans-abolish-feudal-leasehold-system-england-wales.

74 Robert Booth, "England Worst Place in Developed World to Find Housing, Says Report", *Guardian*, 4 October 2023, Society, www.theguardian.com/society/2023/oct/05/england-worst-place-in-developed-world-to-find-housing-says-report.

75 Julia Kollewe, "Why Are Britain's New Homes Built So Badly?", *Guardian*, 11 March 2017, Money, www.theguardian.com/money/2017/mar/11/why-are-britains-new-homes-built-so-badly.

76 Robert Booth, "Housing Ombudsman in England Calls to Re-Establish Link between Housing and Health", *Guardian*, 22 January 2024, Society, www.theguardian.com/society/2024/jan/22/richard-blakeway-ombudsman-england-social-housing-health.

77 Graham Atkins and Stuart Hoddinott, "Neighbourhood Services under Strain: How a Decade of Cuts and Rising Demand for Social Care Affected Local Services" (London: Institute for Government, 2022), www.instituteforgovernment.org.uk/sites/default/files/publications/neighbourhood-services-under-strain.pdf.

78 Freya Thomson, "Joined-up Refuse Planning and Education Key to Reducing Fly-Tipping", Open Access Government (blog), 8 July 2022, www.openaccessgovernment.org/joined-up-refuse-planning-and-education-key-to-reducing-fly-tipping/139445.

79 Matthew Prior, "Fly-Tipping Forces Landowners to Turn Farms into 'forts'", BBC News, 17 January 2022, www.bbc.co.uk/news/science-environment-68007087.

80 Kees Keizer, Siegwart Lindenberg and Linda Steg, "The Spreading of Disorder", *Science* 322, no. 5908 (12 December 2008): 1681–85, https://doi.org/10.1126/science.1161405.

81 Nicholas Crafts, "The Welfare State and Inequality: Were the UK Reforms of the 1940s a Success? " (London: Institute for Fiscal Studies, February 2023), https://ifs.org.uk/inequality/the-welfare-state-and-inequality.

82 Sam Ray-Chaudhuri, Tom Waters, Thomas Wernham and Xiaowei Xu, "Living Standards, Poverty and Inequality in the UK: 2023" (London: Institute for Fiscal Studies, 13 July 2023), https://doi.org/10.1920/re.ifs.2023.0265; Brigid Francis-Devine, "Poverty in the UK: Statistics" (London: House of Commons Library, 1 December 2023), https://researchbriefings.files.parliament.uk/documents/SN07096/SN07096.pdf.

83 Michael Marmot, Jessica Allen, Peter Goldblatt, Tammy Boyce, Di McNeish, Mike Grady and Ilaria Geddes, *Fair Society, Healthy Lives: The*

Marmot Review (London: The Marmot Review, 2010), www.instituteof healthequity.org/resources-reports/fair-society-healthy-lives-the-marmot-review; R. Wilkinson and K. Pickett, *The Spirit Level: Why More Equal Societies Almost Always Do Better* (London: Penguin, 2009); Matthew Thomas Johnson and Elliott Johnson, "Stress, Domination and Basic Income: Considering a Citizens' Entitlement Response to a Public Health Crisis", *Social Theory & Health* 17, no. 2 (June 2019): 253–71, https://doi.org/10.1057/s41285-018-0076-3.

84 Dean Blackburn, "Reassessing Britain's 'Post-War Consensus': The Politics of Reason 1945–1979", *British Politics* 13, no. 2 (June 1, 2018): 203–05, https://doi.org/10.1057/s41293-017-0049-5; Alan Travis, "Margaret Thatcher's Role in Plan to Dismantle Welfare State Revealed", *Guardian*, 28 December 2012, Politics, www.theguardian.com/politics/2012/dec/28/margaret-thatcher-role-plan-to-dismantle-welfare-state-revealed.

85 Paul Johnson and Steven Webb, "Explaining the Growth in UK Income Inequality: 1979–1988", *The Economic Journal* 103, no. 417 (March 1993): 429, https://doi.org/10.2307/2234781.

86 Elliott Johnson and Daniel Nettle, "Fairness, Generosity and Conditionality in the Welfare System: The Case of UK Disability Benefits", Global Discourse 13, no. 2 (5 October 2020): 196–213, https://doi.org/10.1332/204378920X15989751152011.

87 Johnson and Nettle, "Fairness, Generosity and Conditionality".

88 BBC News, "Tax Credits Scandal", 5 June 2003, http://news.bbc.co.uk/1/hi/programmes/working_lunch/2966030.stm.

89 Johnson and Nettle, "Fairness, Generosity and Conditionality".

90 Johnson and Nettle, "Fairness, Generosity and Conditionality".

91 Francis-Devine, "Poverty in the UK".

92 Elliot Johnson, Howard Reed, Daniel Nettle, Graham Stark, Joe Chrisp, Neil Howard, Grace Gregory, Cleo Goodman, Matthew Smith, Jonathan Coates, Ian Robson, Fiorella Parra-Mujica, Kate E. Pickett and Matthew Johnson, "Treating Causes Not Symptoms: Basic Income as a Public Health Measure" (London: Compass, 2023).

93 Hannah Lambie-Mumford, "The Growth of Food Banks in Britain and What They Mean for Social Policy", *Critical Social Policy* 39, no. 1 (February 2019): 3–22, https://doi.org/10.1177/0261018318765855.

94 Department of Health and Social Care and Matt Hancock, "Prevention Is Better than Cure – Matt Hancock's Speech to IANPHI", GOV.UK,

11 May 2018, www.gov.uk/government/speeches/prevention-is-better-than-cure-matt-hancocks-speech-to-ianphi.

95 British Institute of Public Opinion, "The Beveridge Report and the Public" (London: The British Institute of Public Opinion, 1943), www.nationalarchives.gov.uk/education/resources/attlees-britain/survey-beveridge-report.

96 Equality Trust, "The Scale of Economic Inequality in the UK", The Equality Trust, 2023, https://equalitytrust.org.uk/scale-economic-inequality-uk.

What government should do

1 Clare Bambra, "Levelling up: Global Examples of Reducing Health Inequalities", *Scandinavian Journal of Public Health* 50, no. 7 (November 2022): 908–13, https://doi.org/10.1177/14034948211022428.

2 Ashifa Kassam, "'I'm Creating the Tax I Would Want to Pay': Austrian Heiress Marlene Engelhorn on Why She Is Giving Away 90% of Her Wealth", *Guardian*, 23 January 2024, News, www.theguardian.com/news/2024/jan/23/austrian-heiress-marlene-engelhorn-who-is-giving-away-90-per-cent-of-her-wealth-im-creating-the-tax-i-would-want-to-pay.

3 Martin Gilens and Benjamin I. Page, "Testing Theories of American Politics: Elites, Interest Groups, and Average Citizens", *Perspectives on Politics* 12, no. 3 (September 2014): 564–81, https://doi.org/10.1017/S1537592714001595.

4 Patrick Butler, "Gordon Brown Calls for Overhaul of Benefits System as Study Reveals 'Crisis'", *Guardian*, 21 January 2024, Politics, www.theguardian.com/politics/2024/jan/21/gordon-brown-urges-overhaul-benefits-system-study-crisis.

5 Margaret Thatcher, "Speech to Conservative Party Conference", Blackpool, 1975, www.margaretthatcher.org/document/102777.

6 Kevin Hickson, "Equality", in *The Struggle for Labour's Soul: Understanding Labour's Political Thought since 1945*, ed. Raymond Plant, Matt Beech, and Kevin Hickson (London: Routledge, 2004), 127.

7 See Jose Cuesta, Mario Negre, Ana Revenga and Carlos Silva-Jauregui, "Is It Really Possible for Countries to Simultaneously Grow and Reduce Poverty and Inequality ? Going beyond Global Narratives", *Oxford Development Studies* 48, no. 3 (July 2, 2020): 256–70, https://doi.org/10.1080/13600818.2020.1784864.

8 Richard G. Wilkinson and Kate Pickett, *The Spirit Level: Why Equality Is Better for Everyone; with a New Chapter Responding to Their Critics*, republished with a new postscript (London: Penguin, 2010).

9 E.g. Ted Honderich, "The Question of Well-Being and the Principle of Equality", *Mind* 90, no. 360 (1981): 481–504, https://doi.org/10.1093/mind/XC.360.481.

10 Philip Pettit, "Republican Freedom and Contestatory Democratization", in *Democracy's Value*, ed. Ian Shapiro and Casiano Hacker-Cordón (Cambridge: Cambridge University Press, 1999), 165.

11 Johnson and Johnson, "Stress, Domination and Basic Income".

12 Fritz Handerer, Peter Kinderman, Matina Shafti and Sara Tai., "A Scoping Review and Narrative Synthesis Comparing the Constructs of Social Determinants of Health and Social Determinants of Mental Health: Matryoshka or Two Independent Constructs?", *Frontiers in Psychiatry* 13 (14 April 2022): 848556, https://doi.org/10.3389/fpsyt.2022.848556.

13 See Department of Health and Social Care and Hancock, "Prevention Is Better than Cure".

14 HM Revenue and Customs, "Soft Drinks Industry Levy", policy paper (London: Government Digital Service, 5 December 2016), www.gov.uk/government/publications/soft-drinks-industry-levy/soft-drinks-industry-levy.

15 Friedrich A. Hayek, *The Road to Serfdom* (Chicago: The University of Chicago Press, 2001), 124–25.

16 Centre for Local Economic Strategies (CLES) and Preston Council, "How We Built Community Wealth in Preston: Achievements and Lessons" (Manchester: Centre for Local Economic Strategies (CLES) and Preston: Preston Council, May 2019), https://cles.org.uk/publications/how-we-built-community-wealth-in-preston-achievements-and-lessons.

17 Matthew Thomas Johnson, *Evaluating Culture: Wellbeing, Institutions and Circumstance* (London: Palgrave Macmillan, 2013).

A social safety net

1 Sophie Wickham, Lee Bentley, Tanith Rose, Margaret Whitehead, David Taylor-Robinson and Ben Barr, "Effects on Mental Health of a UK Welfare Reform, Universal Credit: A Longitudinal Controlled Study", *The Lancet Public Health* 5, no. 3 (March 1, 2020): e157–64, https://doi.org/10.1016/S2468-2667(20)30026-8.

2 Beveridge, "Social Insurance and Allied Services".
3 Ken Annakin, dir., *It Began on the Clyde* (Moving Image Archive for the Department of Health for Scotland, 1946), https://movingimage.nls.uk/film/0030.
4 Joseph Rowntree Foundation, "UK Poverty 2023: The Essential Guide to Poverty in the UK" (London: Joseph Rowntree Foundation, 2023).
5 Authors' illustration based on data from Reed et al., "Universal Basic Income Is Affordable and Feasible".
6 Howard Robert Reed, Matthew Thomas Johnson, Stewart Lansley, Elliot Aidan Johnson, Graham Stark and Kate E. Pickett, "Universal Basic Income Is Affordable and Feasible: Evidence from UK Economic Microsimulation Modelling", *Journal of Poverty and Social Justice* 31, no. 1 (February 1, 2023): 146–62, https://doi.org/10.1332/175982721X16702368352393.
7 Reed et al., "Universal Basic Income".
8 Johnson et al., "Treating Causes Not Symptoms"; Elliott Aidan Johnson, Matthew Thomas Johnson and Laura Webber, "Measuring the Health Impact of Universal Basic Income as an Upstream Intervention: Holistic Trial Design That Captures Stress Reduction Is Essential", *Evidence & Policy* 18, no. 3 (August 1, 2022): 583–94, https://doi.org/10.1332/174426420X15820274674068.
9 Department for Work and Pensions, "DWP Benefits Statistics: August 2023" (London: Department for Work and Pensions, 2023), www.gov.uk/government/statistics/dwp-benefits-statistics-august-2023/dwp-benefits-statistics-august-2023; Sebastião Viola and Joanna Moncrieff, "Claims for Sickness and Disability Benefits Owing to Mental Disorders in the UK: Trends from 1995 to 2014", *BJPsych Open* 2, no. 1 (January 2016): 18–24, https://doi.org/10.1192/bjpo.bp.115.002246.
10 Daniel Chandler, *Free and Equal: What Would a Fair Society Look Like?* (London: Penguin, 2023).
11 Elliott Johnson and Emma Spring, "The Activity Trap" (Manchester: Activity Alliance, 10 August 2018), www.activityalliance.org.uk/assets/000/002/433/Activity_Alliance_-_The_Activity_Trap_full_report_Accessible_PDF_FINAL_original.pdf?1538668349.
12 Stephen Machin and Costas Meghir, "Crime and Economic Incentives", *The Journal of Human Resources* 39, no. 4 (2004): 958–79, https://doi.org/10.2307/3559034; Benoît de Courson and Daniel Nettle, "Why Do Inequality and Deprivation Produce High Crime and Low Trust?", *Scientific Reports* 11, no. 1 (21 January 2021): 1937,

https://doi.org/10.1038/s41598-020-80897-8; Morgan Kelly, "Inequality and Crime", *Review of Economics and Statistics* 82, no. 4 (November 2000): 530–39, https://doi.org/10.1162/003465300559028.

13 Reed et al., "Universal Basic Income".

14 Ioana Marinescu, "No Strings Attached: The Behavioral Effects of U.S. Unconditional Cash Transfer Programs", working paper (Cambridge, MA: National Bureau of Economic Research, February 2018), https://doi.org/10.3386/w24337; Karl Widerquist, "A Failure to Communicate: What (If Anything) Can We Learn from the Negative Income Tax Experiments?", *The Journal of Socio-Economics* 34, no. 1 (February 1, 2005): 49–81, https://doi.org/10.1016/j.socec.2004.09.050.

15 Jonathan Ostry, Andrew Berg and Charalambos Tsangarides, "Redistribution, Inequality, and Growth" (Washington, DC: International Monetary Fund, 2014), https://elibrary.imf.org/openurl?genre= journal&issn=2617-6750&volume=2014&issue=002.

16 Luca Calafati, Julie Froud, Colin Haslam, Sukhdev Johal, Karel Williams, *When Nothing Works: From Cost of Living to Foundational Livability* (Manchester: Manchester University Press, 2023); Thomas Piketty, *Capital in the Twenty-First Century* (Cambridge, MA: Harvard University Press, 2014).

17 Calafati et al., *When Nothing Works*.

18 A. Advani, E. Chamberlain and A. Summers, "A Wealth Tax for the UK" (London: Wealth Tax Commission, 2020); K. Rowlingson, A. Sood and T. Tu, "Public Attitudes to a Wealth Tax" (London: Wealth Tax Commission, 2020).

19 Matt Padley and Juliet Stone, "A Minimum Income Standard for the United Kingdom in 2023" (York: Joseph Rowntree Foundation, 8 September 2023), www.jrf.org.uk/report/minimum-income-standard-uk-2023; Reed et al., "Universal Basic Income".

20 Reed et al., "Universal Basic Income".

21 David Walsh, Gerry McCartney, Jon Minton, Jane Parkinson, Deborah Shipton and Bruce Whyte, "Deaths from 'Diseases of Despair' in Britain: Comparing Suicide, Alcohol-Related and Drug-Related Mortality for Birth Cohorts in Scotland, England and Wales, and Selected Cities", *Journal of Epidemiology and Community Health* 75, no. 12 (December 2021): 1195–1201, https://doi.org/10.1136/jech-2020-216220.

22 Elliott Johnson, Cleo Goodman, Jack Kellam and Matthew Johnson, "A Big Local Basic Income: Proposal for a Locally-Led Basic Income

Pilot" (Crookham Village: Autonomy, June 2023), https://autonomy. work/portfolio/basic-income-big-local.

23 Elliott Johnson, Cleo Goodman and Matthew Johnson, "A Big Local Basic Income: Resident Perspectives" (Crookham Village: Autonomy, June 2023), https://autonomy.work/wp-content/uploads/2023/06/ BASINCSHORT.pdf.

24 Neil Howard, Grace Gregory, Elliot A. Johnson, Cleopatra Goodman, Jonathan Coates, Ian Robson, Kate Pickett and Matthew T. Johnson, "Designing Basic Income Pilots for Community Development: What Are the Key Community Concerns? Evidence from Citizen Engagement in Northern England", *Local Development & Society*, 11 October 2023, 1–17, https://doi.org/10.1080/26883597.2023.2269483.

25 Johnson et al., "Treating Causes Not Symptoms".

26 L. Bartels, "Political Inequality in Affluent Democracies: The Social Welfare Deficit" (Nashville, TN: Center for the Study of Democratic Institutions, 2017).

27 Bartels, "Political Inequality in Affluent Democracies"; Gilens and Page, "Testing Theories of American Politics".

28 Matthew Johnson, Elliott Johnson and Daniel Nettle, "Are 'Red Wall' Constituencies Really Opposed to Progressive Policy? Examining the Impact of Materialist Narratives for Universal Basic Income", British Politics 18 (18 October 2022): 104–27, https://doi.org/10.1057/ s41293-022-00220-z; Daniel Nettle, Elliot Johnson, Matthew Johnson and Rebecca Saxe, "Why Has the COVID-19 Pandemic Increased Support for Universal Basic Income ?", *Humanities and Social Sciences Communications* 8, no. 1 (17 March 2021): 1–12, https://doi.org/10.1057/ s41599-021-00760-7.

29 Daniel Nettle, Joe Chrisp and Matthew T. Johnson, "What Do British People Want from a Welfare System? Conjoint Survey Evidence on Generosity, Conditionality, Funding, and Outcomes", SocArXiv Papers, 2023, https://doi.org/10.31235/osf.io/zfnuh.

30 Authors' illustration based on data from Nettle et al., "What Do British People Want from a Welfare System?"

31 Howard et al., "Designing Basic Income Pilots"; Elliott A. Johnson, Hannah Webster, James Morrison, Riley Thorold, Alice Mathers, Daniel Nettle, Kate E. Pickett and Matthew T. Johnson "What Role Do Young People Believe Universal Basic Income Can Play in Supporting Their Mental Health?", *Journal of Youth Studies* (8 September 2023): 1–20, https://doi.org/10.1080/13676261.2023.2256236.

A Green New Deal

1 Joshua Emden, Luke Murphy and Russell Gunson, "Net Zero North Sea: A Managed Transition for Oil and Gas in Scotland and the UK after Covid-19" (London: IPPR, 3 December 2020), www.ippr.org/research/publications/net-zero-north-sea.

2 Tianyang Lei, Daoping Wang, Xiang Yu, Shijun Ma, Weichen Zhao, Can Cui, Jing Meng, Shu Tao and Dabo Guan, "Global Iron and Steel Plant CO_2 Emissions and Carbon-Neutrality Pathways", *Nature* 622, no. 7983 (19 October 2023): 514–20, https://doi.org/10.1038/s41586-023-06486-7; Paul Fennell, Justin Drier, Christopher Bataille and Steven J. Davis, "Cement and Steel: Nine Steps to Net Zero", *Nature* 603, no. 7902 (24 March 2022): 574–77, https://doi.org/10.1038/d41586-022-00758-4.

3 Gemma Drake, "How the UK Can Capitalise on Cleaner, Greener Steel", Zero Carbon Academy (blog), 28 September 2023, www.zerocarbon academy.com//posts/how-the-uk-can-capitalise-on-cleaner-greener-steel.

4 Ruth Potts, "The Green New Deal: A Bill to Make It Happen" (London: Green New Deal Group, 20 September 2019), https://greennewdeal group.org/the-green-new-deal-a-bill-to-make-it-happen-2.

5 Elliot Chappell, "Rachel Reeves Pledges £28bn per Year Investment in Green Transition", LabourList, 27 September 2021, https://labourlist.org/2021/09/rachel-reeves-pledges-28bn-per-year-investment-in-green-transition.

6 London Partnership Board, "Retrofit London Board Paper" (London: London Partnership Board, 16 March 2023), www.london.gov.uk/moderngovmb/documents/s76625/07%20Retrofit%20London.pdf.

7 Ben Quinn, "Labour's Plan to Insulate More Homes 'Would Create 4m Job Opportunities'", *Guardian*, 9 July 2023, Environment, www.theguardian.com/environment/2023/jul/09/labours-plan-to-insulate-more-homes-would-create-4m-job-opportunities.

8 Rob Evans, "Half of England Is Owned by Less Than 1% of the Population", *Guardian*, 17 April 2019, Money, www.theguardian.com/money/2019/apr/17/who-owns-england-thousand-secret-landowners-author.

9 United Nations, "The Ocean: The World's Greatest Ally against Climate Change", United Nations, accessed 8 February 2024, www.un.org/en/climatechange/science/climate-issues/ocean.

10 Guy Standing, Blue Commons: Rescuing the Economy of the Sea (London: Penguin, 2023).

11 Economics for the Environment Consultancy Ltd (eftec), "North Devon Marine Protected Areas Cost Evaluation: Final Report" (Woking: WWF-UK, November 2018), https://ukseasproject.org.uk/cms-data/reports/North%20Devon%20Marine%20Protected%20Areas%20Cost%20Evaluation%20-%20%20Final%20Report.pdf.

12 Simply Sustainable, "UK Resources and Waste Strategy: What You Need to Know", Simply Sustainable, December 2018, https://simplysustainable.com/insights/uk-resources-waste-strategy-what-you-need-to-know.

Public utilities

1 Joseph Baines and Sandy Brian Hager, "Profiting amid the Energy Crisis: The Distribution Networks at the Heart of the UK's Gas and Electricity System" (London: Common Wealth, March 2022), www.common-wealth.org/publications/profiting-amid-the-crisis.

2 Carl Shoben, "New Poll: Public Strongly Backing Public Ownership of Energy and Key Utilities", Survation (blog), 15 August 2022, www.survation.com/new-poll-public-strongly-backing-public-ownership-of-energy-and-key-utilities.

3 Le Monde with AFP, "France to Continue Subsidizing Electricity Bills until 2025", Le Monde, 21 April 2023, www.lemonde.fr/en/energies/article/2023/04/21/france-to-continue-subsidizing-electricity-bills-until-2025_6023740_98.html; Paul Bolton and Iona Stewart, "Domestic Energy Prices", Research Briefing (London: House of Commons Library, 4 December 2023), https://researchbriefings.files.parliament.uk/documents/CBP-9491/CBP-9491.pdf.

4 Reuters, "Norway to Further Raise Household Electricity Subsidy", Reuters, 10 January 2022, Commodities, www.reuters.com/markets/commodities/norway-further-raise-household-electricity-subsidy-2022-01-10.

5 Unite, "Unite Investigates: Renationalising Energy. Costs and Savings: Full Report" (London: Unite, February 2023), www.unitetheunion.org/what-we-do/unite-investigates/unplugging-energy-profiteers-the-case-for-public-ownership/unite-investigates-renationalising-energy-costs-and-savings-full-report.

6 Reuters, "Norway to Further Raise Household Electricity Subsidy".

7 PWC, "Norway: Corporate – Taxes on Corporate Income", PWC, 7 July 2023, https://taxsummaries.pwc.com/norway/corporate/taxes-on-corporate-income.

8 Alex Chapman, "The Windfall Tax Was Supposed to Rein in Fossil Fuel Profits. Instead It Has Saved Corporations Billions", New Economics Foundation (blog), 28 November 2023, https://new economics.org/2023/11/the-windfall-tax-was-supposed-to-rein-in-fossil-fuel-profits-instead-it-has-saved-corporations-billions.

9 Ministry of Energy, "Renewable Energy Production in Norway", Government.no, 11 May 2016), www.regjeringen.no/en/topics/energy/renewable-energy/renewable-energy-production-in-norway/id2343462.

10 Jonas Algers and Rainer Kattel, "Equinor and Ørsted: How Industrial Policy Shaped the Scandinavian Energy Giants", IIPP Policy Brief (London: Institute for Innovation and Public Purpose, March 2021), www.ucl.ac.uk/bartlett/public-purpose/sites/public-purpose/files/iipp_pb14_equinor-and-orsted_industrial-policy_final.pdf.

11 Norges Bank, "The Fund's Market Value", Norges Bank Investment Management, 28 April 2017, www.nbim.no/en.

12 Ofgem, "Transmission Licence of National Grid Company PLC", 2011, www.ofgem.gov.uk/sites/default/files/docs/2011/10/nget-rollover-special-conditions.pdf; Ofgem, "Utility Assets Limited: Electricity Distribution Licence", 10 March 2011, https://epr.ofgem.gov.uk; National Grid, "Prospectus: Western Power Distribution Ltd", 2018, www.nationalgrid.co.uk/downloads/16267; Europe Economics, "Implications for Debt-Raising and the Cost of Debt of Changing the Minimum Termination Notice Period for NERL's Licence" (London: Europe Economics, September 2015), www.caa.co.uk/media/mw4jszcr/europe-economics-report.pdf.

13 Louise Butcher, "Railways: Railtrack Administration and the Private Shareholders, 2001–2005" (London: House of Commons Library, 10 August 2010), https://researchbriefings.files.parliament.uk/documents/SN01076/SN01076.pdf.

14 Labour Energy Forum, "Who Owns the Wind, Owns the Future" (London: Labour Party, September 2017), https://transitioneconomics.net/wp-content/uploads/2022/02/who-owns-the-wind.pdf.

15 We Own It, "Guess Which of the Top 10 Green Energy Countries DOESN'T Use Public Ownership?", We Own It (blog), 27 July 2022, https://weownit.org.uk/blog/guess-which-top-10-green-energy-countries-doesnt-use-public-ownership.

16 Bjarne Steffen, Valerie J. Karplus and Tobias S. Schmidt, "State Ownership and Technology Adoption: The Case of Electric Utilities and Renewable Energy", MIT CEEPR Working Paper (Cambridge, MA: MIT CEEPR, August 2020), https://ceepr.mit.edu/wp-content/uploads/2021/09/2020-016.pdf.

17 Lavinia Steinfort and James Angel, "Energy Transition Mythbusters: Myth #5 – Intellectual Property Rights Help Facilitate the Energy Transition", TNI (blog), 19 December 2023, www.tni.org/en/article/energy-transition-mythbusters-myth-5.

18 Business, Energy and Industrial Strategy Committee, "Decarbonisation of the Power Sector" (London: UK Parliament, 28 April 2023), https://publications.parliament.uk/pa/cm5803/cmselect/cmbeis/283/report.html.

19 Steinfort and Angel, "Energy Transition Mythbusters".

20 Matteo Deleidi, Mariana Mazzucato and Gregor Semieniuk, "Neither Crowding In Nor Out: Public Direct Investment Mobilising Private Investment into Renewable Electricity Projects", *Energy Policy* 140 (May 2020): 111195, https://doi.org/10.1016/j.enpol.2019.111195.

21 Sophie Flinders, Chris Hayes and Adrienne Buller, "National Grid: Ownership and Key Financial Indicators" (London: Common Wealth, 16 January 2023), www.common-wealth.org/publications/national-grid-ownership.

22 Vera Weghmann, "Going Public: A Decarbonised, Affordable and Democratic Energy System for Europe" (Brussels: EPSU (European Federation of Public Service Unions, July 2019), www.epsu.org.

23 Energy Networks Association, "Who's My Network Operator?", Energy Networks Association, 2023, www.energynetworks.org/customers/find-my-network-operator.

24 Cheryl Arcibal, "Hong Kong's Richest Family Has US$2.3 Billion of Cash in Its CK Infrastructure Unit to Go on Asset Shopping Spree", *South China Morning Post*, 17 May 2023, www.scmp.com/business/companies/article/3220890/hong-kongs-richest-family-has-us23-billion-cash-its-ck-infrastructure-unit-go-asset-shopping-spree.

25 Becky Mawhood, Adam Clark, Alex Adcock, James Mirza-Davies, Adrienne Buller, Ali Shalchi, Iona Stewart and Timothy Capper, "Energy Bill [HL] 2022–23, Parts 4–6: Electricity and Gas Markets",

Research Briefing (London: House of Commons Library, 4 May 2023), https://commonslibrary.parliament.uk/research-briefings/cbp-9784.

26 Common Wealth, "Grid Is Good: The Case for Public Ownership of Transmission and Distribution" (London: Common Wealth, 8 October 2023), www.common-wealth.org/publications/grid-is-good-the-case-for-public-ownership-of-transmission-and-distribution.

27 Common Wealth, "Grid Is Good".

28 Unite, "Unite Investigates".

29 Carlo V. Fiorio and Massimo Florio, "Electricity Prices and Public Ownership: Evidence from the EU15 over Thirty Years", *Energy Economics* 39 (September 2013): 222–32, https://doi.org/10.1016/j.eneco.2013.05.005.

30 David Hall, "If the UK's Energy Suppliers Were Publicly Owned, Would We Be Having This Crisis?", *Guardian*, 23 September 2021, Opinion, www.theguardian.com/commentisfree/2021/sep/23/uk-energy-suppliers-publicly-owned-crisis.

31 The Energy Shop, "Which Energy Suppliers Have Gone Bust so Far in 2022?", 2023, www.theenergyshop.com/guides/which-energy-suppliers-have-gone-bust.

32 Alex Lawson and Anna Isaac, "Bailing Out Bust Energy Supplier Bulb Will Cost Taxpayers £6.5bn, Figures Show", *Guardian*, 17 November 2022, www.theguardian.com/business/2022/nov/17/bail-out-bust-energy-supplier-bulb-cost-taxpayers-65bn-octopus.

33 TUC, "A Fairer Energy System for Families and the Climate" (London: TUC, July 2022), www.tuc.org.uk/sites/default/files/2022-07/Public%20energy%20public%20paper%20-%20web.pdf.

34 TUC, "A Fairer Energy System".

35 We Own It, "Who Owns Our Water", We Own It, 2023, https://weownit.org.uk/who-owns-our/water.

36 Gill Plimmer, "UK Water Company Dividends Jump to £1.4bn despite Criticism over Sewage Outflows", *Financial Times*, 8 May 2023, www.ft.com/content/ee03d551-8eee-4136-9eeb-7c8b51169a99.

37 Karol Yearwood, "The Privatised Water Industry in the UK: An ATM for Investors" (London: PSIRU, September 2018), https://gala.gre.ac.uk.

38 Gill Plimmer and Ella Hollowood, "Sewage Spills Highlight Decades of Under-Investment at England's Water Companies", *Financial Times*, 27 December 2021, www.ft.com.

39 BBC, "Panorama: The Water Pollution Cover-Up" (BBC, 4 December 2023), www.bbc.co.uk/iplayer/episode/m001t4g5/panorama-the-water-pollution-coverup.

40 Vishala Sri-Pathma, "Water Firms Want Bill Rises to Cut Leaks and Spills", BBC News, 1 October 2023, www.bbc.com/news/business-66979271.

41 Emma Gatten, "Water Companies 'Sold off Reservoirs That Could Have Eased Drought'", *Telegraph*, 9 August 2022, www.telegraph.co.uk/environment/2022/08/09/water-firms-sold-reservoirs-could-have-eased-drought.

42 Richard Murphy, "Cut the Crap: Accounting for Clean Water", Funding the Future (blog), 29 June 2023, www.taxresearch.org.uk/Blog/2023/06/29/cut-the-crap-accounting-for-clean-water.

43 Chas Geiger, "Local Elections 2023: How Sewage Topped the Political Agenda", BBC News, 24 April 2023, www.bbc.com/news/uk-politics-65190097.

44 David Hall, "The UK 2019 Election: Defeat for Labour, but Strong Support for Public Ownership", PSIRU Working Paper (London: PSIRU, 30 January 2020), https://gala.gre.ac.uk.

45 Yearwood, "The Privatised Water Industry in the UK".

46 Scottish Water, "Scottish Water Ranked Best UK Water Company and Utility for Customer Service", Scottish Water (blog), 7 July 2021, www.scottishwater.co.uk/About-Us/News-and-Views/2021/07/070721-Scottish-Water-ranked-best-UK-water-company-and-utility-for-customer-service.

47 Olivier Petitjean, "Remunicipalisation in France: From Addressing Corporate Abuse to Reinventing Democratic, Sustainable Local Public Services", in *Reclaiming Public Services: How Cities and Citizens Are Turning Back Privatisation*, ed. Satoko Kishimoto and Olivier Petitjean (Amsterdam: Transnational Institute, 2017), 24–33.

48 M'Lisa Colbert, "Why Renationalise? Contemporary Motivations in Latin America", in *Reclaiming Public Services: How Cities and Citizens Are Turning Back Privatisation*, ed. Satoko Kishimoto and Olivier Petitjean (Amsterdam: Transnational Institute, 2017), 34–47.

49 Eau de Paris, "Protecting Water Resources", Eau de Paris, 2023, www.eaudeparis.fr/en/protect-water-resources.

50 European Investment Bank, "France: EIB and Eau de Paris Commit to Protecting Biodiversity and Ecosystems in Île-de-France", European

Investment Bank, 18 January 2022, www.eib.org/en/press/all/2022-012-france-eib-and-eau-de-paris-commit-to-protecting-biodiversity-and-ecosystems-in-ile-de-france.

51 David Hall, Emanuele Lobina and Robin de la Motte, "Making Water Privatisation Illegal: New Laws in Netherlands and Uruguay", PSIRU Working Paper (London: PSIRU, November 2004), https://gala.gre.ac.uk.

52 David Hall and Emanuele Lobina, "From a Private Past to a Public Future? The Problems of Water in England and Wales", PSIRU Working Paper (London: PSIRU, November 2007), 22, https://gala.gre.ac.uk.

53 Satoko Kishimoto, Lavinia Steinfort and Olivier Petitjean, eds, *The Future Is Public: Towards Democratic Ownership of Public Services* (Amsterdam: Transnational Institute, 2020), www.tni.org/files/publication-downloads/futureispublic_online_def.pdf.

54 We Own It, "Examples of Successful Public Ownership", We Own It, 2023, https://weownit.org.uk/why-public-ownership/successful-examples.

55 We Own It, "When We Own It: A Model for Public Ownership in the 21st Century" (London: We Own It, 2019), https://weownit.org.uk.

Health and social care

1 Danielle Jefferies, Dan Wellings, Jessica Morris, Mark Dayan and Cyril Labont, "Public Satisfaction with the NHS and Social Care in 2023: Results from the British Social Attitudes Survey" (London: The King's Fund and Nuffield Trust, 27 March 2024), www.kingsfund.org.uk/insight-and-analysis/reports/public-satisfaction-nhs-social-care-2023.

2 PHIN, "PHIN Private Market Update: March 2024", 5 March 2023, www.phin.org.uk/news/phin-private-market-update-march-2024.

3 BMA, "NHS Backlog Data Analysis", October 2023, www.bma.org.uk.

4 Royal College of Emergency Medicine, "RCEM Explains: Long Waits and Excess Deaths", February 2023, https://rcem.ac.uk/wp-content/uploads/2023/02/RCEM_Explains_long_waits_and_excess_mortality.pdf.

5   Jefferies et al., "Public Satisfaction with the NHS and Social Care in 2023", 42–46.

6   Peter Roderick and Allyson M. Pollock, "Dismantling the National Health Service in England", International Journal of Health Services (25 July 2022), https://doi.org/10.1177/00207314221114540.

7   Leo Ewbank, James Thompson, Helen McKenna, Siva Anandaciva and Deborah Ward, "NHS Hospital Bed Numbers: Past, Present, Future", The King's Fund, 5 November 2021, www.kingsfund.org.uk.

8   NHS England, "Discharge Delays (Acute)", NHS England, March 2024, www.england.nhs.uk/statistics/statistical-work-areas/discharge-delays-acute-data; Michael Anderson, Emma Pitchforth, Nigel Edwards, Hugh Alderwick, Alistair McGuire, and Elias Mossialos, "United Kingdom: Health System Review 2022", Health Systems in Transition 24, no. 1 (2022): 88.

9   "NHS England Increasing Capacity Framework Agreement: Refresh", GOV.UK, 15 August 2022, www.contractsfinder.service.gov.uk.

10 "Health and Social Care Act" (2012), section 164, www.legislation.gov.uk/ukpga/2012/7/contents.

11 David Rowland, "Pounds for Patients? How Private Hospitals Use Financial Incentives to Win the Business of Medical Consultants" (London: Centre for Health and the Public Interest (CHPI), June 2019), https://chpi.org.uk; CHPI, "Mapping the Joint Venture Relationship between Private Healthcare Companies and NHS Medical Consultants" (London: Centre for Health and the Public Interest (CHPI), 2022), https://chpi.org.uk.

12 Shailen Sutaria, Graham Kirkwood and Allyson M Pollock, "An Ecological Study of NHS Funded Elective Hip Arthroplasties in England from 2003/04 to 2012/13", Journal of the Royal Society of Medicine 112, no. 7 (July 2019): 292–303, https://doi.org/10.1177/0141076819851701; G. Kirkwood and A.M. Pollock, "Patient Choice and Private Provision Decreased Public Provision and Increased Inequalities in Scotland: A Case Study of Elective Hip Arthroplasty", Journal of Public Health 39, no. 3 (2017): 593–600, https://doi.org/10.1093/pubmed/fdw060.

13 Justin Cumberlege, "Bidding for NHS Contracts: APMS Contract Terms and Conditions" (London: Carter Lemon Camerons LLP Solicitors, 2010), www.cartercamerons.com.

14 NHS Digital, "NHS Payments to General Practice, England 2021/22", NHS Digital, 25 November 2022, table 1a, https://digital.nhs.uk.

15 Centene Corporation, "Form 10–K for the Fiscal Year Ended December 31, 2022" (Washington, DC: Securities and Exchange Commission, 2023), www.sec.gov.

16 NHS England, "Annual Report and Accounts 2022/23 (London: NHS England, 25 January 2024), www.england.nhs.uk/publication/nhs-england-annual-report-and-accounts-2022-to-2023.

17 Caroline Fraser, Jake Beech and Estera Mendelsohn, "General Practice Tracker", The Health Foundation, 2023, www.health.org.uk/news-and-comment/charts-and-infographics/general-practice-tracker.

18 Jacqui Wise, "Serco Pulls out of Out-of-Hours Care in Cornwall", *BMJ* 347 (2013), https://doi.org/10.1136/bmj.f7549; Public Accounts Committee, "House of Commons: The Provision of the Out-of-Hours GP Service in Cornwall" (London: House of Commons, 24 June 2013), https://publications.parliament.uk/pa/cm201314/cmselect/cmpubacc/471/47102.htm.

19 MH Services International Holdings (UK) Limited, "Annual Report and Financial Statements for the Year Ended 31 December 2019" (London: Companies House, 11 January 2021), 1, https://find-and-update.company-information.service.gov.uk/company/10926063/filing-history.

20 Jake Beech, Caroline Fraser, Tim Gardner, Luisa Buzelli, Skeena Williamson and Hugh Alderwick, "Stressed and Overworked: What the Commonwealth Fund's 2022 International Health Policy Survey of Primary Care Physicians in 10 Countries Means for the UK" (London: The Health Foundation, March 2023), www.health.org.uk.

21 Paul King, "Why GPs May Feel Forced to Go Private", *Guardian*, 28 February 2021, www.theguardian.com/society/2021/feb/28/why-gps-may-feel-forced-to-go-private.

22 Royal College of General Practitioners, "RCGP Brief: Access to GP Appointments and Services in England" (London: Royal College of General Practitioners, November 2022), www.rcgp.org.uk.

23 British Medical Association, "General Practice Responsibility in Responding to Private Healthcare", BMA, 31 August 2023, www.bma.org.uk/advice-and-support/gp-practices/managing-workload/general-practice-responsibility-in-responding-to-private-healthcare.

24 Beech et al., "Stressed and Overworked", 26–27.

25 National Audit Office, "Adult Social Care at a Glance" (London: National Audit Office, July 2018), www.nao.org.uk/wp-content/uploads/2018/07/Adult-social-care-at-a-glance.pdf.

26 Competition and Markets Authority, "Care Homes Market Study" (London: Competition and Markets Authority, 2017), www.gov.uk/cma-cases/care-homes-market-study.

27 Office for National Statistics, "Healthcare Expenditure, UK Health Accounts: 2021", 17 May 2023, www.ons.gov.uk/peoplepopulation andcommunity/healthandsocialcare/healthcaresystem/bulletins/ukhealthaccounts/2021.

28 BBC Panorama Reporting Team, "Overseas Staff 'exploited and Trapped' at UK Care Home", BBC News, 18 December, 2023, www.bbc.com/news/uk-67684417.

29 Skills for Care, "The State of the Adult Social Care Sector and Workforce in England" (Leeds: Skills for Care, 2023), 57, www.skillsforcare.org.uk/Adult-Social-Care-Workforce-Data/Workforce-intelligence/documents/State-of-the-adult-social-care-sector/The-State-of-the-Adult-Social-Care-Sector-and-Workforce-2023.pdf.

30 Skills for Care, "The State of the Adult Social Care Sector", 52, 126.

31 Carers UK, "The Experiences of Black, Asian and Minority Ethnic Carers during and beyond the COVID-19 Pandemic" (London: Carers UK, August 2022), www.carersuk.org/media/c5ifvjio/carersukbame covidreport2022.pdf; Derek Wanless, "Securing Good Care for Older People: Taking a Long-Term View" (London: King's Fund, 2006), 137–52, www.kingsfund.org.uk/sites/default/files/field/field_publication_file/securing-good-care-for-older-people-wanless-2006.pdf; Carers UK, "State of Caring 2022: A Snapshot of Caring in the UK" (London: Carers UK, November 2022), www.carersuk.org/reports/state-of-caring-2022-report.

32 Age UK, "Lack of Social Care Has Led to 2.5 Million Lost Bed Days in the NHS between the Last Election and This One", Age UK (blog), 5 December 2019, www.ageuk.org.uk/latest-press/articles/2019/december/lack-of-social-care-has-led-to-2.5-million-lost-bed-days-in-the-nhs-between-the-last-election-and-this-one.

33 Chris Thomas, "Resilient Health and Care: Learning the Lessons of Covid-19 in the English NHS" (London: IPPR, 27 July 2020), www.ippr.org/research/publications/resilient-health-and-care.

34 King's Fund, "The NHS Budget and How It Has Changed".

35 Note that these calculation are for NHS funding only and do not address the shortfall in local authority social care budgets, which are discussed later in chapter 12.

36 David Finch and Myriam Vriend, "Public Health Grant: What It Is and Why Greater Investment Is Needed", The Health Foundation, 17 March 2023, www.health.org.uk/news-and-comment/charts-and-infographics/public-health-grant-what-it-is-and-why-greater-investment-is-needed.

37 Benjamin Goodair and Aaron Reeves, "Outsourcing Health-Care Services to the Private Sector and Treatable Mortality Rates in England, 2013–20: An Observational Study of NHS Privatisation", *The Lancet Public Health* 7, no. 7 (July 2022): e638–46, https://doi.org/10.1016/S2468-2667(22)00133-5.

38 Calum Paton, "At What Cost? Paying the Price for the Market in the English NHS" (London: Centre for Health and the Public Interest, February 2014), https://chpi.org.uk/papers/analyses/at-what-cost-paying-the-price-for-the-market-in-the-english-nhs.

39 Sid Ryan, "Is Treating Private Patients a Net Benefit to NHS Trusts? We May Never Know", CHPI (blog), 28 November 2022, https://chpi.org.uk/blog/is-treating-private-patients-a-net-benefit-to-nhs-trusts-we-may-never-know.

40 Sarah Walpole, "NHS Treatment of Private Patients: The Impact on NHS Finances and NHS Patient Care", CHPI (blog), 12 March 2018, https://chpi.org.uk/papers/reports/nhs-treatment-of-private-patients-the-impact-on-nhs-finances-and-nhs-patient-care.

41 Department of Health and Social Care, "DHSC Annual Report and Accounts", 390.

42 Department of Health and Social Care, Steve Barclay and Will Quince, "Government Boosts Use of Independent Sector Capacity to Cut NHS Waits", GOV.UK, accessed 20 December 2023, www.gov.uk/government/news/government-boosts-use-of-independent-sector-capacity-to-cut-nhs-waits.

43 Chris Thomas, "The 'Make Do and Mend' Health Service: Solving the NHS' Capital Crisis" (London: IPPR, 18 September 2019), www.ippr.org/news-and-media/press-releases/nhs-hospitals-under-strain-over-80bn-pfi-bill-for-just-13bn-of-actual-investment-finds-ippr.

44 Denis Campbell, "NHS across UK Spends a 'Staggering' £10bn on Temporary Staff", *Guardian*, 16 January 2024, Society, www.theguardian.com/society/2024/jan/16/nhs-across-uk-spends-a-staggering-10bn-on-temporary-staff.

45 NHS Professionals, "Our Services", NHS Professionals, 2023, https://rg-sitecore-prd-173860-cd.azurewebsites.net/partners/our-services.

46 NHS England, "NHS Long Term Workforce Plan" (Leeds: NHS England, June 2023), www.england.nhs.uk/publication/nhs-long-term-workforce-plan.

47 Joe Lewis, "The Cap on Medical and Dental Student Numbers in the UK" (London: House of Commons Library, 20 December 2023), https://commonslibrary.parliament.uk/research-briefings/cbp-9735/.

48 NHS England, "NHS Long Term Workforce Plan".

49 Lewis, "The Cap on Medical and Dental Student Numbers".

50 NHS England, "NHS Long Term Workforce Plan".

51 British Medical Association, "NHS Medical Staffing Data Analysis", BMA, 30 November 2023, www.bma.org.uk/advice-and-support/nhs-delivery-and-workforce/workforce/nhs-medical-staffing-data-analysis.

52 BMA, "NHS Medical Staffing Data Analysis".

53 NHS England, "Record Recruitment and Reform to Boost Patient Care under First NHS Long Term Workforce Plan", NHS England (blog), 30 June 2023, www.england.nhs.uk/2023/06/record-recruitment-and-reform-to-boost-patient-care-under-first-nhs-long-term-workforce-plan.

54 Benjamin Cooper, "Jeremy Hunt Again Pushes Plans to Train More Doctors and Nurses", *Evening Standard*, 26 December 2021, News, www.standard.co.uk/news/uk/jeremy-hunt-care-quality-commission-health-care-government-b973830.html.

55 Cooper, "Jeremy Hunt Again Pushes Plans".

56 British Medical Association, "Tax Relief for Locum Doctors", BMA, 5 April 2023, www.bma.org.uk/pay-and-contracts/tax/tax-relief/tax-relief-for-locum-doctors.

57 Parliamentary Office of Science and Technology, "Drug Pricing" (London: Parliamentary Office of Science and Technology, October 2010), www.parliament.uk/globalassets/documents/post/postpn_364_Drug_Pricing.pdf.

58 MIMS, "Drug Shortages", December 2023, www.mims.co.uk/drug-shortages.

59 Jeffrey K. Aronson, Carl Heneghan and Robin E. Ferner, "Drug Shortages. Part 2: Trends, Causes and Solutions", *British Journal of Clinical Pharmacology* 89, no. 10 (October 2023): 2957–63, https://doi.org/10.1111/bcp.15853.

60 Aronson, Heneghan and Ferner, "Drug Shortages. Part 2"; Mohamed Obiedalla, Nilesh Patel and Parastou Donyai, "Exploring Drug Shortages in the United Kingdom", *Pharmacy* 11, no. 5 (18 October 2023): 166, https://doi.org/10.3390/pharmacy11050166.

61 Obiedalla, Patel and Donyai, "Exploring Drug Shortages"; Jeffrey K. Aronson, Carl Heneghan and Robin E. Ferner, "Drug Shortages. Part 1. Definitions and Harms", *British Journal of Clinical Pharmacology* 89, no. 10 (October 2023): 2950–56, https://doi.org/10.1111/bcp.15842; Obiedalla, Patel and Donyai, "Exploring Drug Shortages".

62 Mariana Mazzucato, Henry Lishi Li and Ara Darzi, "Is It Time to Nationalise the Pharmaceutical Industry?", *BMJ* (4 March 2020): m769, https://doi.org/10.1136/bmj.m769.

63 Diego Tonelli and Valeria Iansante, "Health Solutions: Gearing up Pharmaceutical Manufacturing", European Investment Bank, 22 December 2021, www.eib.org/en/essays/gearing-up-pharmaceutical-manufacturing.

64 Tonelli and Iansante, "Health Solutions".

65 Office for National Statistics, "Research and Development Expenditure by the UK Government: Dataset", 30 March 2023, www.ons.gov.uk/economy/governmentpublicsectorandtaxes/researchanddevelopmentexpenditure/datasets/scienceengineeringandtechnologystatisticsreferencetables.

66 Michele Boldrin and David K. Levine, "The Pharmaceutical Industry", in *Against Intellectual Monopoly* (Cambridge: Cambridge University Press, 2008), https://doi.org/10.1017/CBO9780511510854.

67 Press Association, "Nationalised Drug Companies May Be Needed to 'Fix Antibiotics Market'", *Guardian*, 27 March 2019, Business, www.theguardian.com/business/2019/mar/27/nationalised-drug-companies-may-be-needed-to-fix-antibiotics-market.

68 Fran Quigley, "Tell Me How It Ends: The Path to Nationalizing the U.S. Pharmaceutical Industry", *University of Michigan Journal of Law Reform* 53, no. 4 (2020): 755, https://doi.org/10.36646/mjlr.53.4.tell.

69 Press Association, "Nationalised Drug Companies".

70 Dzintars Gotham, Chris Redd, Morten Thaysen, Tabitha Ha, Heidi Chow and Katy Athersuch, "Pills and Profits: How Drug Companies Make a Killing out of Public Research" (London: Global Justice Now and STOPAIDS, October 2017), www.globaljustice.org.uk/wp-content/uploads/2018/12/pills-and-profits-report-web.pdf.

71 Zachary Brennan, "Do Biopharma Companies Really Spend More on Marketing Than R&D?", *Regulatory Focus*, 24 July 2019, www.raps.org/news-and-articles/news-articles/2019/7/do-biopharma-companies-really-spend-more-on-market.

72 Azeem Majeed and Simon Hodes, "Has the Covid Pandemic Changed the Debate about Nationalising GPs?", *BMJ* (2 March 2022): 0406, https://doi.org/10.1136/bmj.0406.

73 Royal College of General Practitioners (RCGP), "The Future of the Partnership Model", RCGP, 27 April 2023, www.rcgp.org.uk/gp-frontline/spring-2023-policy-focus-partnerships.

74 Eliza Parr, "Over 250 Fewer FTE GPs Since Last Year as Appointment Activity Rises", *Pulse Today*, 26 October 2023, www.pulsetoday.co.uk/news/workforce/over-250-fewer-fte-gps-since-last-year-as-appointment-activity-rises.

75 Costanza Potter, "GPs Could Be Incentivised to Work under Hospital Trusts, Reports Claim", *Pulse Today*, 31 January 2022, www.pulsetoday.co.uk/news/politics/gps-could-be-incentivised-to-work-under-hospitals-trusts-reports-claim.

76 RWT Primary Care Network, "The Royal Wolverhampton Trust: Primary Care Network", RWT Primary Care Network, 2023, www.rwtprimarycare.nhs.uk; RWT Primary Care Network, "The Royal Wolverhampton Trust".

77 Lizzie Roberts, "Labour's Plan to 'Nationalise' GPs Would Cost More than £7bn", *Telegraph*, 15 January 2023, www.telegraph.co.uk/politics/2023/01/15/labours-plan-nationalise-gps-would-cost-7bn.

78 Eren Waitzman, "Free NHS Prescriptions: Eligibility for Benefit Claimants" (London: House of Lords Library, 24 November 2023), https://lordslibrary.parliament.uk/free-nhs-prescriptions-eligibility-for-benefit-claimants.

79 Nick Hex, James Mahon and Anne Webb, "Prescription Charges Coalition: Economic Evaluation of the Benefits of Extending Free Prescriptions to People with Long-Term Conditions" (York: York Health Economics Consortium, May 2018), www.prescriptionchargescoalition.org.uk/uploads/1/2/7/5/12754304/economic_evaluation_report.pdf.

80 Richard Partington, "Care Services Must Now Be Nationalised, Says John McDonnell", *Guardian*, 20 July 2020, Politics, www.theguardian.com/politics/2020/jul/20/care-services-must-be-nationalised-post-coronavirus-urges-labours-john-mcdonnell.

81 Harry Quilter-Pinner and Dean Hochlaf, "Social Care: Free at the Point of Need – the Case for Free Personal Care in England" (London: IPPR, May 2019), www.ippr.org/research/publications/social-care-free-at-the-point-of-need.

82 Centre for International Corporate Tax Accountability and Research (CICTAR), "Lifting the Lid on Offshore Care Home Landlords"

(Geneva: CICTAR, July 2022), https://cictar.org/all-research/lifting-the-lid-on-offshore-care-home-landlords; CICTAR and Public Services International, "Darkness at Sunrise: UK Care Homes Shifting Profits Offshore?" (Geneva: CICTAR and Public Services International, February 2021), https://cictar.org/all-research/uk-care-homes-shifting-profits.

83 Quilter-Pinner and Hochlaf, "Social Care".

84 London Borough of Tower Hamlets, "Pay Policy Statement 2023/2024" (London: London Borough of Tower Hamlets, 1 June 2023), https://democracy.towerhamlets.gov.uk.

Healthy and flourishing children

1 Nelson Mandela, "Address by President Nelson Mandela at the Launch of the Nelson Mandela Children's Fund, Pretoria", mandela.gov.za, 8 May 1995, www.mandela.gov.za/mandela_speeches/1995/950508_nmcf.htm.

2 Anna Gromada, Gwyther Rees and Yekaterina Chzhen, "Worlds of Influence: Understanding What Shapes Child Well-Being in Rich Countries", Innocenti Report Card 16 (Florence: UNICEF Office of Research, 2020).

3 OECD, "Infant Mortality Rates (Indicator)", 2023, https://doi.org/10.1787/bd12d298-en.

4 David C. Taylor-Robinson, Eric T. Lai, Margaret Whitehead, W.H. Duncan and Ben Barr, "Child Health Unravelling in UK", *BMJ* 364 (2019): l963, https://doi.org/10.1136/bmj.l963.

5 Office for National Statistics, "Child and Infant Mortality in England and Wales: 2020", *Statistical Bulletin*, 17 February, 2022.

6 Gromada, Rees and Chzhen, "Worlds of Influence".

7 OECD, "Infant Mortality Rates (Indicator)", 2024, https://doi.org/10.1787/bd12d298-en.

8 Carl Baker, "Obesity Statistics", research briefing (London: House of Commons Library, 12 January 2023). https://researchbriefings.files.parliament.uk/documents/SN03336/SN03336.pdf.

9 Gromada, Rees and Chzhen, "Worlds of Influence".

10 F. Marcheselli, T. Newlove-Delgado, T. Williams, D. Mandalia, J. Davis, S. McManus, M. Savic, W. Treloar and T. Ford, "Mental Health of Children and Young People in England, 2022" (Leeds: NHS Digital, 2022).

11 Gareth Iacobucci, "Covid-19: Pandemic Has Disproportionately Harmed Children's Mental Health, Report Finds", *BMJ* 376 (2022): o430, https://doi.org/10.1136/bmj.o430.

12 Wilkinson and Pickett, *The Spirit Level*; R. Wilkinson and K. Pickett, *The Inner Level: How More Equal Societies Reduce Stress, Restore Sanity and Improve Everybody's Wellbeing* (London: Allen Lane, 2018); Kate E. Pickett and Richard G. Wilkinson, "Child Wellbeing and Income Inequality in Rich Societies: Ecological Cross Sectional Study", *BMJ* 335, no. 7629 (22 November 2007): 1080, https://doi.org/10.1136/bmj.39377.580162.55; K.E. Pickett and R.G. Wilkinson, "The Ethical and Policy Implications of Research on Income Inequality and Child Well-Being", *Pediatrics* 135, Suppl 2 (March 2015): S39–47, https://doi.org/10.1542/peds.2014-3549E.

13 Sophie Wickham, Elspeth Anwar, Ben Barr, Catherine Law and David Taylor-Robinson, "Poverty and Child Health in the UK: Using Evidence for Action", *Archives of Disease in Childhood* 101, no. 8 (2016): 759–66; Rose Atkins, Luke Munford and Clare Bambra, "The Economic Impacts of Child Health", in *Child of the North: Building a Fairer Future after COVID-19*, ed. Davara Bennet, Hannah Davies, Kate Mason, Stephen Parkinson, Kate Pickett and David Taylor-Robinson (Manchester: Northern Health Sciences Alliance and N8 Research Partnership, 2021).

14 J. Bradshaw, S. Wickham, A. Alexiou and C. Webb, "Child Poverty, Inequality and Deprivation", in *Child of the North: Building a Fairer Future after COVID-19*, ed. K. Pickett and D. Taylor-Robinson (Manchester: Northern Health Sciences Alliance and N8 Research Partnership, 2021).

15 Gromada, Rees and Chzhen, "Worlds of Influence".

16 University of York Cost of Living Research Group, "Sticking Plasters and Systemic Solutions: Cost of Living Responses in the UK" (York: University of York, 2023).

17 Food Foundation, "Food Insecurity Tracking", The Food Foundation, 2023, https://foodfoundation.org.uk/initiatives/food-insecurity-tracking.

18 Greater Manchester Independent Inequalities Review, "The Next Level: Good Lives for All in Greater Manchester" (Manchester: Greater Manchester Combined Authority, 2021), www.greatermanchester-ca.gov.uk/media/4605/the-next-level-good-lives-for-all-in-greater-manchester.pdf.

19 Amy Jane Elizabeth Barnes, Carolyn Jane Snell, Amanda Bailey, Rachel Loopstra, Mandy Cheetham, Steph Morris, Madeleine Power, Hannah Davies, Matthew Scott, David Taylor-Robinson and Kate Pickett, "APPG Child of the North: Child Poverty and the Cost of Living Crisis. A Report Prepared for the APPG Child of the North" (York: University of York, 2023).

20 David Taylor-Robinson, "Child Health Inequalities", UK Covid-19 Inquiry, 6 October 2023, https://covid19.public-inquiry.uk/documents/inq000280060-expert-report-titled-child-health-inequalities-by-professor-david-taylor-robinson-dated-21-september-2023.

21 Image from Greater Manchester Independent Inequalities Commission, "The Next Level: Good Lives for All in Greater Manchester" (Manchester: Independent Inequalities Commission, 2021).

22 Taylor-Robinson et al., "Child Health Unravelling in UK"; D. Taylor-Robinson and R. Gosling, "English North–South Divide: Local Authority Budget Cuts and Health Inequalities", *BMJ* 342 (8 March 2011): d1487, https://doi.org/10.1136/bmj.d1487; D. Taylor-Robinson, M. Whitehead and B. Barr, "Great Leap Backwards", *BMJ* 349 (2 December 2014): g7350, https://doi.org/10.1136/bmj.g7350; D. Taylor-Robinson, S. Wickham and B. Barr, "Child Health at Risk from Welfare Cuts", *BMJ* 351 (13 October 2015): h5330, https://doi.org/10.1136/bmj.h5330.

23 K. Pickett and D. Taylor-Robinson, eds, *Child of the North: Building a Fairer Future after COVID-19* (Manchester: Northern Health Sciences Alliance and N8 Research Partnership, 2021), www.thenhsa.co.uk/app/uploads/2022/01/Child-of-the-North-Report-FINAL-1.pdf.

24 Mark Mon-Williams, Megan Wood and David Taylor-Robinson, "Addressing Education and Health Inequity: Perspectives from the North of England. A Report Prepared for the Child of the North APPG" (Health Equity North, 2023).

25 University of York Cost of Living Research Group, "Sticking Plasters and Systemic Solutions".

26 Atkins, Munford and Bambra, "The Economic Impacts of Child Health".

27 Future Generations Commissioner for Wales, "The Future Generations Commissioner for Wales: Acting Today for a Better Tomorrow", 2023, www.futuregenerations.wales.

28 James J. Heckman, "Invest in Early Childhood Development: Reduce Deficits, Strengthen the Economy" (Chicago: The Heckman Equation, July 2013), https://heckmanequation.org/wp-content/uploads/2013/07/F_HeckmanDeficitPieceCUSTOM-Generic_052714-3-1.pdf.

29 End Child Poverty Coalition, "Child Povertyin Your Area – Data Tables" (End Child Poverty Coalition, 2023), https://endchildpoverty.org.uk/wp-content/uploads/2023/06/Child-Poverty-AHC-estimates-2015-2022_final.xlsx.

30 Yassaman Vafai, Rebecca Benson, Alex Albert, Claire Cameron and Kate Pickett, "Child and Family Health and Wellbeing in Bradford and Tower Hamlets: An ActEarly Report" (Bradford: ActEarly, February 2023), https://actearly.org.uk/wp-content/uploads/2023/02/55843_HL_Act-Early-Report_v10-1.pdf.

31 FixOurFood, "FixOurFood in Schools: Initatives", Fix Our Food, 2023, https://fixourfood.org/what-we-do/our-activities/schools-and-nurseries/fixourfood-in-schools-initatives.

32 Child of the North, "Child of the North", Health Equity North, 2023, www.healthequitynorth.co.uk/child-of-the-north; Cost of Living Research Group, "Cost of Living Research Group", University of York, 8 September 2023, www.york.ac.uk/policy-engine/cost-of-living.

33 Changing Realities, "What Is Life Really Like on a Low Income in the UK?", 2023, https://changingrealities.org; Larger Families Study, "Welcome to the Larger Families Project", 2023, https://largerfamilies.study.

34 IPPR, "Boost Child Benefit by Extra £20 and Ditch Benefit Limits to Lift 900,000 Children from Poverty, Ministers Urged", 16 November 2022, www.ippr.org/news-and-media/press-releases/boost-child-benefit-by-extra-20-and-ditch-benefit-limits-to-lift-900-000-children-from-poverty-ministers-urged.

A fairer education system

1 Howard Reed and Jonathan Portes, "The Cumulative Impact on Living Standards of Public Spending Changes", research report (Manchester: Equality and Human Rights Commission, November

2018), www.equalityhumanrights.com/sites/default/files/cumulativeimpact-on-living-standards-of-public-spending-changes.pdf; Howard Reed and Jonathan Portes, "The Impact of Public Spending Changes in Northern Ireland" (Belfast: Northern Ireland Human Rights Commission, September 2021), https://nihrc.org/uploads/publications/Northern-Ireland-Public-Spending-report_FULL.pdf.

2 OECD, "Education at a Glance 2021: OECD Indicators" (Paris: OECD, 2021), https://doi.org/10.1787/b35a14e5-en.

3 The Children's Society, "The Good Childhood Report 2022" (London: The Children's Society, 2022), 32, www.childrenssociety.org.uk/sites/default/files/2022-09/GCR-2022-Full-Report.pdf.

4 The Children's Society, "The Good Childhood Report 2022", 38.

5 Björn Bremer and Reto Bürgisser, "Public Opinion on Welfare State Recalibration in Times of Austerity: Evidence from Survey Experiments", *Political Science Research and Methods* 11, no. 1 (January 2023): 34–52, https://doi.org/10.1017/psrm.2021.78.

6 Paul Gregg and Lindsey Macmillan, "Intergenerational Joblessness across Europe: The Role of Labour Markets, Education and Welfare Generosity", CEPEO Working Paper Series (London: UCL Centre for Education Policy and Equalising Opportunities (CEPEO), 2020), https://ideas.repec.org/p/ucl/cepeow/20-11.html.

7 Luke Sibieta, "Tax, Private School Fees and State School Spending" (London: Institute for Fiscal Studies, July 2023), https://ifs.org.uk/sites/default/files/2023-07/IFS-Report-R263-Tax-private-schoolfees-and-state-school-spending.pdf.

8 Sibieta, "Tax, Private School Fees and State School Spending".

9 Francis Green, "Private Schools and Inequality" (London: IFS, 16 August 2022), https://ifs.org.uk/inequality/private-schools-andinequality.

10 Melissa Benn, "The Only Way to End the Class Divide: The Case for Abolishing Private Schools", *Guardian*, 24 August 2018, News, www.theguardian.com/news/2018/aug/24/the-only-way-to-end-the-classdivide-the-case-for-abolishing-private-schools.

11 Imran Tahir, "The UK Education System Preserves Inequality: New Report", *The Conversation*, 18 August 2022, https://theconversation.com/the-uk-education-system-preserves-inequality-new-report-188761.

12 National Education Union, "The Crisis in School Funding", National Education Union, 3 April 2023, https://neu.org.uk/latest/press-releases/crisis-school-funding.

13 OECD, "Education at a Glance 2021"; Department for Education, "Schools, Pupils and Their Characteristics, Academic Year 2022/23", GOV.UK, 8 June 2023, https://explore-education-statistics.service.gov.uk/find-statistics/school-pupils-and-their-characteristics/2022-23.

14 Peter Blatchford and Anthony Russell, *Rethinking Class Size* (London: UCL Press, 2020), www.jstor.org/stable/j.ctv15d7zqz.

15 Philip M. Nicholson, "Pedagogy, Culture and Transition: A Qualitative, Collective Case Study Exploring Pedagogies of the Transition from Reception to Year One in England" (Leicester, University of Leicester, 2022), https://doi.org/10.25392/leicester.data.20309592.v1.

16 Carol Goodenow and Kathleen E. Grady, "The Relationship of School Belonging and Friends' Values to Academic Motivation among Urban Adolescent Students", *The Journal of Experimental Education* 62, no. 1 (1993): 60–71; Place2Be, "Let's Connect: The Role of School Connectedness in Mental Health", 10 February 2023, www.childrens mentalhealthweek.org.uk/news-and-blogs/2023/february/let-s-con-nect-the-role-of-school-connectedness-in-mental-health.

17 Wendy Wallace, "Schools within Schools: Human Scale Education in Practice" (London: Calouste Gulbenkian Foundation, 2009), https://cdn.gulbenkian.pt/uk-branch/wp-content/uploads/sites/18/2009/09/Schools-with-Schools-low-res-1-9-09.pdf.

18 Nigel Wyatt, "Three Tiers for Success: A System Designed to Meet the Needs of Children as They Grow and Develop" (National Middle Schools' Forum, January 2018), https://middleschools.org.uk/download/advantages/Three-tiers-for-success.pdf.

19 Madeleine Arnot and Diane Reay, "A Sociology of Pedagogic Voice: Power, Inequality and Pupil Consultation", *Discourse: Studies in the Cultural Politics of Education* 28, no. 3 (1 September 2007): 311–25, https://doi.org/10.1080/01596300701458814.

20 Deborah Wilson and Gary Bridge, "School Choice and Equality of Opportunity: An International Systematic Review" (London: Nuffield Foundation, April 2019), www.nuffieldfoundation.org/sites/default/files/files/Wilson%20and%20Bridge%20report%20April%202019.pdf.

21 Ruth Lupton and Debra Hayes, *Great Mistakes in Education Policy and How to Avoid Them in the Future* (Bristol: Policy Press, 2021).

22 Nicholson, "Pedagogy, Culture and Transition", 202.

23 Andy Daly-Smith, Matthew Hobbs, Jade L. Morris, Margaret A. Defeyter, Geir K. Resaland and Jim McKenna, "Moderate-to-Vigorous Physical Activity in Primary School Children: Inactive Lessons Are Dominated by Maths and English", *International Journal of Environmental Research and Public Health* 18, no. 3 (22 January 2021): 990, https://doi.org/10.3390/ijerph18030990.

24 Open Society Institute Sofia, "Media Literacy Index 2023" (Sofia: Open Society Institute Sofia, June 2023), https://osis.bg/wp-content/uploads/2023/06/MLI-report-in-English-22.06.pdf.

25 Clare Sambrook and Warwick Mansell, "Revealed: The Brexit-Backing Businessmen Taking Control of England's Schools", *openDemocracy*, 11 December 2019, www.opendemocracy.net/en/shine-a-light/revealed-the-brexit-backing-businessmen-taking-control-of-englands-schools.

26 Jo Littler, "What's Wrong with Meritocracy?", *The Political Quarterly* 92, no. 2 (April 2021): 372–75, https://doi.org/10.1111/1467-923X.12979.

27 Benjamin Kentish, "The Vast Majority of Students Never Repay Their Tuition Fee Debts", *Independent*, 16 November 2017, News, www.independent.co.uk/news/education/education-news/student-debt-finance-majority-never-pay-back-study-findings-a8057156.html.

28 Paul Bolton, "Student Loan Statistics" (London: House of Commons Library, 25 October 2023), https://researchbriefings.files.parliament.uk/documents/SN01079/SN01079.pdf.

29 Social Mobility Commission, "State of the Nation 2021: Social Mobility and the Pandemic" (London: HMSO, July 2021), www.gov.uk/government/publications/state-of-the-nation-2021-social-mobility-and-the-pandemic.

30 Sam Friedman and Daniel Laurison, *The Class Ceiling: Why It Pays to Be Privileged* (Bristol: Policy Press, 2020).

31 Sarah Cattan, Kjell G. Salvanes and Emma Tominey, "Mixing with Better Educated Families Improves Life Chances of Lower Income Children", Institute for Fiscal Studies (blog), 7 June 2023, https://ifs.org.uk/news/mixing-better-educated-families-improves-life-chances-lower-income-children.

Housing

1 Social Housing Policy Working Group, "Social Housing Policy Working Group", CaCHE (UK Collaborative Centre for Housing Evidence), 2022, https://housingevidence.ac.uk/our-work/social-housing-policy-working-group; The Housing Executive, "The Housing Selection Scheme", NI Housing Executive, 2023, www.nihe.gov.uk/-help/apply-for-a-home/the-housing-selection-scheme.

2 Rightmove, "The Rightmove Rental Trends Tracker: Q3 Report (July–September 2023)" (London: Rightmove, 5 October 2023), www.rightmove.co.uk/news/content/uploads/2023/10/Rental-Trends-Tracker-Q3-2023-FINAL.pdf.

3 Adam Peggs, "To Fix the Housing Crisis, We Need Better Public Housing, Not More Homeowners", *Jacobin*, 4 July 2023, https://jacobin.com/2023/07/uk-housing-crisis-labour-party-homeownership-policy-mortgage-public-housing.

4 Adam Peggs, "What Is Housing Policy for? And Why We Need a Radical Approach", LabourList, 21 September 2022, https://labourlist.org/2022/09/what-is-housing-policy-for-and-why-we-need-a-radical-approach.

5 Danny Dorling, "House Prices: Should We Welcome a Crash?", UK in a Changing Europe (blog), 24 July 2021, https://ukandeu.ac.uk/long-read/house-prices-crash.

6 James Riding, "City Council Confirms Plan to Close One of the UK's Largest ALMOs", *Inside Housing*, 4 December 2023, www.insidehousing.co.uk/news/city-council-confirms-plan-to-close-one-of-the-uks-largest-almos-84184.

7 Image from Oxford City Council, 2019.

8 D. Dorling, R. Goulding, N. Gray, S. Hodkinson, J. Penny, G. Robbins, S. Smyth and P. Watt, "Council Housing: Time to Invest (Now, More than Ever), Submission of Evidence to the All Party Parliamentary Group for Council Housing" (Defend Council Housing and Homes for All, 6 July 2023), www.dannydorling.org/?page_id=9790.

9 Nancy Kwak, *A World of Homeowners: American Power and the Politics of Housing Aid* (Chicago: The University of Chicago Press, 2015).

10 Snapshot by Danny Dorling of one of the many TV reports in the immediate aftermath of the fire.

11 D. Dorling, "A Letter from Helsinki", *Public Sector Focus* 41 (2022): 12–15.

12 Dale Spridgeon, "'Plenty of Money' from Holiday Homes Tax to Help Gwynedd Locals on Ladder", North Wales Live, 3 February 2023, www.dailypost.co.uk/news/north-wales-news/plenty-money-holiday-homes-tax-26153519.

13 Communities and Local Government Committee, "Third Report: Housing and the Credit Crunch", House of Commons, 10 February 2009, https://publications.parliament.uk/pa/cm200809/cmselect/cmcomloc/101/10102.htm.

14 Adriana Elgueta, "Rough Sleeping up 9% in London in a Year", BBC News, 31 July 2023, www.bbc.com/news/uk-england-london-66360501.

15 Danny Dorling, All That Is Solid: The Great Housing Disaster (London: Allen Lane, 2014).

16 Wandsworth Borough Council, "Council's New Administration Unveils A raft of Radical New Housing Policies", 19 July 2022, https://wandsworth.gov.uk/news/2022-news/news-july-2022/council-s-new-administration-unveils-raft-of-radical-new-housing-policies.

17 George Monbiot, Robin Grey, Tom Kenny, Laurie Macfarlane, Anna Powell-Smith, Guy Shrubsole and Beth Stratford, "Land for the Many: Changing the Way Our Fundamental Asset Is Used, Owned and Governed" (London: The Labour Party, June 2019), https://labour.org.uk/wp-content/uploads/2019/06/12081_19-Land-for-the-Many.pdf.

18 Mark Fransham, "Population by Ward, 2011 Census" (Oxford: Oxford Council, 2011), https://mycouncil.oxford.gov.uk/documents/s12211/EE%20-%20Appendix%20C.pdf.

19 Oxford City Council, "How Many More Homes Will Oxford Need?", Oxford.Gov.Uk (blog), 28 September 2023, www.oxford.gov.uk/news/article/2526/how_many_more_homes_will_oxford_need.

20 Image from Fransham, "Population by Ward, 2011 Census" (Oxford Council, 2011). Population data from www.visionofbritain.org.uk. Maps contain Ordnance Survey data © Crown Copyright and database right 2015. Ordnance Survey 100019348.

21 Jim Armitage, "Persimmon's £40m Boss Quits Just Over a Year after the £75 Million One", Evening Standard, 27 February 2020, Business, www.standard.co.uk/business/persimmons-ps40m-boss-quits-little-over-a-year-into-the-job-a4373321.html.

Transport and infrastructure

1 Department for Transport, "Creating Growth, Cutting Carbon: Making Sustainable Local Transport Happen White Paper" (London: TSO, January 2011), https://assets.publishing.service.gov.uk/media/5a797a 7d40f0b63d72fc62ae/making-sustainable-local-transport-happen-whitepaper.pdf.

2 Transport for the North, "Transport-Related Social Exclusion in the North of England" (Manchester: Transport for the North, 22 September 2022), https://transportforthenorth.com/reports/transport-related-social-exclusion-in-the-north-of-england.

3 Foundational Economy Research Ltd, "Jobs and Liveability" (Manchester: Foundational Economy Research Ltd, September 2022), https://foundationaleconomyresearch.com/wp-content/uploads/2022/12/FERL-Report-Jobs-Liveability-for-Karbon-Homes-Sept-2022.pdf.

4 John Ellmore, "What Is The Cost Of Owning A Car In The UK?", NerdWallet UK (blog), 19 July 2021, www.nerdwallet.com/uk/personal-finance/cost-of-car-ownership.

5 Department for Energy Security and Net Zero, "DUKES 2023 – Chapter 1: Energy" (London: Government Digital Service, 24 August 2023), www.gov.uk/government/statistics/energy-chapter-1-digest-of-united-kingdom-energy-statistics-dukes.

6 RAC Foundation, "Motoring FAQs: Mobility", RAC Foundation, 2023, www.racfoundation.org/motoring-faqs/mobility.

7 Transformative Urban Mobility Initiative, "Passenger Capacity of Different Transport Modes", September 2021, https://transformative-mobility.org/multimedia/passenger-capacity-of-different-transport-modes.

8 Office for National Statistics, "Family Spending in the UK: April 2021 to March 2022" (London: Government Digital Service, 31 May 2023). www.ons.gov.uk/peoplepopulationandcommunity/personaland householdfinances/expenditure/bulletins/familyspendingintheuk/april2021tomarch2022.

9 Rachel Griffith, "The Costs of Obesity: An Update" (London: IFS, 13 July 2023), https://doi.org/10.1920/re.ifs.2023.0265b.

10 Jamie Driscoll, "Regional Wealth Generation: Focusing on Local Wealth Generation", Levelling up Briefings (London: The RSA, October

2021), www.thersa.org/globalassets/_foundation/new-site-blocks-and-images/reports/2021/10/regional_wealth_generation.pdf.

11 London Finance Commission, "Devolution: A Capital Idea. The Report of the London Finance Commission" (London: London Finance Commission, January 2017), www.london.gov.uk/programmes-strategies/business-and-economy/promoting-london/london-finance-commission.

12 Daniel Keane, "Avanti West Coast Caught Joking That Taxpayer Funding Is 'Free Money'", *Evening Standard*, 16 January 2024, www.standard.co.uk/news/transport/avanti-west-coast-joking-taxpayer-funding-free-money-b1132759.html.

13 Jess Warren and PA Media, "LNER: Train Fares 'Simplified' in Bid to Boost Passenger Numbers", BBC News, 16 January 2024, www.bbc.com/news/uk-england-london-67993208.

14 Government Finance Function and HM Treasury, "The Green Book (2022)" (London: TSO, 18 November 2022), www.gov.uk/government/publications/the-green-book-appraisal-and-evaluation-in-central-governent/the-green-book-2020.

Democracy, power and security

1 Hayek, The Road to Serfdom.

2 John Kenneth Galbraith, *The Good Society: The Humane Agenda* (London: Sinclair-Stevenson, 1996).

3 Parth Patel, Ryan Swift and Harry Quilter-Pinner, "Talking Politics: Building Support for Democratic Reform" (London: IPPR, June 2023), www.ippr.org/files/2023-06/talking-politics-june23.pdf.

4 Will Doig, "The Coronavirus-Proof Nation", Reasons to Be Cheerful, 16 March 2020, https://reasonstobecheerful.world/the-coronavirus-proof-nation.

5 Electoral Reform Society, "The 2019 General Election: Voters Left Voiceless" (London: Electoral Reform Society, 2 March 2020), www.electoral-reform.org.uk/latest-news-and-research/publications/the-2019-general-election-voters-left-voiceless.

6 Elise Uberoi and Neil Johnston, "Political Disengagement in the UK: Who Is Disengaged?", research briefing (London: House of Commons Library, 21 November 2022), https://researchbriefings.files.parliament.uk/documents/CBP-7501/CBP-7501.pdf.

7 Joel Kotkin, "Welcome to the End of Democracy", *The Spectator*, 8 January 2022, www.spectator.co.uk/article/welcome-to-the-end-of-democracy.

8 Oliver Hawkins, Richard Keen and Nambassa Nakatudde, "General Election 2015", briefing paper (London: House of Commons Library, 28 July 2015), https://commonslibrary.parliament.uk/research-briefings/cbp-7186.

9 Liberal Democrats, "Fair Votes Now", 2023, www.libdems.org.uk/fairvotes; Green Party, "Public Administration and Government", September 2021, https://policy.greenparty.org.uk/our-policies/long-term-goals/public-administration-and-government; UKIP, "Reform Voting System with PR", 9 December 2019, www.ukip.org/reform-voting-system-with-pr.

10 Oonagh Gay, "Voting Systems: The Jenkins Report", research paper (London: House of Commons Library, 10 December 1998), https://researchbriefings.files.parliament.uk/documents/RP98-112/RP98-112.pdf.

11 Benjamin Reilly and Jack Hudson Stewart, "Compulsory Preferential Voting, Social Media and 'Come-from-Behind' Electoral Victories in Australia", *Australian Journal of Political Science* 56, no. 1 (2 January 2021): 99–112, https://doi.org/10.1080/10361146.2021.1879010.

12 Harold J. Jansen, "The Political Consequences of the Alternative Vote: Lessons from Western Canada", *Canadian Journal of Political Science* 37, no. 3 (September 2004): 647–69, https://doi.org/10.1017/S0008423904030227; David Kimball and Joseph Anthony, "Public Perceptions of Alternative Voting Systems: Results from a National Survey Experiment", *SSRN Electronic Journal*, 28 May 2021, https://doi.org/10.2139/ssrn.3854047.

13 Margaret Wilson, "Electoral Reform in the United Kingdom: Lessons from New Zealand", *The Round Table 100*, no. 416 (October 2011): 509–17, https://doi.org/10.1080/00358533.2011.609691.

14 Neil Johnston, "Who Can Vote in UK Elections?" research briefing (London: House of Commons Library, 16 November 2023), https://researchbriefings.files.parliament.uk/documents/CBP-8985/CBP-8985.pdf.

15 e-Estonia, "E-Governance", e-Estonia, 2023, https://e-estonia.com/solutions/e-governance/e-democracy.

16 Commission on the UK's Future, "A New Britain: Renewing Our Democracy and Rebuilding Our Economy" (London: Labour Party, December 2022), https://labour.org.uk/wp-content/uploads/2022/12/Commission-on-the-UKs-Future.pdf.

17 Nicolaus Tideman, "The Single Transferable Vote", *Journal of Economic Perspectives* 9, no. 1 (1 February 1995): 27–38, https://doi.org/10.1257/jep.9.1.27: Electoral Reform Society, "Single Transferable Vote", 2023, www.electoral-reform.org.uk/voting-systems/types-of-voting-system/single-transferable-vote.

18 Scottish Government, "Organisations", myscot.gov, accessed 6 January 2024, www.mygov.scot/organisations; Local Government Association, "Combined Authorities", 2023, www.local.gov.uk/topics/devolution/devolution-online-hub/devolution-explained/combined-authorities.

19 PolicyMogul, "Rayner to Set out Labour's Plan to Ensure Politicians Serve the Public, Not Themselves, with Creation of New Government Ethics Watchdog", *PolicyMogul*, 12 July 2023, https://policymogul.com/key-updates/29924/rayner-to-set-out-labour-s-plan-to-ensure-politicians-serve-the-public-not-themselves-with-creation-of-new-government-ethics-watchdog.

20 Office for National Statistics, "Employee Earnings in the UK", 1 November 2023, www.ons.gov.uk/employmentandlabourmarket/peopleinwork/earningsandworkinghours/bulletins/annualsurveyofhoursandearnings/2023.

21 Holger Döring and Philip Manow, "Is Proportional Representation More Favourable to the Left? Electoral Rules and Their Impact on Elections, Parliaments and the Formation of Cabinets", *British Journal of Political Science* 47, no. 1 (January 2017): 149–64, https://doi.org/10.1017/S0007123415000290.

22 Torben Iversen and David Soskice, "Electoral Institutions and the Politics of Coalitions: Why Some Democracies Redistribute More Than Others", *American Political Science Review* 100, no. 2 (May 2006): 165–81, https://doi.org/10.1017/S0003055406062083.

23 Jonathan Rodden, "The Geographic Distribution of Political Preferences", *Annual Review of Political Science* 13, no. 1 (1 May 2010): 321–40, https://doi.org/10.1146/annurev.polisci.12.031607.092945; Graham Gudgin and Peter J. Taylor, *Seats, Votes, and the Spatial Organisation of Elections* (London: Pion, 1979).

24 Johnson, Johnson and Nettle, "Are 'Red Wall' Constituencies Really Opposed to Progressive Policy?"
25 Josiah Mortimer, "Major Political Reform Could Secure Key Labour Target Voters, Study Suggests", *Byline Times*, 12 November 2023, https://bylinetimes.com/2023/12/11/major-political-reform-could-secure-key-labour-target-voters-study-suggests.

A new economy with a fully costed and fully funded plan

1 John Burn-Murdoch, "Britain and the US Are Poor Societies with Some Very Rich People", *Financial Times*, 16 September 2022, www.ft.com.
2 Authors' illustration based on GDP data from ONS, "Gross Domestic Product at Market Prices: Current Price: Seasonally Adjusted £m", 11 August 2023, www.ons.gov.uk/economy/grossdomesticproductgdp/timeseries/ybha/pn2; UK population data from ONS, "National Population Projections: 2020-Based Interim", 12 January 2022, www.ons.gov.uk/peoplepopulationandcommunity/populationandmigration/populationprojections/bulletins/nationalpopulationprojections/2020basedinterim.
3 Authors' illustration based on data from ONS, "Labour Productivity Time Series", 24 October 2023, www.ons.gov.uk/employmentandlabourmarket/peopleinwork/labourproductivity/datasets/labourproductivity.
4 Issam Samiri and Stephen Millard, "Why Is UK Productivity Low and How Can It Improve?" NIESR (National Institute of Economic and Social Research) (blog), 26 September 2022, www.niesr.ac.uk/blog/why-uk-productivity-low-and-how-can-it-improve.
5 Krishnan Shah and Gregory Thwaites, "Minding the (Productivity and Income) Gaps: Decomposing and Understanding Differences in Productivity and Income across Countries", (London: Resolution Foundation, 3 February 2023), https://economy2030.resolutionfoundation.org/wp-content/uploads/2023/02/Minding-the-productivity-and-income-gaps.pdf.
6 Samiri and Millard, "Why Is UK Productivity Low?"
7 Rob Mallows, "Long Term Review Sets out Pressing Need to Modernise Infrastructure to Support Economic Growth and Climate

Action", National Infrastructure Commission (blog),18 October 2023, https://nic.org.uk/news/long-term-review-sets-out-pressing-need-to-modernise-infrastructure-to-support-economic-growth-and-climate-action.

8 Ian Brinkley and Elizabeth Crowley, "From 'Inadequate to 'Outstanding': Making the UK's Skills System World Class" (London: Chartered Institute of Personnel and Development (CIPD), April 2017), www.cipd.org.

9 Harry Farmer and Madeleine Gabriel, "Innovation after Lockdown: Using Innovation to Build a More Balanced, Resilient Economy" (London: Nesta, June 2020), https://media.nesta.org.uk/documents/Innovation_after_Lockdown_v5_2.pdf.

10 Resolution Foundation, "Britain Must Get Serious about Its Toxic Combination of Low Growth and High Inequality That Has Left Typical Families £8,800 Poorer Than Their Counterparts in Comparable Countries", Resolution Foundation, 13 July 2022, www.resolution foundation.org/press-releases/britain-must-get-serious-about-its-toxic-combination-of-low-growth-and-high-inequality-that-has-left-typical-families-8800-poorer-than-their-counterparts-in-comparable-countries.

11 Dirk Bezemer, Michael Hudson and Howard Reed, "Exploring the Capital Gains Economy: The Case of the United Kingdom" (Washington, DC: The Democracy Collaborative, forthcoming).

12 Intergovernmental Panel on Climate Change (IPCC), "Global Warming of 1.5°C", Special Report (Geneva: IPCC, 2018), www.ipcc.ch/sr15.

13 Labour Party, "A National Investment Bank for Britain: Putting Dynamism into Our Industrial Strategy" (London: Labour Party, October 2017), https://labour.org.uk/wp-content/uploads/2017/10/National-Investment-Bank-Plans-Report.pdf.

14 HM Treasury and Infrastructure Bank, "UK Infrastructure Bank Framework Document" (London: Government Digital Service, 17 June 2021), https://assets.publishing.service.gov.uk.

15 George Cooper, "People's Quantitative Easing Is Both Dangerous and Necessary", *Independent*, 15 September 2015, www.independent.co.uk/voices/comment/people-s-quantitative-easing-may-be-the-best-way-to-undo-the-mistakes-of-the-first-round-of-qe-10501479.html.

16 New Economy Brief, "The Inequality of Interest Rates", *New Economy Brief*, 25 October 2023, www.neweconomybrief.net/the-digest/the-inequality-of-interest-rates.

17 Ben Chapman, "£575,000-a-Year Bank of England Boss Defends 'Wage Restraint' Comments", *Independent*, 23 February 2022, News, www.independent.co.uk/news/business/bank-england-boss-andrew-bailey-wage-restraint-b2021380.html.

18 Ed Conway, "Bank of England Head Andrew Bailey Denies Role in Liz Truss's Downfall", Sky News, 14 November 2022, https://news.sky.com/story/bank-of-england-head-andrew-bailey-denies-role-in-liz-trusss-downfall-12747640.

19 Positive Money, "Positive Money – Written Evidence IBE0013 – Bank of England: How Is Independence Working?" Written Evidence (London: Economic Affairs Committee, 2 May 2023), https://committees.parliament.uk/writtenevidence/120469/pdf.

20 Stephen Millard, "Macroeconomic Effects of the Move to Net Zero", NIESR, 2023, www.niesr.ac.uk/projects/macroeconomic-effects-move-net-zero.

21 Nettle et al., "What Do British People Want from a Welfare System?"

22 "Tax on Dividends", GOV.UK, accessed 12 February 2024, www.gov.uk/tax-on-dividends.

23 Howard Reed, "Options for Increasing Taxes in Scotland to Fund Investment in Public Services" (Glasgow: Scottish Trades Union Congress, December 2022, https://stuc.org.uk/files/Reports/Scotland_Demands_Better_Fairer_Taxes_for_a_Fairer_%20Future.pdf.

24 ONS, "Wealth and Assets Survey QMI", 25 February 2022, www.ons.gov.uk/peoplepopulationandcommunity/personalandhouseholdfinances/debt/methodologies/wealthandassetssurveyqmi.

25 Josh Burke, Sam Fankhauser, Alex Kazaglis, Louise Kessler, Naina Khandelwal, Peter O'Boyle and Anne Owen, "Distributional Impacts of a Carbon Tax in the UK" (London: The Grantham Research Institute on Climate Change and the Environment, 2020), www.lse.ac.uk.

26 Ella Blom and Lyndsay Walsh, "Payment Overdue: Fair Ways to Make UK Polluters Pay for Climate Justice" (Oxford: Oxfam, 18 September 2023), https://doi.org/10.21201/2023.621539.

27 Alex Chapman, Leo Murray, Griffin Carpenter, Christiane Heisse and Lydia Prieg, "A Frequent Flyer Levy: Sharing Aviation's Carbon Budget In A Net Zero World" (London: New Economics Foundation, July 2021), https://neweconomics.org/uploads/files/frequent-flyer-levy.pdf.

28 Blom and Walsh, "Payment Overdue".

29 Office for Budget Responsibility, "Policy Measures Database: December 2023", 21 December 2023, https://obr.uk/download/policy-measures-database-6/?tmstv=1707806964.

30 Sean Bray, "2023 Corporate Income Tax Rates in Europe", Tax Foundation, 14 February 2023, https://taxfoundation.org/data/all/eu/corporate-tax-rates-europe-2023.

31 Fairer Share, "Proportional Property Tax", 2022, https://fairershare.org.uk/proportional-property-tax; Reed, "Options for Increasing Taxes in Scotland to Fund Investment".

32 The discrepancy in PPT rate between Scotland and England and Wales arises because average council tax bills in Scotland are significantly lower than in England and Wales.

33 Howard Reed, "Raising Taxes to Deliver for Scotland" (Glasgow: Scottish Trades Union Congress, November 2023), https://stuc.org.uk/files/Scottish_Tax_options.pdf.

34 House of Commons Treasury Committee, "Tax Reliefs: Twentieth Report of Session 2022–23", HC 723 (Westminster: House of Commons Library, 2023), https://committees.parliament.uk/publications/41067/documents/200054/default.

35 HM Revenue & Customs, "Tax Relief Statistics" (London: HMRC, 2023), www.gov.uk/government/collections/tax-relief-statistics.

36 Fiorella Parra-Mujica, Elliott Johnson, Howard Reed, Richard Cookson and Matthew Johnson, "Understanding the Relationship between Income and Mental Health among 16– to 24–Year-Olds: Analysis of 10 Waves (2009–2020) of Understanding Society to Enable Modelling of Income Interventions", *PLOS ONE* 18, no. 2 (28 February, 2023): e0279845, https://doi.org/10.1371/journal.pone.0279845.

37 Paul Johnson, "Lots More People Are Working, but in Jobs That Keep Them in Poverty", *The Times*, 8 May 2023, www.thetimes.co.uk/article/lots-more-people-are-working-but-in-jobs-that-keep-them-in-poverty-5sq6nzp2d; Antonia Keung and Jonathan Bradshaw, "Who Are the Fuel Poor? Post-Budget Update" (York: Social Policy Research Unit, University of York, 24 March 2023), https://cpag.org.uk/policy-and-campaigns/briefing/who-are-fuel-poor-post-budget-update.

38 Stephen Rocks, Giulia Boccarini, Anita Charlesworth, Omar Idriss, Ruth McConkey and Laurie Rachet-Jacquet, "Health and Social Care Funding Projections 2021" (London: The Health Foundation, 30 September 2021), https://doi.org/10.37829/HF-2021-RC18.

39 ONS, "Healthcare Expenditure, UK Health Accounts Provisional Estimates: 2022", 17 May 2023, www.ons.gov.uk/peoplepopulation andcommunity/healthandsocialcare/healthcaresystem/bullet ins/healthcareexpenditureukhealthaccountsprovisionalestimates/ 2022.

40 The King's Fund, "Social Care 360: Expenditure", 2 March 2023, www.kingsfund.org.uk/publications/social-care-360/expenditure.

41 David McDaid and A-La Park, "The Economic Case for Investing in the Prevention of Mental Health Conditions in the UK" (London: Mental Health Foundation and LSE, February 2022), www.mentalhealth.org. uk/explore-mental-health/publications/economic-case-investing-prevention-mental-health-conditions-UK.

42 Jonathan Portes, Howard Reed and Andrew Percy, "Social Prosperity for the Future: A Proposal for Universal Basic Services" (London: UCL Institute for Global Prosperity, 2017), www.ucl.ac.uk.

43 Andrew O'Brien and Howard Reed, "The Better Business Bounce: The Economic Benefits of Purpose-Led Businesses" (London: Demos, forthcoming).

44 Chappell, "Rachel Reeves Pledges £28bn".

45 Emden, Murphy and Gunson, "Net Zero North Sea".

46 Quinn, "Labour's Plan to Insulate More Homes".

47 Green Finance Institute, "Finance Gap for UK Nature Report", Green Finance Institute, 12 October 2021, www.greenfinanceinstitute. com/news-and-insights/finance-gap-for-uk-nature-report.

48 eftec, "North Devon Marine Protected Areas Cost Evaluation".

49 Simply Sustainable, "UK Resources and Waste Strategy".

50 HM Revenue and Customs, "Statistics of Government Revenues from UK Oil and Gas Production September 2023" (London: Government Digital Service, 27 September 2023), www.gov.uk/government/statistics/ government-revenues-from-uk-oil-and-gas-production–2/statistics-of-government-revenues-from-uk-oil-and-gas-production-september-2023.

51 Blom and Walsh, "Payment Overdue".

52 Unite, "Unite Investigates".

53 TUC, "A Fairer Energy System".

54 Department of Health and Social Care, "Aligning the Upper Age for NHS Prescription Charge Exemptions with the State Pension Age: Government Response" (Westminster: Department of Health and Social Care, 2023), www.gov.uk.

55 Roberts, "Labour's Plan to 'Nationalise' GPs".

56 Scottish Government, "The Case for a National Care Service (NCS)", in *Adult Social Care: Independent Review* (Edinburgh: Scottish Government, 2021), 5, www.gov.scot/publications/independent-review-adult-social-care-scotland/pages/7.

57 Reed et al., "Universal Basic Income Is Affordable and Feasible"; Johnson et al., "Treating Causes Not Symptoms".

58 IPPR, "Boost Child Benefit".

59 IPPR, "Boost Child Benefit".

60 Bryony Hirsch, "Expanding Free School Meals: A Cost Benefit Analysis" (London: Impact on Urban Health, 10 October 2022), https://urbanhealth.org.uk/insights/reports/expanding-free-school-meals-a-cost-benefit-analysis.

61 Department for Education, "Holiday Activities and Food Programme 2023" (London: Government Digital Service, 22 December 2022), www.gov.uk/government/publications/holiday-activities-and-food-programme/holiday-activities-and-food-programme-2023.

62 House of Lords Public Services Committee, "Children in Crisis: The Role of Public Services in Overcoming Child Vulnerability", House of Lords, 2021, https://ukparliament.shorthandstories.com/public-services-children-vulnerability.

63 National Education Union, "The Crisis in School Funding"; Elaine Drayton, Christine Farquharson, Kate Ogden, Luke Sibieta, Imran Tahir, and Ben Waltmann, "Annual Report on Education Spending in England: 2023" (London: IFS, December 2023), https://ifs.org.uk/sites/default/files/2023-12/IFS-Annual-report-on-education-spending-in-England-2023-new.pdf.

64 Paul Bolton, Joe Lewis and Colin Harrison, "Estimates: Spending of the Department for Education on Adult Education, Post-16 Education, Further Education and Colleges", debate pack (London: House of Commons Library, 30 June 2023), https://researchbriefings.files.parliament.uk/documents/CDP-2023-0147/CDP-2023-0147.pdf.

65 Labour Party, "Funding Real Change" (London: Labour Party, November 2019), https://labour.org.uk/wp-content/uploads/2019/11/Funding-Real-Change-1.pdf.

66 Labour Party, "Funding Real Change".

67 Shelter, "Executive Summary: A Vision for Social Housing" (London: Shelter, 2019), https://england.shelter.org.uk/support_us/campaigns/a_vision_for_social_housing/executive_summary.

68 Shelter, "Three Million New Social Homes Key to Solving Housing Crisis", Shelter, 14 January 2019, https://england.shelter.org.uk/media/press_release/three_million_new_social_homes_key_to_solving_housing_crisis2.

69 Hugh Macknight, "New North East Devolution Deal Brings Billions of Pounds to the North East", North of Tyne Combined Authority (blog), 28 December 2022, www.northoftyne-ca.gov.uk/news/devo.

70 Department for Transport, "North East to Benefit from £19.8 Billion Transport Investment", GOV.UK, 4 October 2023, www.gov.uk/government/news/north-east-to-benefit-from-198-billion-transport-investment.

71 Isobel White, "AV and Electoral Reform", Standard Note (London: House of Commons Library, 12 July 2011), https://researchbriefings.files.parliament.uk/documents/SN05317/SN05317.pdf.

72 David Cowling, "What Price Democracy? Counting the Cost of UK Elections", BBC News, 8 November 2013, www.bbc.com/news/uk-politics-24842147.

73 Electoral Reform Society, "Revealed: The True Cost of the House of Lords", Electoral Reform Society, 15 November 2017, www.electoral-reform.org.uk/latest-news-and-research/media-centre/press-releases/revealed-the-true-cost-of-the-house-of-lords.

74 "List of United Kingdom MPs by Seniority (2019–Present)", Wikipedia, 10 January 2024, https://en.wikipedia.org/w/index.php?title=List_of_United_Kingdom_MPs_by_seniority_(2019%E2%80%93present.

75 "MPs' Severance Pay to Double at next General Election", BBC News, 25 August 2023, www.bbc.com/news/uk-politics-66612463.

76 Aubrey Allegretti, "Parliament Renovation Could Take 76 Years and Cost £22bn, Report Says", *Guardian*, 23 February 2022, Politics, www.theguardian.com/politics/2022/feb/23/parliament-renovation-could-take-76-years-and-cost-22bn-report-says.

77 Scott MacNab, "Scottish Parliament at 20: £414m, Endless Recrimination, and Finally, an Iconic Building", *The Scotsman*, 7 May 2019, www.scotsman.com/news/scottish-news/scottish-parliament-at-20-ps414m-endless-recrimination-and-finally-an-iconic-building-1418185.

78 Allegretti, "Parliament Renovation".

79 Electoral Commission, "Public Funding for Political Parties", Electoral Commission, 6 October 2023, www.electoralcommission.org.uk/political-registration-and-regulation/financial-reporting/donations-and-loans/public-funding-political-parties.

80 Independent Parliamentary Standards Authority (IPSA), "The Scheme of MPs' Staffing and Business Costs 2023–24" (London: IPSA, 16 March 2023), https://theipsa.org.uk.

81 The Parliamentary Commissioner for Standards, "The Parliamentary Commissioner for Standards Annual Report 2022–23" (London: House of Commons, 12 July, 2023), www.parliament.uk.

82 Matteo Deleidi, Francesca Iafrate and Enrico Sergio Levrero, "Public Investment Fiscal Multipliers: An Empirical Assessment for European Countries" (London: UCL Institute for Innovation and Public Purpose, 2019), www.ucl.ac.uk.

83 Johnson et al., "Treating Causes Not Symptoms".

Conclusion and a call to action

1 Elliott Aidan Johnson, Irene Hardill, Matthew T. Johnson and Daniel Nettle, "Breaking the Overton Window: On the Need for Adversarial Co-Production", *Evidence & Policy*, 23 October 2023, 1–13, https://doi.org/10.1332/17442648Y2023D000000005.

2 Nicholas Timmins, ed., *Rejuvenate or Retire? Views of the NHS at 60* (London: The Nuffield Trust, 2008), 47.

3 Dan Degerman, Elliott Johnson, Matthew Flinders and Matthew Johnson, "After Nudging: Pandemocracy, Fear and Social Safety Nets", Humanities and Social Sciences Communications, forthcoming; Dan Degerman, Matthew Flinders and Matthew Thomas Johnson, "In Defence of Fear: COVID-19, Crises and Democracy", *Critical Review of International Social and Political Philosophy* 26, no. 6 (19 September 2023): 788–809, https://doi.org/10.1080/13698230.2020.1834744.

4 Matthew T. Johnson, Elliott Aidan Johnson, Howard Reed and Daniel Nettle, "Can the 'Downward Spiral' of Material Conditions, Mental Health and Faith in Government Be Stopped? Evidence from Surveys in 'Red Wall' Constituencies", *The British Journal of Politics and International Relations* 26, no. 1 (10 January 2023), https://doi.org/10.1177/13691481221146886.

5 Johnson, Johnson and Nettle, "Are 'Red Wall' Constituencies Really Opposed to Progressive Policy?"

6 Milton Friedman, *Capitalism and Freedom* (Chicago: The University of Chicago Press, 1962), xiv.

INDEX